AT THE ALTAR OF

SEXUAL
IDOLATRY

STEVE GALLAGHER

COMING NOVEMBER 2003!
Out of the Depths of Sexual Sin: The Story of My Life and Ministry

Also available by Steve Gallagher:
At The Altar Of Sexual Idolatry Workbook
Living in Victory
Break Free from the Lusts of this World
The Walk of Repentance
How to Run a Successful Support Group
Irresistible to God

For these books and other teaching materials contact:
Pure Life Ministries
P.O. Box 410
Dry Ridge, KY 41035
(888) 293-8714 - to order
(859) 824-4444 - office
(859) 824-5159 FAX
www.purelifeministries.org
info@purelifeministries.org

ISBN 0-9702202-0-0

ACKNOWLEDGMENTS

My deepest appreciation to Tiffany McCormick and Justin Carabello who provided much help in the editing of this book.

My special gratitude to Bradley Furges whose commitment and tireless efforts made such a difference in the quality of this work.

*This book is dedicated to my wife Kathy who
"bears all things, believes all things,
hopes all things, endures all things."
Her love has never failed me.*

TABLE OF CONTENTS

FOREWORD

WHEN STEVE ASKED ME TO WRITE the foreword for this book, I was honored at first, then struck with anxiety concerning what I could say, when he is the source of truth concerning this subject. Then I remembered that I had just written something the Holy Spirit had impressed upon me, and realized it would help in the solution to addiction.

The text of "washing the mind with the water of the Word" is found in a passage concerning marital relationships.

> "Husbands, love your wives, even as Christ also loved the church, and gave himself for it; That he might sanctify and cleanse it with the washing of water by the Word, that he might present it to himself a glorious church, not having spot, or wrinkle, or any such thing; but that it should be holy and without blemish."

> "The apostle, having mentioned Christ's love to the church, enlarges upon it, assigning the reason why he gave himself for it, namely, that he might sanctify it in this world, and glorify it in the next: That he might

sanctify and cleanse it, with the washing of water by the word (v. 26)—that he might endue all his members with a principle of holiness, and deliver them from the guilt, the pollution, and the dominion of sin." (Matthew Henry)

The reason for books such as this one of Steve's is to clarify, amplify or make understandable the Word of God to those in need, so that it can become at once the foundation for their faith, and the solution to their torments.

I wrote once, "The torment of the temptation to sin is nothing compared with the consequences of sin." The consequences can last for a lifetime or an eternity. It's the consequences that are so terribly tormenting.

The solution of course, as in every thing with the Lord, is in the Word of God. God's Word is where every solution is found to every problem or issue that a man or woman faces. There is no place for help like the Word of God. All God's healing work begins with His Word.

The subjective emotion and thinking of the addict is, "I'm too unclean, too unworthy, too unholy, too undeserving to read the Bible." That is a lie! God's Word is written for such people, to show them the way Jesus Christ has made for them to get out of the pit or hole they dug for themselves.

Or they say, "I have failed so badly. How can I ever be good enough again so God can hear me?" You don't get good and get to God, you get to God and God makes you good. Getting to God is getting into His Word.

The Word does the work!

Read it when you feel guilty; read it when you don't get anything from it; read it in the face of the devil and his accusations against you; read it when you are not even sure you believe it, just read it!!

The Word does the work!

The Word of God washes the mind as soap does the

hands. The Word is like soap in that it is only effective when used.

All you have is the Word!

Life's greatest failure is not your sin, but in failure to read the Word.

The only way the Word can wash your mind is when you read it. Reading the Word is the only way God can do His work in your life.

Christianity is not difficult to live, it's impossible. It is Christ living in you that is real Christianity. That is where the life of Christ is. Not what you try to do, but what He does in you.

The Word pays no attention to your sin, emotions, or actions; it merely does its work when you read it.

God's Word never changes, we do.

It doesn't make us feel guilty, we do that to ourselves. It gives us a way out of our feelings, habits, desires and wants. God's Word is our source of life and blessing.

The reason I am writing this foreword for Steve is that he has based everything in this book on God's Word. It is foundational, inspirational, confrontational—just what you need. I'm not talking just about you and your problem, but I am writing to you who desires to be a problem solver.

This is your book. Put the Bible and this book side by side—reading them—and let the Word do the work.

But if we confess our sins to him, he can be depended on to forgive us and *cleanse* us from every wrong. [And it is perfectly proper for God to do this for us because Christ died to wash away our sins.]

When you do your part, God will do His. You can't do His part, and He won't do yours. Yours is to act on His Word, and let His Word do the work.

Thank God for a man like Steve Gallagher, who will tell the truth, and let the truth make us free. Live Free!

Dr. Edwin Louis Cole, Founder
Christian Men's Network

INTRODUCTION

THIS BOOK ADDRESSES THE ISSUE of sexual addiction and its powerful hold on countless Christian and non-Christian men alike. It was purposely written to draw back the curtain and expose the secret workings of this evil which is not only pervasive in the American culture at large but is a festering sore within the Church itself—from the pulpit to the pews. Most of us have been motivated and mislead in the past by an inflated perspective of who we are as people and as believers. Consequently, with itching ears we have gravitated to those teachings which coddle us and make us feel good. Unfortunately, we discover sooner or later that such teachings offer only a temporary reprieve at best and ultimately fail at helping us to obtain the freedom we desire.

As you read this book, you will be enlightened to the struggles of the sex addict and the harsh consequences of his sinful behavior. If you are one who struggles yourself, it is very likely that there will be those times when the piercing truths presented here will be extremely painful. I understand this, having experienced the process myself. If this happens, simply set the book aside. You can pick it up again in a couple of days when you regather your courage. Even though seeing what you are like inside may be extremely agonizing at times, the good news is that once you face *yourself,* you will then be able to go through this difficult process and come out on the other side— free!

I must mention that there are certain true stories contained in this book about the behavior of those in habitual sexual sin which might provoke your mind to think on or recall some past sexual experience. Initially, I was hesitant to include them. However, after prayerfully considering how this could affect you and seeking the advice of others, I decided to keep the stories for two reasons: First, and foremost, it is vital that you, the reader, see yourself in this book. Identifying your own struggles will help you to see yourself in the answers which this book provides. Secondly, the stories written in this book are no more graphic than can be read in the newspaper on any given day. Most men involved with sexual sin are accustomed to far worse!

I pray that this book will be a blessing to you and that the truths it presents will draw you closer to God and to the freedom which He offers.

Steve Gallagher

PART ONE

THE PROBLEM

one

SEXUAL ADDICTION

Like a dog that returns to its vomit is a fool who repeats his folly. (Proverbs 26:11)

His own iniquities will capture the wicked, and he will be held with the cords of his sin. (Proverbs 5:22)

...and especially those who indulge the flesh in its corrupt desires... having eyes full of adultery and that never cease from sin... they entice by fleshly desires, by sensuality, those who barely escape from the ones who live in error, promising them freedom while they themselves are slaves of corruption; for by what a man is overcome, by this he is enslaved. (II Peter 2:10-19)

For the lips of an adulteress drip honey... do not go near the door of her house, lest you give your vigor to others, and your years to the cruel one.

Suddenly he follows her, as an ox goes to the slaughter, or as one in fetters to the discipline of a fool, until an arrow pierces through his liver; as a bird hastens to the snare, so he does not know that it will cost him his life. (Proverbs 5:3, 9; 7:22-23)

JIMMY WAS INTRODUCED TO PORNOGRAPHY when he was seven years old. One day his older brother took him to a friend's house whose father sold pornographic movies. As Jimmy watched the movies with much fascination, the other two disappeared into a bedroom for what he later realized was a homosexual encounter. Jimmy would never be the same. This initial exposure ushered him into a lifetime of slavery to pornography which transformed him into a full-fledged sex addict. (Jimmy's brother, also a sex addict, would be convicted of raping and murdering two women and a young girl years later.)

Richard was introduced to sex for the first time as a young teenager when he was invited over to a friend's house to participate in a wild orgy. For years he lived a life obsessed with sex. Shortly after he got married, with much manipulation and relentless "guilt trips," he managed to convince his wife to incorporate the "swinging life-style" into their marriage. For twelve years Rebecca, his wife, lived in constant degradation and shame, until she met Jesus Christ and her whole life changed. It would be several years later before Richard made the same discovery.

One day, as a young teenager, Glen was walking down a country road on his way home from school. As he nonchalantly tramped along, a car pulled over about a half of a mile in front of him. Glen became very curious when he saw a box being thrown from the car. When he reached the box, he opened it up and found an assortment of several hundred pornographic magazines. His life would never be the same. Even after becoming a Christian while in college, years of sexual addiction followed. Glen became the general manager of a Christian radio station, in spite of his ongoing struggle with pornography. The truth about his secret life eventually came out when he left his godly wife and ran off with the wife of a pastor.

Bob was introduced to pornography for the first time when

he discovered explicit magazines under his father's bed. Years of bondage followed. When pornography no longer thrilled him, he started sneaking around houses to peek into windows. He would spend hours at a window hoping to catch just a glimpse of flesh. After ruining one marriage and almost another, Bob finally sought help.

Sexual Bondage

All of these individuals shared one thing in common: they became addicted to compulsive sexual behavior. An addiction is a constellation of unbiblical habits of thinking and acting that have become a lifestyle. Thus, there are those who develop a lifestyle of sexual gratification and become addicted to the "high" associated with sexual activity just as others become addicted to the euphoria of alcohol or drugs. When people over-emphasize the importance of sex in their lives, it begins to dictate a lifestyle to them, and they become obsessed with thoughts of sex. Eventually they lose control of how often, with whom, and under what circumstances they will engage in sex. They become enslaved to compulsive sexual behavior. What begins as "just having a little fun" or "satisfying normal urges," gradually lures them deeper and deeper into the mire of bondage. If continued without repentance, God will give them over to a reprobate mind. (Romans 1:28)

As the neighborhood drug pusher entices someone with free marijuana, with the intention of leading him in the direction of hard core drugs, so will Satan subtly lure an unwitting victim into his clutches with a few satisfying sexual experiences. However, the Bible promises that the pleasure of sin will last only for a season. (Hebrews 11:25) In a later chapter, I will discuss how Satan masterfully uses fantasy, especially through pornography, to dangle the proverbial carrot in front of his victim's nose.

SPECIAL ROUTINES

As the addiction tightens its grip on the victim, he enters into special routines or rituals to which he becomes accustomed. The man in the habit of watching pornographic movies might begin by browsing the magazine racks in an adult bookstore for awhile. As his lust heightens, he may venture to the movie arcade, a dimly lit room located in the rear of the bookstore. From there he might go from booth to booth, searching for the perfect movie (his ultimate fantasy) until he finally satisfies his lust. I can personally identify with this particular ritual. I, too, would go into an adult bookstore and "size it up" by walking around the video booths, looking at the movie advertisements for each one. Then I would methodically go from booth to booth, saving the one that most appealed to me for last.

A step-father who is a practicing child molester would have a completely different routine. He may (or may not) start off by looking at pornography. Eventually, though, he will sneak into the child's bedroom where he will act out his lust.

Lew began molesting his oldest daughter from the time she was ten. Each time he would spend several moments coaxing and comforting her to convince her that it was his way of showing his "special love" for her and that it would be their little secret. She reluctantly went along with it until he tried to molest her younger sister. Having lived with the horror of molestation, she could not bear to see her sister go through what she had endured. Out of desperation, she told her teacher, who immediately alerted the authorities.

An exhibitionist usually acts out his routine in the confines of a car. He might be driving to a store when the idea of exposing himself to a girl enters his mind. He immediately becomes preoccupied with the thought until finally he acts out his fantasy in front of some unsuspecting victim.

Sam was a young teenager when he began sensing a desire to expose himself. Every morning, when a group of teenage girls would walk through his backyard on their way to school, he would masturbate while watching them through his window. Although he never dared to make himself visible, the thought of the girls seeing him masturbate would arouse him. As he grew older this nagging urge continued to plague him. He would repeatedly dismiss it, yet it would not disappear. One day, he pulled his car over and masturbated while a woman walked by. He did a good job of hiding himself, but the thought of her seeing him was what was exciting to him. He repeated this same routine occasionally over the next several months until finally his lust overcame him, and he gave in to the temptation. He allowed a woman to see him as he climaxed. Even though it frightened him terribly, he found himself repeating the act over and over again. Masturbation alone was no longer enough to fulfill him.

The indecent phone caller's routine closely resembles that of the exhibitionist's, except that his ritual is done over the phone. As he dials telephone numbers, the caller will become aroused at the thought of reaching some woman who is naive enough to listen to what he says. This is when his lust will be fulfilled.

Take Stan for example. His problems began with "dial-a-porn." He would get himself worked up with pornography and then call a special number where a girl would talk sexually with him. But this was too easy. Rather than allow himself to end it with her, he would start breezing through the local telephone book calling numbers until he found a woman who would listen to his lewd suggestions and the graphic description of his subsequent climax.

The voyeur, "peeping Tom," will cruise streets for hours in hopes of finding a window that might provide some excitement.

After he anxiously waits, for perhaps hours at a time, finally a glimpse of flesh will enter his visual field. This eyeful brings about the culmination of his lust.

Bob would be sitting in his house at night watching television when the thought of all of those potential windows would start to entice him. After everyone went to bed, he would sneak out of the house and down the street, searching for a window with open curtains. After finding one, he might stay for a long period of time until he could get a glimpse of anything exciting.

The woman addicted to fornication might act out her routine in bars, going from man to man, night after night. She might attempt to see how many men she can flirt with or tease in a given night until she chooses one to sleep with. Then she will finish the night's buildup.

Betty, a woman of average attractiveness at best, was a nightclub singer who loved to seduce men. She enjoyed the attention she received from the audience while singing. During her performance, she would pick one man out to "come on to." Ending up in bed with that man would make her feel incredibly desirable and sexy as a woman. If a man in the bar did not pay enough attention to her, perhaps because he was married, she would take that as a challenge to seduce him. All such conquests gave her tremendous satisfaction. Eventually Betty married, but soon came to miss the attention of men and started having secret affairs. No matter how many men she managed to seduce, she could not reach the point where she was really content with herself as a person. However, that all began to change for her when she met Jesus Christ as her Savior.

A "John" may act out his routine by cruising the "red-light" district, a haven for prostitutes. Captivated by the whole scene, he slowly cruises by each girl, carefully examining her. He begins to fantasize and lust builds up in his heart. Finally, one will catch his interest for whatever reason, and he will seek out her services for the evening.

Jody would spend hours driving down streets teeming with prostitutes. This was half of the excitement for him. Occasionally, he might pull over and talk with one for awhile, but usually he was not ready for his routine to end yet; so he would drive on and continue his cruising. Finally, after his desire to have sex approached its peak, he would select one of the girls to take back to his hotel room. This is where his routine would find its climax.

The compulsive homosexual might act out his routine in one of several ways. Usually he will go to the local "gay" bar where he will flirt around until he finds the "right" person. Or he might choose to go to an adult movie arcade where there will be "straight" or bisexual men who will welcome his services. There he will go from man to man throughout the night until he finally tires and finds some way to achieve enjoyment for himself.

Rick did both. Some nights he would go to the gay bars or gay bathhouses, seeking out another homosexual who attracted him. The two of them might have several drinks together as they got to know each other, and would then end up in bed for the night. Other nights he would go to the adult bookstores. He would offer to "take care of" straight men who were watching pornographic movies in small booths. In any given night, he might have sex with a dozen or more men in that booth. Although he was driven to do this, it was confusing to him how little satisfaction he received.

All of these different people share one thing in common: they have allowed unbiblical thinking to dominate their lives to the point that they have become addicted to their behavior. Their actual routines may differ but they all have a distinct or observable pattern which eventually leads to their "acting out" sexually.

Vicious Cycle of Sin

Once an individual becomes addicted to sex, he enters into a vicious cycle of self-destruction and degradation. It appears that the more compulsive or perverted his sexual behavior is, the harsher society is in labeling and judging him because of it. Consequently, his whole life is consumed with guilt and shame. This is especially true of those persons who come from a Christian background or who are actively involved in their local church. As time progresses, many things begin to happen in the sex addict's life. His sense of confidence and self-worth continually diminish, and the emptiness inside of him is magnified. As a result, he begins an intense and desperate search to fill this void in his life. Since sex has been his personal elixir to which he has turned during previous times of despair, just as a drunk turns to his liquor bottle, the sex addict will pursue the object(s) of his desire. Unfortunately, after fleeing to sex to find comfort or simply a "quick-fix," he only manages to heap more shame and despair upon himself—the pit becomes deeper, the darkness even blacker.

He starts building up walls around himself. As the need to protect himself grows, he further alienates himself from his loved ones; thus, they begin to feel helpless in reaching him. They cannot understand what is happening to him or why they are unable to communicate with him. This is one of the differences between an alcoholic and a sexual addict. It is a rare thing for an alcoholic's drinking to be a secret. It generally does not take long for people to discover an alcoholic's drinking problem. They can even understand why the drunk alienates himself; with the sexual addict, people often have no idea of what is going on and cannot understand his behavior. Hal describes what happened in his family:

The alienation of my family began long before I ever realized it. It was only in retrospect that I could see the situation for what it really was. Initially, this involved only my immediate family. My self-centered obsession with sex resulted in my wife not getting the love and attention which she truly deserved. Her understandable frustration with this void in our relationship resulted in countless arguments—many of them severe.

BLAMESHIFTING

The man who has become bound by habits of sexual sin often starts blaming all of his troubles on other people. To accept responsibility for his life and his own failures would mean having to come to grips with his addiction. Unwilling to accept responsibility for his actions, he must find others to blame. He is in a constant state of denial, even if he understands his addiction. The more he denies the sinfulness of his life or actions, the more he blames those around him. "It's my dad's fault." "It's because my wife doesn't take care of me." It seems as though the problem always lies elsewhere.

This blameshifting process might be taking place in a sex addict's mind as he seeks to justify his actions or to simply direct the blame toward those around him as they attempt to approach him on some related subject. He not only fails to admit the wrongness of his sexual behavior, but he may even deny any other wrong-doing in his life. The writer of Hebrews knew of the effects of sin when he said, "Take care, brethren, lest there should be in any one of you an evil, unbelieving heart, in falling away from the living God. But encourage one another... lest any one of you be hardened by the deceitfulness of sin." (Hebrews 3:12-13)

MANIPULATING OTHERS

In addition to blameshifting, the addict becomes manipulative. Since it is always someone else's fault, he justifies his actions and his manipulation. His selfish maneuvering might include laying "guilt trips" on his wife every time she questions his behavior. "You're always on my back about something!" "You just don't trust me!" These are favorites of anyone in habitual sin. Often the poor wife thinks that she is losing her mind. His guilt trips are so convincing, even he himself believes them. If he should somehow fail to convince himself that his problems are everyone else's fault, he would have to deal with his own guilt.

Richard used his manipulating skills with his wife to get her involved in his perverted lifestyle. At first he would make comments about other men as he made love to her. Then he stepped up his efforts. He would either be sweet and cajoling as he tried to persuade her to become involved, or he would attack her for her stand for decency. He tried one tactic after another as he sought to break her down. Once she realized that as long as she resisted him she would never have a happy home, she quit caring. It was not long before she gave in and became involved in the "swinging lifestyle" with him. If she would try to protest, he would use vicious sarcasm to belittle and degrade her. Only after coming to the Lord did she have the determination to re-establish her commitment to decency.

Solomon could have been describing Richard when he said, "A worthless person, a wicked man, is the one who walks with a false mouth, who winks with his eyes, who signals with his feet, who points with his fingers; who with perversity in his heart devises evil continually, who spreads strife." (Proverbs 6:12-14)

CRITICAL AND ATTACKING

The sexual addict will also become very critical and

judgmental of those around him. Since he has placed himself on a pedestal through the process of denial, he sees himself as incapable of wrong-doing. Again, to admit that he is vulnerable to failure or imperfections would require his coming to grips with the reality of his actions. This is all part of "the deceitfulness of sin."

Inside, the man who has developed a lifestyle of sexual gratification knows that what he is doing is wrong so he lashes out at others with criticism. His insults keep others beneath him, thereby making him feel better about himself as well as convincing others (at least in his warped thinking) that they are more to blame for any problems that might exist than he is. As a Los Angeles Deputy Sheriff assigned to a maximum security jail facility, I often became a dispenser of vigilante justice. I did not spend much time examining the filth in my own life, but I was quick to inflict punishment on troublesome inmates for their infractions!

The sex addict also lashes out at loved ones in order to protect himself from their probing questions. If he is unapproachable, he will not have to answer for his actions. If his wife attempts to question him about his personal life, his vicious defensiveness wilts her best intentions, and she quickly learns to keep her mouth shut. In the back of his mind, he knows that his temper is his "ace in the hole" if she starts scrutinizing his behavior. Surely Solomon saw all this when he said, "He who corrects a scoffer gets dishonor for himself, and he who reproves a wicked man gets insults for himself. Do not reprove a scoffer, lest he hate you, reprove a wise man, and he will love you." (Proverbs 9:7-8)

The man who is being controlled by sin will often be overly sensitive to criticism, blowing every imagined slight out of proportion. All the while, his deep sense of shame over his actions reinforces his sense of unworthiness. However, instead of coming to the cross of Jesus Christ with that great need he will try to deal with it by attempting to create an inflated sense of his own worth. His sexual sin creates a vicious cycle that stirs up a whirlwind of destruction. The more sin the sex addict indulges in, the deeper the shame and the worse he feels about himself. He overcompensates for the shame by becoming more prideful. Dominated by pride, he becomes an extremely touchy individual. As we will discuss in Chapter Seven, much of this arrogance and self-centeredness dissipates as the man begins to humble himself.

Sam, the exhibitionist, was this way. He felt a deep shame because of his behavior. Although he was cocky and arrogant to those around him, inside he felt like a "weirdo." He knew he was betraying his wife, but instead of humbling himself to her, he made himself unapproachable. Sam was so overly-sensitive that she could not make mention of any of his shortcomings or faults. However, the truth of his sin came to light when he exposed himself to her best friend.

THE CONTROLLING FLESH

Sin affects people in different ways. In general, sin tends to amplify a person's fallen nature. If the person is naturally withdrawn, sin will drive him deeper into isolation. Mark was an Air Force sergeant, assigned to an elite para-rescue team. While serving in Korea for a number of years, he became increasingly isolated to everyone around him. He could never bring himself to ask a girl out on a date. The more involved he became in his sexual sin, the more his shame destroyed his confidence as a man. However, he did not have any problem frequenting massage parlors and go-go bars because it was unnecessary for him to have a relationship with those girls in order to have fun; he only needed money. In the end, a deep hatred for women consumed him. (Only after coming to PLM years later and learning to humble himself, was he able to be set free from this hatred.)

Many men handle the frustration of their misery by becoming "super control-freaks." They seek to control every detail of life around them. The least crossing of their wills causes great agitation and frustration. Len was a man who recognized his need to come to the Pure Life Live-In Program for sexual addicts. However, he also had several preconceived notions of what life should be like for him there. Instead of coming into the program humbled by his sin and desperate for help, he came with an attitude expecting to have everything his way. In fact, he actually sent a list of demands to the program director! Once he actually made it to the facility, Len became increasingly frustrated because he was unable to manipulate his environment and those around him as he had been accustomed to doing. His attitude became unbearable to the fellow students. Although he wanted help and tried to endure the program, he was simply unwilling to surrender the reins of his life to the Lord. The director of the live-in program eventually explained to him that his attitude was making it impossible for the staff to help him. Even though the program director was gentle and humble in his approach, it was too much for Len. He stormed out of the office in a rage. For many, a situation like this would have sent them over the edge and back into sin. However, Len got a motel room and thought about things. The next morning he called the director and humbled himself. He was allowed to return to the live-in program, where he eventually had a life-changing breakthrough with the Lord.

Charlie was a completely different type of person. His gregarious and lovable nature made him one of the most adorable people you could ever meet. No one knew he was a peeping Tom, though. As a result, he carried a deep sense of guilt and humiliation over his secret sin. Charlie was by no means an angry person by nature, nor was he controlling or introverted. He was a "people person" who seemed to gain momentum in life by gaining the admiration and affection of those around him. His lovable nature only served to disguise an extremely arrogant spirit. The more he gave over to his sin, the more high-minded he became. Charlie's happy-go-lucky attitude masked his arrogance and lack of reverence for authority of any kind. In fact, he was able to get away with a lot in his home church because the people liked him so much. When Charlie came to the live-in program, God dealt very severely with his mocking, rebellious spirit; and after he had been humbled and sobered, his life turned around.

Although each case is different, a man's true nature will be magnified by his sin. Sin, like war, only brings out the worst in people. The answers provided in the latter part of this book will help to suppress the old, carnal nature and diminish the person's shortcomings.

PARANOID

Another phenomenon the sexual addict faces is paranoia, imagining that others know about his secret behavior. I remember once leaving an adult bookstore, after committing an act of lust, when a police car went screaming by me in the direction from which I had come. In my twisted thinking I imagined that they were after me! Another time, while on the way to an adult bookstore, I saw a carload of my friends. Although I steered the car away from the bookstore, I just knew that I would be branded a pervert from that day on. In reality, neither the police nor my friends had any idea of what I was doing.

Ted was really paranoid of people knowing about his secret life. He was convinced that everybody on his job knew about his abnormal behavior. He would describe in great detail the things that had happened at his work to convince himself that they knew. He was also sure that the police had him staked out, twenty-four hours a day. It took quite a bit of talking on my part to convince him that the police cannot afford to set up surveillance on one exhibitionist!

In addition to paranoia, there is the deep shame that sexual addicts live with daily. I felt like such a hypocrite when I would go to church. I always had a nagging feeling that the people in church somehow knew what I was doing in secret. When I finally began walking in victory, it was liberating to be able to look people right in the eye, knowing I had nothing to hide. As Solomon describes, "The wicked flee when no one is pursuing, but the righteous are bold as a lion." (Proverbs 28:1)

ALL GROUPS AFFECTED

Sexual addiction/bondage transcends all socioeconomic, racial and ethnic groups. The idea of the sexual deviant being a filthy little man that crawls out from under some rock has been dispelled in recent years as increasingly more "respectable" personalities are discovered in compromising situations. In fact, the more highly respectable an addict is in his outward life, the more shame he is likely to incur and the greater his fear of discovery and exposure.

Sexual addiction also goes beyond sexual preference lines. Not all homosexuals are addicted to compulsive sexual behavior. Some live with one mate and have no need to venture out into the life of multiple partners. However, this is generally a rare exception. Homosexuality, by its nature, promotes variety in sex. The homosexual who wishes to repent of his behavior must face additional problems. He has viewed himself as being "gay" for many years. It is his identity as a person. When I was in the midst of my sin, I simply viewed myself as a normal, albeit oversexed man. However, a man who has been involved in the "gay" life-style often views himself as a homosexual first and a man second. He must not only overcome the sexual addiction, but also hope that somehow his sexual preference will change. His mannerisms and often his entire self-identity will need to be transformed. Can it really happen? Absolutely! Promise of change and freedom from sin is at the very heart of the gospel. "If therefore the Son shall make you free, you shall be free indeed." (John 8:36) two

THE SPIRAL OF DEGRADATION

Yes, they knew about him all right, but they wouldn't admit it or worship him or even thank him for all his daily care. And after awhile they began to think up silly ideas of what God was like and what he wanted them to do. The result was that their foolish minds became dark and confused. Claiming themselves to be wise without God, they became utter fools instead... So God let them go ahead into every sort of sex sin, and do whatever they wanted to—yes, vile and sinful things with each other's bodies. Instead of believing what they knew was the truth about God, they deliberately chose to believe lies. So they prayed to the things God made, but wouldn't obey the blessed God who made these things. That is why God let go of them and let them do all these evil things, so that even their women turned against God's natural plan for them and indulged in sex sin with each other. And the men, instead of having a normal sex relationship with women, burned with lust for each other, men doing shameful things with other men and, as a result, getting paid within their souls with the penalty they so richly deserved. So it was that when they gave God up and would not even acknowledge Him, God gave them up to doing everything their evil minds could think of... They were fully aware of God's death penalty for these crimes, yet they went right ahead and did them anyway, and encouraged others to do them, too. (Romans 1:21-22, 24-28, 32 Living Bible)

IN THIS LARGE PORTION OF SCRIPTURE, we can clearly see the downward spiral into sexual bondage. No where else in Scripture is the vileness of sin more vividly contrasted with the glory of God. What a tragedy it is when someone comes to know God and yet remains in sexual sin. Some grow up in the church, but start dabbling in sin because they do not want to truly surrender to the Lord. Before long, they are falling headlong into the great abyss of perversion. Others have been in bondage to sexual sin for years before coming to the Lord. The tantalizing call comes forth and the person is quickly pursuing the sin again. Often they will go even deeper into sin than before their conversion.

Something happens spiritually to the person who turns away from the light. Peter said, "For if after they have escaped the defilements of the world by the knowledge of the Lord and Savior Jesus Christ, they are again entangled in them and are overcome, the last state has become worse for them than the first. For it would be better for them not to have known the way of righteousness, than having known it, to turn away from the holy commandment delivered to them. It has happened to them according to the true proverb, 'a dog returns to its own vomit,' and, 'a sow, after washing, returns to wallowing in the mire.'" (II Peter 2:20-22) Whether the person grew up in the church and became involved in sin or came to the Lord but returned to his old habits, the pattern of sin presented in Romans chapter 1 still occurs. There are seven steps downward into sexual bondage. Let us take a look.

NUMBER ONE: FAILURE TO GLORIFY GOD

"Yes, they knew about him all right, but they wouldn't admit it or worship him..."

Losing a reverential, worshipful spirit is the first step down into the spiral of degradation. When a person gets saved, he falls in love with Jesus. Jesus becomes his "first love." Should the new believer remain living in that love for Jesus, many fruitful years can be expected. However, Romans 1:21 describes a person who has begun to turn away from that first love. He may still continue to go through the outward motions of a believer, but something within him is drying up. He is losing his sense of adoration for the God who has saved him. This waning of this first love is enough to allow an altar of sexual idolatry to be erected in a person's heart, and once established, he will turn from worshipping God to worshipping the perversion of sexual lust.

Another aspect is the old prideful nature which begins to reemerge. The person who once was broken in the awareness of his great need for God loses that poverty of spirit and begins to rise up in pride. Once someone is saved, it does not take him long to learn a few spiritual truths and then think that such newfound knowledge has somehow made him a spiritual giant. Before he realizes what is happening, he begins losing the awe (and the fear that accompanies it) he once had of God, and he starts to develop a terrible pattern of *self-glory*. The honor and reverence that is due to God, and God alone, is soon swallowed up in self-exaltation, or as expressed by the King James version, "...they glorified him not as God." Man's love for self replaces love for God. Belief in self supplants belief in God. Self-glory substitutes the glory that belongs to the Lord. Thus, the wandering away from God begins.

NUMBER TWO: THE LOSS OF A GRATEFUL SPIRIT

"...they wouldn't admit it or worship him or even thank him
for all his daily care."

Once that first step downward has been taken, the next becomes easier. The second step is the failure to thank God—an attitude of ungratefulness. Paul is specifically targeting the spirit these people were in toward God. Ingratitude is what infuriated the Lord with the Israelites as He led them toward the Promised Land. They were dissatisfied with what God had given them. They "murmured" against the Lord. Even after He had miraculously delivered them out of the hands of their cruel oppressors, they still had the audacity to complain. Their lack of thankfulness almost brought God to the point of annihilating the Israelites.

It is this attitude which sneaks in very subtly once a person takes his eyes off of God. If God's wonderful presence alone does not capture their devotion, how will they ever be satisfied with anything else? Such a sense of dissatisfaction leads people to seek other ways of satisfying perceived needs. It is a dangerous spirit to be in, for if God's wonderful provisions are not enough to hold a person's attention, what will it take?

Bill's life is a perfect example of what happens to the person who lives in dissatisfaction. Brought up in a Christian home and spoiled in many ways, he took his Christian walk for granted. He loved God, or at least he thought he did, and he wanted to serve Him. However, he failed to appreciate His salvation since it was something he took for granted he always had. As the years rolled on, Bill started developing a fascination with the idea of having a homosexual relationship. At first, he would quickly put those thoughts out of his mind. But gradually this desire began gaining a foothold in Bill's heart, and eventually he left his wife to pursue another man. In his mind, only this fantasy would really meet his needs. Bill never cultivated an attitude of thanksgiving toward God, thus, he was easily enticed into a sin he believed would offer him true satisfaction. After several months in sin, and thanks to the fasting and praying of his dedicated wife, Bill eventually realized he had been deceived by a lie. He saw the emptiness of the "gay" lifestyle and returned home.

NUMBER THREE: THE DARKENING HEART

"And after awhile they began to think up silly ideas of what God was like and what he wanted them to do. The result was that their foolish minds became dark and confused."

When a person turns away from God in his heart, he becomes vulnerable to carnal thinking. Paul said they "...became vain in their imaginations, and their foolish heart was darkened." (Romans 1:21 KJV) He looks around for something to give meaning to his life, something that will offer pleasure and satisfaction, and then he allows his mind to speculate, to daydream and to fantasize.

For the sexual addict, the thought life becomes dominated with wonderful affairs and liasons with other people. Perhaps this all started when he was a teenager flipping through a *Playboy* magazine, filling his mind with the thoughts of having sex with all those apparently willing partners. Or maybe it was a youthful homosexual encounter with a friend which introduced him to sex. For Bill, like most men, it began with only an occasional lustful thought. Wherever it starts, it only leads in one direction and that is down the slippery path toward darkness. Unfortunately, most never turn away from this path.

It is also important to note how darkness begins to take over a person's heart. A turning point in the man's life is when he gives himself over to vain imaginations. Bill's life is an example of someone who allowed fantasy to gain a stronghold in his mind, actually giving up his precious mind for adoption to demonic forces.

Up to this point, Bill initiated the steps into darkness. Now sin began to exercise its dominion over his life, the dominion that he gave it. He voluntarily made the decision to place God second in his life, choosing not to be thankful to Him, deciding to speculate about things other than the Lord, and, thus, he lost control. Darkness consumed his heart and Bill suddenly disappeared into the homosexual community. It was then that sin had free reign in his life.

Paul speaks of the dangers of this:

> Do not let sin control your puny body any longer; do not give in to its sinful desires. Do not let any part of your bodies become tools of wickedness, to be used for sinning; but give yourselves completely to God—every part of you—for you are back from death and you want to be tools in the hands of God, to be used for his good purposes... Don't you realize that you can choose your own master? You can choose sin (with death) or else obedience (with acquittal). The one to whom you offer yourself—he will take you and be your master and you will be his slave. (Romans 6:12-13; 16; Living Bible)

Those strong words indicate the power that we can give sin in our lives. Once sin is the master over a person's life, darkness prevails; where darkness reigns, evil forces dominate and control.

As a person's mind becomes controlled by sin, he becomes less sensitive to the voice of the Holy Spirit. In another epistle Paul uses some of the same terminology that is found in Romans chapter 1 to describe this phenomena.

> This I say therefore, and affirm together with the Lord, that you walk no longer just as the Gentiles also walk, in the futility of their mind, being darkened in their understanding, excluded from the life of God, because of the ignorance that is in them, because of the hardness of their heart; and they, having become callous, have given themselves over to sensuality, for the practice of every kind of impurity with greediness. (Ephesians 4:17-19)

Darkness of mind signifies the lack of light in a person's thinking. The more a person gives himself over to the power of sin, the harder he grows toward God. He may still attend church, sing all of the songs of worship, and even enjoy good preaching, but there is a thick callous around his heart that keeps him from *feeling* the Holy Spirit nudge him toward repentance. The more a person sins, the thicker that callous grows. Eventually he will find himself so hardened that he can no longer discern truth for himself. Although he is likely to still have some comprehension for doctrinal truth, the Truth has been effectively shut out of his heart.

NUMBER FOUR: THE SUPPRESSION OF TRUTH

"Instead of believing what they knew was the truth about God, they deliberately chose to believe lies."

Paul says that these people "suppress the truth in unrighteousness." (Romans 1:18) Literally, he means to hold the truth down, or hold it in check. The picture here is that God is trying desperately to break through the darkness of their thinking with the light of Jesus. However, something rises up inside the person which causes him to turn away from the truth. The Holy Spirit keeps introducing convicting thoughts into the man's mind, but he turns a deaf ear to them. He does not want to hear the voice of the Lord because he knows it would mean giving up what he wants. Not only is truth ignored, but deception now enters the scene. The following statements are typical of what the deceived person tells himself in order to justify his sin or to keep from coming to grips with it.

"I'm walking with God. I just have this one little problem." This is the mentality of someone who wishes to minimize the evil of his sin so that he may hold on to it. Let us take the monstrous evil of pornography for example. Even the person who has gone no farther than occasionally viewing pornography and masturbating, is still giving up his mind and heart to wickedness. No one who is looking at pornography is walking with God! The man

may occasionally have experiences with the Lord, but as we shall see later in this book, he certainly is not walking with Him. He is simply flattering his own ego and deceiving himself.

"I'm going through a difficult period of my life right now. I'll come out of it." This is someone who is simply waiting to repent, imagining that he can shut his sin down whenever he wishes. Perhaps he does not realize that sexual sin is a beast that grows in direct proportion to how much it is fed. The more the man gives over to sin, the more it demands. "... now is 'the acceptable time,' behold, now is 'the day of salvation.'" (II Corinthians 6:2) The longer a person puts off repentance, the less likely he is to ever come to repent of his sin.

"I've tried to quit. I've tried to follow the steps this book outlines. Nothing changes. I'm just as addicted as I have ever been." Many men who have vacillated between their love for God and their love of sin have honestly believed that they have done everything they could to find freedom, but it just did not work. Those who are honest with themselves realize they have only made half-hearted attempts at changing. They might try to convince themselves that they really tried but the truth is that they did not.

Tim was an example of this. He had a wealth of biblical "head knowledge" and knew the truth. When I told him that he needed to faithfully put the principles of this book into his daily life, he insisted that he had, but to no avail. He left Pure Life Ministries having convinced himself that he needed special therapy to "work through this." After wasting a couple of years, he humbly came back to us, although he returned in worse condition than when he had left. It was then that he admitted he had never really tried doing things God's way. Initially he had deceived himself into believing what he wanted to believe.

"God understands that I am a man and that I have natural passions.

Masturbation is God's provision for me until I get married." Some of the leading Christian psychologists in the nation have said that masturbation is a normal function that, unless carried on into marriage, usually proves to be harmless.* I believe this was said in order to alleviate some of the guilt and condemnation associated with it. However, something cannot be condoned because it makes people feel guilty. It may be normal for fallen man to masturbate, but that does not make it acceptable in the eyes of a holy God! These natural passions are called "the lusts of the flesh." As we will discover later in this book, the Lord has graciously given us answers to help us to overcome such carnal desires.

God does not, nor will He ever, condone the carnal and selfish gratification of masturbation. He created sexuality as a way for two married people to express love for one another and to enjoy mutual satisfaction. Sex outside of this context becomes something sordid and dirty. For instance, what is a person thinking about when he is masturbating? Masturbation revolves around lust and fantasy, neither of which God approves. Furthermore, it is masturbation that opens the door to further bondage. To attempt to justify it spiritually is just more self-deception.

NUMBER FIVE: THE TIGHTENING OF THE CHAIN

"That is why God let go of them and let them do all these evil things... as a result, getting paid within their souls with the penalty they so richly deserved."

As a person continues in pursuit of sexual fantasy, he finds that each sin he becomes involved in will eventually lose the power to satisfy him. As he repeatedly indulges himself in his

* One even suggested that adolescent acts of homosexuality are also "normal."

particular routine, the level of temptation is less pronounced because the sinful act loses its ability to gratify him. Once he has given over to the impurity of lust, nothing will be able to keep him satisfied. He will plunge from one depth of darkness to the next until he is eventually saturated in despicable behavior. Sin is tightening its grip.

First, the addict increasingly desires more of one specific activity. It may be fornication, adultery, masturbation, and so on. As the initial sex act begins to lose its thrill, the addict will attempt to maintain the high level of excitement he is accustomed to achieving by increasing the frequency of his behavior. Each time he goes back for more, the clutches of sin are strengthened. The more he does it, the more he wants it.

Eventually, however, repetition will not be enough to keep the man interested. He will begin to crave something darker, more degrading, more forbidden, and more evil. He becomes driven to recapture the exuberance he once felt in the beginning of his sin. Undaunted by any fear of consequences, his only aim is pleasure.

Whereas he was once gratified looking at *Playboy,* he now finds himself drawn to hard core pornography. Perhaps he may have even cringed at the thought of homosexuality, but he now finds himself drawn to it. The thought of his wife sleeping with another man repulsed him at one time, now he finds himself fantasizing about it. As the person crosses the barrier of fantasy and enters into actual behavior he discovers that he views things differently. He will eventually begin to have thoughts that are directly opposed to what he knows to be right. For instance, he might actually start thinking that most women really do want immoral sex but are just inhibited by the constraints of society. Once a person reaches this point, his life quickly begins to be governed almost exclusively by his sin. He no longer can be counted on to make sound decisions and his life is likely to quickly unravel. Sinful pleasure now dominates his mind.

Consequently, he is getting paid within his soul the penalty he so richly deserves.

NUMBER SIX: GIVEN OVER

"So it was that when they gave God up and would not even acknowledge Him, God gave them up to doing everything their evil minds could think of..."

One of the terrifying realities about this being, Jehovah, that we serve, is that He will give people what they have shown they desire. This can be seen over and over again in Scripture. Consider the time the Hebrews were wandering in the wilderness. God was trying to reveal His marvelous ways to them, but instead they repeatedly demanded to have the carnal lifestyle of Egypt. They did not want to be delivered from the darkness of Egypt until they had paid the price of slavery. But even then, they only remembered their time in the country of the Nile with fondness instead of with horror. They longed for the "flesh pots" of Egypt. "Oh that someone would give us meat to eat. For we were well-off in Egypt... Why did we ever leave Egypt?" (Numbers 11: 18, 20)

After having endured this attitude for so long, God finally became angry and said, "You shall eat, not one day, nor two days, nor five days, nor ten days, nor twenty days, but a whole month, until it comes out of your nostrils and becomes loathsome to you; because you have rejected the LORD...'" (Numbers 11:19-20) They were given exactly what they wanted. God is extremely longsuffering with His people, but a time will come, if they continue to resist His promptings and insist on sinning, that He will give them over to what they desire. Three times in this chapter in Romans we find the words, "God gave them over..."

This phrase is a translation of the Greek word *paradidomai*, which literally means to betray or give someone up. We find it used in the words Judas spoke to the high priest when he said, "What are you willing to give me to *deliver Him up to you?*" (Matthew 26:15) Jesus used the same word when describing the persecution of the last days, "Then they will *deliver you* to tribulation..." (Matthew 24:9) The exact meaning of this word, as used in the context of Romans chapter 1 is this: If you insist on having your sin, the time will come when God will surrender you up to the power of the enemy.

The picture being painted here is of a traitor being left to the enemy to fend for himself. The person having deserted the Lord, actually finds *himself* to be the deserted one. What the apostle is illustrating is not so much the action of one handing another over, but rather the withdrawing of one's protection over another. In the case of the believer, God withdraws the grace to keep him from sin. More than most realize, the Lord keeps people restrained from plunging themselves into unfathomable sin by His grace. Rejected once too often, that protective grace is eventually withdrawn and the person is allowed to have what he has shown he truly wants. This does not mean that God has totally given up on him, but that the Holy Spirit's conviction no longer affects him. His mind no longer thinks sanely; his thinking has become twisted. He finds himself doing things that are literally insane because his mind has become depraved.

NUMBER SEVEN: FILLED WITH ALL UNRIGHTEOUSNESS

> "They were fully aware of God's death penalty for these crimes, yet they went right ahead and did them anyway..."

Left to himself, the sinner hurls himself into sin. Burning with an intense flame of lust, he finds himself no longer able to restrain himself. Deeper and deeper he sinks into the foul cesspool of depravity. Nothing is too gross, shameful, or forbidden. The cup of iniquity is now full. Sin has been given complete reign over the man's mind. Rather than overflowing with the love of Jesus, the man finds himself brimming over with depravity. The only thing that keeps him in check is whatever fear he might still retain for God, the law, or the possible loss of loved ones.

Having reached this place, he finds himself enjoying the company of others who live in the same degradation. They have their filthy desires in common. They not only enjoy each other's company, but give hearty approval to the degrading acts of others. They all have found a way to rationalize their lifestyles. Swingers talk about how they have the "courage" to step out and have some fun, while the rest of society is too inhibited. Homosexuals convince each other that they were born "that way." Pedophiles claim that children have minds of their own and have the right to decide whether or not they want to have sex. They surround themselves with others who will help them escape responsibility for their sin and support their ways of thinking. They have all gone over the edge. Their minds have become depraved and their consciences seared. They have allowed darkness to rule their lives; thus they are filled with all unrighteousness.

This entire section of Scripture is a giant arrow pointed downward. Jesus said, "Truly, truly, I say to you, everyone who commits sin is the slave of sin." (John 8:34) Paul said, "Do you not know that when you present yourselves to someone as slaves for obedience, you are slaves of the one whom you obey, either of sin resulting in death, or of obedience resulting in righteousness?" (Romans 6:16) Solomon said, "His own iniquities will capture the wicked, and he will be held with the cords of his sin." (Proverbs 5:22) And the Psalmist said, "There were those who dwelt in darkness and in the shadow of death, prisoners in misery and chains, because they had rebelled against the words of God, and spurned the counsel of the Most High." (Psalms 107:10-11)

Could there be a more terrible picture of slavery than that of the believer who worships the idol of sensuality inwardly and serves its lusts outwardly? There is no slavery worse than that of lust. It is impossible to satisfy its demands. Sin is never satisfied.

three

THE FOUR PRIMARY MOTIVES

SOLOMON GIVES US FOUR MOTIVES for illicit sex. In this chapter we will examine each of these in detail.

NUMBER ONE: THE FORBIDDEN

The woman of folly is boisterous, she is naive, and knows nothing. And she sits at the doorway of her house, on a seat by the high places of the city, calling to those who pass by, who are making their paths straight: "Whoever is naive, let him turn in here," and to him who lacks understanding she says, "Stolen water is sweet; and bread eaten in secret is pleasant." But he does not know that the dead are there, that her guests are in the depths of Sheol. (Proverbs 9:13-18)

In this passage of Scripture, Solomon gives us an excellent illustration of the first motive: the forbidden. He shows us a prostitute sitting in the doorway to lure unsuspecting men. Solomon tells us that the simple will be caught in her trap. The Hebrew word used for simple here is *peti*. According to scholars: "The basic verb idea is to 'be open, spacious, wide,' and might relate to the immature or simple one who is open to all kinds of enticement, not having developed a discriminating judgment as to what is right or wrong."[1] This accurately describes the way I once was. I was always *open* to try new experiences regardless of the dangers or possible consequences involved. If it was forbidden, it was all the better.

One of the most captivating features of illicit sex is its forbidden nature. Seemingly, the more forbidden it is, the more alluring it tends to be. This is one reason why a married Christian man addicted to sex feels the need to be with other women. He is not supposed to. It is "off-limits." Thus, for the Christian who feels pressured to live a righteous life and is constantly struggling to resist the demands of his flesh, it can be overwhelmingly irresistible because of this. Desiring that which is forbidden is part of man's fallen nature. Just try leaving a four-year old alone in a room with a box that he has been told not to open!

Genesis tells of Eve being tempted to eat fruit from the one tree that was forbidden by God. Apparently because it was prohibited, it was more desirable. Such is the case with sex, the more forbidden, the more desired. This is one of the things that excites a man. If he knows, without a doubt, that he can have a woman, it will only be of ordinary excitement usually. However, if a certain woman teases him and then pretends that she is uninterested in going to bed with him, he becomes greatly aroused. The mere question in his mind about whether or not she will give in to him, is enough to keep him enthralled. Many people are prevented from pursuing "the forbidden" by morals, governmental law, or divine law. Otherwise, people would be unable to restrain themselves. Again this is all due to the fallen nature of man. This motivation especially comes into play with rapists, pedophiles (child molesters), those who take indecent liberties and voyeurs (peeping Toms).

The rapist, although motivated by a spirit of power and usually anger, desires to have that which is unlawful. He sees a woman walking down the street, and the idea of overpowering her, forcing her to do what he wants, excites him immensely. She has not consented for him to enjoy her charms. Instead, they are for the man of her choosing. The urge to take that which is unlawful, is a powerful, driving force in his life. Otherwise, he would simply pay a prostitute to let him overpower her. As this would dampen the excitement, he prefers to forcibly take what does not belong to him.

Ray was a convicted rapist. He admitted that he had raped several women before he was caught. The satisfaction of taking "ownership" over the women, even if for only but a short time, motivated him. None of these women were so gorgeous that he just *had* to have her nor was he so overly sexually aroused that he had to actually have sex with a woman. Rather, it was the heightened stimulation he experienced when pondering the thought of overpowering a woman and taking possession of her body. He simply wanted to enjoy what was strictly off-limits to him.

The pedophile's motives are slightly different than those of a rapist. He too seeks what is forbidden to him, but it is not the act of overpowering another that excites him. In fact, he will almost always attempt to gain what he wants by convincing, alluring, or bribing his victims. He is not interested in fighting for what he wants; he craves willing victims. His motive comes from having the most forbidden thing in our society: a child. He does not stop to examine his feelings. He does not take the time to determine why he is sexually drawn to a child. He just knows that he is. But why is he? Why would the flesh of a young girl excite him more than that of a perfectly developed woman? It is because it is forbidden. The younger the child, the more forbidden the act. This is the force which drives the pedophile.

The next type of addict enthralled with the forbidden, is the man who enjoys taking indecent liberties with women, especially in crowded places. He purposefully gets himself in positions of cramped quarters with women. It may be on a crowded bus or standing in a line. He will carefully time his arrival to coincide with that of a woman of his choosing. If he is lucky, the bus will turn sharply, and he will "accidently" brush up against her. He might even be brazen enough to position his hand so that it will touch some part of her body.

Finally, the most obvious seeker of the forbidden is the voyeur. He will spend hours upon hours walking through neighborhoods looking for the perfect window to peer into hoping to get an "eyeful." Just a glimpse of flesh is well worth his wait.

Take Bob, for instance. He would drive around at night looking for potential windows. What excited him most was being able to watch someone in their normal activities unbeknownst to them. The anticipation of seeing someone undress or have sex would keep him stationed at the window. Why not simply go to a strip show? Bob too was mesmerized by the forbidden.

Number Two: Ego Fulfillment

To keep thee from the evil woman, from the flattery of the tongue of a strange woman. Lust not after her beauty in thine heart; neither let her take thee with her eyelids. For by means of a whorish woman a man is brought to a piece of bread: and the adulteress will hunt for the precious life... Can one go upon hot coals, and his feet not be burned? (Proverbs 6:24-28)

The second motivating factor associated with illicit sex is ego fulfillment. The attention of a beautiful woman can quickly spark the interests of almost any man. Women are often vulnerable to this enticement, as well. The man who visits prostitutes is often duped by this ploy of the devil. He does not consider the fact that prostitutes will only put on an act to get his money. He knows it subconsciously but does not care. He wants to be noticed. He likes to feel needed. He desires to feel like a real man. Thus, she is instrumental in flattering his ego, making him feel good and virile all at the same time—for a small fee of course. Though it is only an act, he is still willing to pay, simply because of the way she makes him feel.

For this sex addict, the prostitute reinforces his grandiose thinking of "being someone special that people just do not understand." In reality, deep inside he feels very inferior and overcompensates for this by playing himself up to be more than he is. The flattering words of a prostitute temporarily soothe his fragile ego. He feels better about himself for awhile: however, it is short-lived because it does not change the deep feelings of inferiority he has about himself. For a man who feels unlovable, a rendezvous with a sweet-talking prostitute is like a "quick fix" to boost his self-esteem.

The "Don Juan" type has somewhere in his past mistakenly come to believe that seducing women will make him feel better about himself. He imagines that "conquering" a woman will convince others how desirable he must be. I can remember countless times waking up the next morning with a new woman and feeling as though I was on top of the world. The actual sex act may have been only mediocre, but I had managed to possess her body with my charm. The woman-chaser feels that he has accomplished something significant, i.e. a notch-on-the-belt.

The woman in habitual sexual sin may go through her routine for a slightly different reason. She, like the womanizer, initiates her behavior in order to reinforce her sense of self-worth. The difference is that she is also attempting to satisfy the need to feel loved. She may or may not experience pleasure from sex. What is most important to her is to have an experience which makes her feel wanted as a woman. A case in point is Martha, who found herself in bed with men repeatedly. She had been raped and molested as a child and came to see herself as dirty and unworthy of real love. She felt her only worth as a human was to gratify men; so that is what she did. Deep inside, she was trying to gain self-acceptance by pleasing men. If she made them appreciate her, she somehow felt better about herself.

While women-chasers and "Johns" are the primary victims of the enticement of ego fulfillment, there are others who also fall victim. In their twisted thinking, a rapist, child molester or exhibitionist, will achieve ego fulfillment from their activity as they imagine their victims enjoying the experience. Pornographic movies showing girls who are being raped and who gradually begin to enjoy it may reinforce or cause some men to justify their perverted behavior. They assume that their victims will respond in like manner—resisting initially but eventually enjoying what is being done to them.

There is one more person who is seduced by the enemy into this lie of ego-fulfillment. This person is not even a sex addict and can have a seemingly wonderful relationship with God and be unaware that she is experiencing this problem. I am referring to the average girl who has become "addicted" to the trap of being noticed by men. Women today are under tremendous pressure by our society (through the media and the advertisers) to look alluring, sexy, and attractive to men. They compete with each other to look fashionable and to attract the stares of men. What is especially a shame is that such competitiveness runs rampant in the Church today. It is shocking sometimes to see what Christian girls wear. Unfortunately, they have allowed the world to infringe upon or even replace their own morals because of the strong desire to acquire attention from men. Illicit sex and attention from the opposite sex never have and never will fulfill an individual's primary needs. Only by accepting oneself as God accepts us, will one truly experience a sense of self-worth. This comes as we learn to love God and love others.

Frank Worthen writes:

> The image we hold of ourselves is of vital importance to the change process. It is, however, interwoven with our image of God and of others. Until we have a personal relationship with God, loving and trusting Him, we can never relate well to others. We will have no real love to share. Only when we love God and share His love can we feel right about ourselves. In a sense, our self image is the result of a filtering down process.[2]

NUMBER THREE: REWARDING ONESELF

> I said to myself, "Come now, I will test you with pleasure. So enjoy yourself." And behold, it too was futility....
>
> Also, I collected for myself... many concubines. Then I became great and increased more than all who preceded me in Jerusalem. My wisdom also stood by me. And all that my eyes desired I did not refuse them. I did not withhold my heart from any pleasure, for my heart was pleased because of all my labor and this was my reward for all my labor. Thus I considered all my activities which my hands had done and the labor which I had exerted, and behold all was vanity and striving after wind and there was no profit under the sun. (Ecclesiastes 2:1, 8-11)

The third motive for illicit sexual activity is to reward oneself. There are several things that will initiate an addict's decision to move toward his place of sin. One contributing factor is the feeling of justification that comes as the addict tells himself that he deserves to have some fun. For the person who gets temporary fulfillment out of compulsive behavior, it is easy to use this excuse as a reward. In the past my wife would justify her struggle with compulsive spending.

She would tell herself that she had worked hard all week and that she deserved to treat herself to a new dress. "After all, why am I working at all if I can't enjoy the money?" she would ask. (What she did not consider were the credit card bills and the debt she currently owed for such gifts to herself. She would simply dismiss it as "just another bill.")

Let us examine Solomon who did many great and wonderful things with the kingdom he inherited. It was God who blessed Israel during that time, but Solomon effectively managed its affairs. David brought Israel into power, but Solomon brought the nation into prominence. He not only brought her to a position of economic greatness, but he constructed the temple of God. As he looked at his great accomplishments, he convinced himself that he deserved a reward. His first mistake was to take credit for God's work. Rather than being grateful to God for all the wonderful things He had done, Solomon took credit for those blessings himself. He dishonored God, robbing Him of the glory that belonged only to the Lord. Next, he began lusting after the foreign women living in Israel. He entertained "futile speculations" and dove into the world of fantasy. As he allowed his fantasies to take control of his mind, darkness was ushered into his heart. Consequently, he rewarded himself by taking hundreds of foreign wives and concubines which was outlawed by God. He knew it to be wrong, but justified it in his mind by telling himself that he deserved them. As a result, Solomon experienced the spiral of degradation described in the previous chapter.

No one deserves sin. Sin is not something to be deserved or desired, but is something to avoid at all cost. God blesses obedience and richly gives rewards as He sees fit. In fact, He takes great pleasure in rewarding His children when they obey Him. To seek one's own reward, especially to satisfy one's sinful lust, will only heap trouble upon oneself.

NUMBER FOUR: VARIETY

My son, attend unto my wisdom, and bow thine ear to my understanding: that thou mayest regard discretion, and that thy lips may keep knowledge. For the lips of a strange woman drop as an honeycomb, and her mouth is smoother than oil: but her end is bitter as wormwood, sharp as a twoedged sword. Her feet go down to death; her steps take hold on hell... And why wilt thou, my son, be ravished with a strange woman, and embrace the bosom of a stranger? (Proverbs 5:1-5, 20)

The fourth motive for illicit sexual activity is variety. Solomon compares the lips of a strange woman to honey and smooth oil. Why does he make so much of the beauty of a strange woman? It is probably because she is different. God instilled in us a natural attraction toward the opposite sex, but we can defile it by our sin. Solomon's life told of this motive:

Now King Solomon loved many foreign women along with the daughter of Pharaoh: Moabite, Ammonite, Edomite, Sidonian, and Hittite women, from the nations concerning which the LORD had said to the sons of Israel, "You shall not associate with them, neither shall they associate with you, for they will surely turn your heart away after their gods." Solomon held fast to these in love. And he had seven hundred wives, princesses, and three hundred concubines, and his wives turned his heart away. (I Kings 11:1-3)

A person's desire for variety often manifests itself through obsessive behavior. One never becomes satisfied, as proven by the excesses of Solomon's life. I can remember once spending all night with two girls, and not fifteen minutes after leaving them the next morning, I spotted a prostitute that I was drawn to and bought her services—I had not had my fill of pleasure.

Anyone addicted to variety will never become satisfied. Each pornographic movie will be exciting only until it has been "captured" or somehow experienced, allowing the novelty to dwindle. These same feelings could be said of the "Don Juan" who wants to conquer women. Each one will be used until he has finished with her, and then he will search for new adventures.

Variety is probably the biggest lie Satan gives for illicit activity. When I was in my life of sin I would become obsessed with the thought of a certain type of girl, a blond for instance. After I would seduce one, and had experienced her enough to be "satisfied," I would find myself mesmerized with the thought of a different type of girl, maybe a tall brunette. After I would seduce a brunette, I would be back to thinking about blondes, or redheads, or whoever. I continued to be deceived, believing that if I could just have one particular type of girl, I would be satisfied. In reality, I was never satisfied nor would I ever have been. Variety is undoubtedly the primary reason for most illicit sexual behavior. The world promotes variety as the spice of life. I say it is an empty lie from Satan.

four

THE NEED TO LIVE IN THE LIGHT

TIM HAD BEEN THE YOUTH PASTOR of a thriving Baptist church for six years when allegations surfaced that he had been sexually involved with one of the high school girls in his youth group. When Pastor Thomas confronted him about such accusations, Tim admitted that they were true, and tearfully asked the church leadership for forgiveness. The pastor went on to question him further about other possible incidents with girls in the church. Tim sincerely denied that there were any other relationships. The church board accepted his apology at face value and decided that exposing Tim's sin to the congregation was unnecessary. It was dismissed as temporary weakness in the face of temptation, and Tim was allowed to remain as the youth pastor.

Close to three years later more incidents began to come to light. Once again, the pastor confronted Tim with the information he had received. And again Tim (just as before) admitted only to that on which he was questioned. This time, Pastor Thomas asked him to resign his position. Upon his request, he was allowed to make a statement to the congregation at a church business meeting. Because the charming young minister painted such a wrenching, yet believable, picture of contrition, the church immediately voted to continue his salary as he went through a process of restoration and counseling. However, it was discovered later that even during this period of rehabilitation Tim continued having sexual encounters with other teenage girls.

Henry ran one of the most successful drug rehabilitation ministries in the country. He was very articulate and had a natural ability to conduct himself in a professional manner. Charismatic and brimming with confidence, he was a picture of the new leadership rising up in the Church of the nineties. Unbeknownst to those around him, he was regularly visiting prostitutes and having sexual relationships with women in his community.

Keith, a third generation Pentecostal minister, was one of the promising young preachers of his denomination. He had such an ability to touch people emotionally that he was constantly in demand as a speaker. Everyone loved Keith. Even the superintendent of his denominational district took him under his wing as his personal protege. If he had been aware of Keith's secret life, things would have been quite different. After most of his speaking engagements, Keith would "reward" himself at the local massage parlor. He had also began to drink, carrying a flask around with him wherever he went. His wife knew of his secret life but covered for him in fear of damaging their reputation within the denomination.

These stories represent a massive underworld that is currently thriving within the realm of American Christianity. A recent survey taken by *Promise Keepers* revealed that sixty-five percent of the men questioned reported the regular usage of pornography.[1] I suspect this large percentage reflects the fact that men struggling with sexual sin tend to be drawn to *Promise Keepers*. Nevertheless, sexual sin is undoubtedly a problem of enormous proportions in the body of Christ, and is usually unreported. There are numerous reasons why these men keep their sin hidden.

First, sexual sin is shameful to admit. In our society, a person can be glorified for being a "Don Juan," but just about any other sexual behavior that is out of control is looked upon with suspicion and even disdain. If a man admits his struggles to his pastor, from that day he wonders what his pastor thinks of him. "Is he thinking I'm weird? Is he concerned about me being around the teenagers, or worse, the children? Was that sermon about lust aimed at me? Has he told others in the church about my problem?" These concerns make it difficult for the struggling believer to confide in his pastor, let alone others in the church.

Secondly, even though our society does not consider fornication or even adultery to be shameful, these sins are considered big "no-nos" in the evangelical movement. A woman can have a terrible habit of spreading gossip in the church, a man can be obsessed with his work at the expense of his family, or someone can be extremely critical of those around them, but these, as well as many other sins, are overlooked in the Church. However, if a man admits to committing adultery, he is instantly judged as someone who is far from God. Although that is probably the truth, there is certainly a double standard within the body of Christ.

Another factor that contributes to a man keeping his sin covered, is that it is fairly easy to live a double life of outward religion and secret sexual sin. Unlike alcohol or drug abuse, a man can maintain an outwardly normal life without being discovered. There is a lifestyle that goes with getting high. Drugs and alcohol affect a person's ability to function. Most are unable to keep this kind of a habit secret. But with sexual addiction, a man can be a president, a celebrity, even a famous evangelist, and still maintain an outward facade of respectability.

WHEN THE INWARD AND OUTWARD DO NOT LINE UP

We all have an inside world that is made up of the different parts of our inner man: the heart, soul, mind, spirit, will, intellect and emotions. It is the life that goes on inside of us: our thoughts, feelings, attitudes, sentiments and opinions. This is where dreams are born and failures grieved, the place where intricate processes are put into motion and life's decisions are contemplated. Here we also find the conflicting emotions of love and hate, like and dislike, attraction and repulsion. Our inside world is where we live our daily existence. Some people are considered "open" because they are not afraid to show their thoughts and feelings with other people. Others are thought to be "closed," feeling anxious when people become too intimate. Regardless of how willing a person is to talk about his feelings, the truth is, he will never completely allow another to intimately know the deepest part of his inner man. This is an extremely private place, an inner sanctum—a holy of holies, so to speak.

The outward life stands in contrast to the inside world. This is how we speak and act in front of other people. We all have an image which we attempt to maintain—a way in which we want other people to view us. One person might want to be seen as someone who is intellectual and cultured. Another might want to portray himself as being tough, while yet another will want to be seen as sweet. The impressions we wish to project are woven into everything we say and do in the presence of other people.

The tendency to project ourselves the way we want others to view us also carries over into the spiritual life where we encounter the overwhelming temptation to make ourselves appear in a favorable light. If we are Christians surrounded by other Christians, we tend to project ourselves as being "spiritual." Why? In Christian circles, looking "spiritual" is what causes others to admire and respect us. For someone to admit fault, defeat or (horror of horrors) flagrant sin, would be to admit to being a failure at Christianity.

Because Jesus understood the fears people wrestle with, He took the time to address this issue one day. Turning to His closest followers, He gave them this sober warning:

> "Beware of the leaven of the Pharisees, which is hypocrisy. But there is nothing covered up that will not be revealed, and hidden that will not be known. Accordingly, whatever you have said in the dark shall be heard in the light, and what you have whispered in the inner rooms shall be proclaimed upon the housetops. And I say to you, My friends, do not be afraid of those who kill the body, and after that have no more that they can do. But I will warn you whom to fear: fear the One who after He has killed has authority to cast into hell; yes, I tell you, fear Him!" (Luke 12:2-5)

We all have, to some degree, a fear of what other people think of us. I suppose it begins on the playground where kids can be so cruel to one another. The fear is deepened during the awkward teenage years and becomes embedded during adulthood. Jesus says that we must overcome these fears and instead concentrate our fears upon God, "the One who after He has killed has authority to cast into hell; yes, I tell you, fear Him!" In other words, we should be more concerned about the reality of our inward spiritual condition than how we look outwardly in the eyes of man.

The conflict between the way we present ourselves outwardly and the way we live our lives inwardly is a predominant theme in Scripture. Paul said, "For he is not a Jew who is one outwardly; neither is circumcision that which is outward in the flesh. But he is a Jew who is one inwardly; and circumcision is that which is of the heart, by the Spirit, not by the letter; and his praise is not from men, but from God." (Romans 2:28-29) Peter told the Christian women of his day, "Your beauty should not come from outward adornment, such as braided hair and the wearing of gold jewelry and fine clothes. Instead, it should be that of your inner self, the unfading beauty of a gentle and quiet spirit, which is of great worth in God's sight." (I Peter 3:3-4 NIV) God said through the prophet Isaiah, "These people come near to me with their mouth and honor me with their lips, but their hearts are far from me. Their worship of me is made up only of rules taught by men." (Isaiah 29:13) And to the prophet Samuel He said, "God sees not as man sees, for man looks at the outward appearance, but the LORD looks at the heart." (I Samuel 16:7)

There are over two thousand direct references to the inner life in the Bible, but it is indirectly referred to on almost every page. It is clear that Scripture places an enormous emphasis on what goes on inside us. Many Christians today closely resemble the Pharisees, addressed by Jesus in Luke 11:39, who "...clean the outside of the cup and of the platter; but inside of (them, they) are full of robbery and wickedness." In essence, they ignore the importance of the inward life and choose to concentrate on presenting the most favorable outward appearance.

The Apostle John also observed this happening around him. In his first epistle, he said the following in regard to this dichotomy:

> If *we say* that we have fellowship with Him and yet walk in the darkness, we lie and do not practice the truth; but if we walk in the light as He Himself is in the light, we have fellowship with one another, and the blood of Jesus His Son cleanses us from all sin. If *we say* that we have no sin, we are deceiving ourselves, and the truth is not in us. If we confess our sins, He is faithful and righteous to forgive us our sins and to cleanse us from all unrighteousness. If *we say* that we have not sinned, we make Him a liar, and His word is not in us. (I John 1:6-10)

	What we say	What we do	Results or reality of situation
vs. 6	we have fellowship with Him	walk in darkness	we lie; do not practice truth
vs. 7	----------------	walk in light	we have fellowship; blood of Jesus cleanses us
vs. 8	we have no sin	deceive ourselves	truth is not in us
vs. 9	confess our sin	----------------	He forgives and cleanses us
vs. 10	we have not sinned	make Him a liar	The word is not in us

Figure 4-1

In the chart above, we can see a breakdown of those verses in John's epistle. There are three categories. The first, *what we say*, is simply what we convey to those around us. The second classification is *what we do*. Our actions speak of our true condition, what we are really like. The third category describes the *result*, the consequence of what we say and what we do. When a person blameshifts, minimizes or conceals his sin, the message he sends to those around him is that he has no sin. Of course, he may never actually say the words, "I have no sin." He simply tries to convince others of his innocence by masking it or minimizing it. When John wrote these words he was simply referring to all Christians. Everyone certainly has some degree of sin—no one is exempt. Those who are in unrepentant sexual sin are all the more guilty of hypocrisy because their sin is much deeper than that of the average believer.

John clearly shows us how vitally important it is to bring our sin into the "light" through open confession. The Greek word for confession, *homologeo*, literally means "to be of one mind, to bring oneself into agreement with another." Whether or not we acknowledge, to ourselves or to others, that our sin is present, it still exists and God sees it. When we confess our sin, or "walk in the light," the blood of Christ graciously cleanses us from guilt, and we come into fellowship with the believer we opened up to. It is not enough for a person to come to grips with his sin. He must come into the light with others. Darkness is the devil's domain. Those who refuse to come into the light about their sin are choosing to remain in darkness.

EXPOSURE

The Christian who thinks he can continue hiding his sin will eventually discover that God loves him too much to allow him to remain bound to his secret sin. It may become evident in his speech (Proverbs 12:13), by his leering at girls (Matthew 6:23) or his mannerisms. At some point, his secret life will be exposed to those around him. Jesus promised this when He said, "For nothing is hidden that shall not become evident, nor anything secret that shall not be known and come to light." (Luke 8:17)

Tom was a pastor of a small church in Iowa. He was also addicted to pornography and often frequented prostitutes in a nearby city. It became increasingly difficult for him to lead this double life. People respected him as their spiritual leader, and yet there were times when the filth of his mind was quite obvious to others. Because he was watching pornographic movies regularly, he was well accustomed to their sexual language. Once, while amongst some of the church women, he dropped a dish, which shattered when it hit the floor, and before he knew it, he had uttered a curse word. On another occasion, his eyes followed a scantily dressed girl as she walked by, and when he turned back around he discovered one of his deacons observing him.

The Christian who is involved in sexual sin will only be able to hide his true identity for so long. God has been known to bring humiliation upon one of His children in order to get his attention. If He feels that He needs to do so, He will. He is very patient and gentle with us, but He loves us too much to leave us in our sin.

This was the case for a minister who was having an

adulterous affair with one of the women in his church. One day he was talking to his girlfriend on his office telephone. They were having a sexual conversation when somehow, without him being aware of it, he accidently flipped on the intercom button. The whole conversation ended up being piped throughout the church. Later, he was able to look back and see how God had repeatedly tried to get his attention, but to no avail.

Another man's sin, who was a deacon in a large church, was discovered in an entirely unforeseeable way. His church was filming a short documentary on teenage runaways. As they filmed one of the girls posing as a prostitute for the movie, this man drove up to solicit her. Imagine his surprise and utter embarrassment when he found out that the entire youth group of his church saw that movie.

Needless to say, God will use any method to get one's attention—even public humiliation. God will not strive with man forever!

THE DECEPTION OF SEXUAL SIN

People are prone to overlook their deeply embedded sin because it has an extremely deceptive nature. There exists an interesting correlation between a person's involvement with sin and his awareness of it. The more a person becomes involved in sin, the less he sees it. Sin is a hideous disease that destroys a person's ability to comprehend its existence. It could be compared to a computer virus that has the ability to hide its presence from the user while it systematically destroys the hard drive. Typically, those who are the most entangled in sin are the very ones who cannot see its presence at work inside them. Sin has the ability to mask itself so well that it can actually make the person who deals with it the least, think he is the most spiritual.

On the other hand, the more a person overcomes sin in his life and draws closer to God, the more glaringly his *nature of sin* stands out. God "dwells in unapproachable light" (I Timothy 6:16) and so consequently, every remnant of selfishness, pride, and sin is going to be exposed to the sincere seeker. The intense, brilliant light of God exposes what is in a person's heart. Those who want to draw near to Him rejoice because of this. They love the Light and so they embrace it, even though it means their true selves will be unmasked. Jesus said, "And this is the judgment, that the light is come into the world, and men loved the darkness rather than the light; for their deeds were evil. For everyone who does evil hates the light, and does not come to the light, lest his deeds should be exposed. But he who practices the truth comes to the light, that his deeds may be manifested as having been wrought in God." (John 3:19-21)

If an individual who is bound by sexual sin hopes to turn his life around, it is crucial that he comes into the light with "the sin which doth so easily beset" him, so that he may finally "lay aside every weight" and walk in victory through Jesus Christ. (Hebrews 12:1)

If it appears that I am promoting the idea that one should walk around berating himself or beating himself down, nothing could be further from the truth. I am however, advocating the need for a person to come into reality about where he is spiritually. His only hope is to have something real in God. Keeping himself hyped up in a false sense of security will only keep him buried under the burden of unconfessed sin, which in turn will further the delusion about his spirituality.

On the back of the application for the Pure Life Live-In Program for sexual addicts is the following:

Please rate yourself on a scale of 1 to 10 in the following areas ("10" being very godly and "1" being very carnal):

Loving others___ Relationship to God___ Prayer Life___ Obedience___ Humility___ Generosity___ Kindness___ Joy___ Self-Discipline___ Zeal___ Maturity___ Honesty___

Men who come to us for help are often struggling with the deepest perversions imaginable. With this in mind, it would probably surprise you to see how they rate themselves spiritually. Typically, the applicants rate themselves fairly high on everything except self-discipline. It is not uncommon to see six's, seven's, and even eight's across the board in their self-evaluation. How can this be? The majority of them come into the program thinking of themselves as being fairly godly people with only "one small problem."

It takes months of patient work on the part of our counselors to help a man see that he is not as godly as he has thought he was and that there is much work to be done in his life. It is only then that his hardened heart begins to soften, and he finally sees his need for the Lord. The attitude he entered the program with, that he was fairly godly with only one small problem, gradually dissipates, and we can begin to help him. Why is it so important for him to come to this realization? If he believes that he is in fairly good shape spiritually, he will not see his need to change, grow, mature, or even repent. We have occasionally had to ask men who have come to the program with such an attitude, "If you're so godly and have it so together, why are you here?" This question is not meant to insult them, but it quickly brings them into some sort of reality; humility is now produced so that we can begin to lead them onto the path of victory.

LIVING IN THE LIGHT

Being honest is an extremely important issue for the man struggling with sexual sin. Honesty begins with examining one's own heart, thought life, and actions. In this process, the man who wants God will humble and brace himself for the unavoidable conclusion: "I am not nearly as godly as I imagined myself to be. If I'm ever going to change, I must quit fooling myself and others. I am where I am, spiritually. Keeping an inflated perspective of my spirituality is only hindering any real growth. The truth is that my heart is full of wickedness. My thinking has become increasingly warped. I have hurt God and my family by my actions. I need to repent." Being brutally honest with oneself is crucial, but it is only the beginning. One man who had been convicted for attempted rape but later struggled his way out of sexual addiction said, "If you don't want to get rid of the problem, confess it only to God. If you want to get rid of the problem, confess it to another person. And if you *really* want to get rid of the problem, keep yourself accountable!" Yet another man who is now living in victory said, "I confessed my sin to God for years. I mean I poured my heart out, begging for His forgiveness, but it was within weeks of starting to confess to another brother, that I obtained victory!"

A man who is struggling needs to be honest with himself and at least one other person. That person should be a godly Christian who is strong in the Word. He should also be the kind of man who is willing to lovingly confront the confessor about his sin as well as encourage him in his growth in righteousness. The pastor of a Bible believing, preaching, practicing church would be a good place to start.

There is great healing in confession (James 5:16), and it only benefits a person in his commitment to change. Just knowing that there is someone who is aware of his secret life and is exhorting him toward victory is a tremendous help. Solomon said, "He who conceals his transgressions will not prosper, but he who confesses and forsakes them will find compassion." (Proverbs 28:13)

One thing that tends to exacerbate the problem further is that sexual addicts are very prone to isolating themselves from other people. As we will discover later, fantasy plays a huge part in their daily lives. This keeps them in a closed-in world of extreme self-centeredness. Breaking out of that isolation is a key step toward coming out of the darkness of sexual sin.

The double life must be dismantled no matter what. Satan knows the power he has within secrecy. The man who wants to remain in his sin avoids exposure at all cost. However, the man who is serious about overcoming it, exposes his sin so that he is less likely to succumb to the temptations when they arise later. Living in a double life prevents a solid foundation of godliness from being formed. James said that the double minded man is "unstable in all of his ways." (James 1:8) He will never experience real spiritual stability.

I have heard people tell me many times that they do not have anyone to confess to. What they were really saying is that they themselves were not desperate enough to seek out someone that might be able to assist them. As mentioned earlier, if a man is determined to break free from the hold of sexual sin, he will do whatever it takes. Making oneself transparent to another person is one of the difficult things that *must* be done. A man may institute all of the other steps outlined in this book into his life, but if he hedges on this one, all other efforts might prove to have been in vain.

We must ask the question of the ninth chapter: "How much do you care?" When you get to the place that you are truly sick of the sin in your life, will you be willing to do *anything*, even making yourself vulnerable to another person? What could stop you? Only the desire to save face, to save reputation, and protect self. *Real deliverance from sexual sin can never be possible until the heart is opened up and exposed.* Glossing over, hiding and masking one's true inner person will only keep oneself locked into darkness.

Find someone in your church to open up to. If you do not know who would be best, go to your pastor and explain to him that you want to make yourself accountable to someone and ask him for guidance to identify who would be most trustworthy. You will find that on-going accountability will prove to be a very important step in the overcoming process.

Secondly, if you are a married man it is important to open up to your wife. I have had men tell me that they could not bear to hurt their wives who are unaware of their problem. I only reply, "If you were all that concerned about your wife, you wouldn't have committed the sin in the first place. And not only that, but it's your sin that is hurting your wife. She may not know about it, but you are destroying your home because of it." Truthfully, the man is not concerned about hurting his wife as much as he is about making the painful confession to her of what he is really like. It is not the knowledge of the sin that is hurting the wife but the sin itself! In countless different ways, a person with illicit sex in his life hurts his loved ones. Yes, truth hurts, but it is far more preferable over sin when one compares the consequences of both. Hiding his sin is just another way that the self-centered lifestyle of a sexual addict manifests itself. In truth, he is far more concerned about the cost *he* will have to pay for his transparency than the possible harm done to his loved ones.

While it is important that a man opens up to his wife, she should *not* be his "accountability partner." Such a responsibility of sharing the details of his failures is asking too much of her. Primarily, he needs to bring the essence of the sin out in the open to her so that she is aware of his secret life. She will then be able to hold him accountable with his time and money. Once she is aware of his struggles, she will be much more alert to his schemes to acquire money or time for his sin. A godly wife, who will help her husband in this way, is priceless to the man who wants freedom.

True Biblical Accountability

As I mentioned before, bringing secret sin into the open is vital. But biblical accountability was never meant to be a group of men sitting in a circle discussing their failures. Such a setting may be somewhat helpful to men who need to bring their sin out into the open with others, but there is no power in such a situation to bring about their needed deliverance.

A person can only lead another spiritually as far as he has gone himself. Jesus said, "...if a blind man guides a blind man, both will fall into a pit." (Matthew 15:14) It is helpful to a certain extent to open up with other people about one's struggles. But there is a biblical principle that is far more powerful in its ability to change lives. What men greatly need is to be discipled. "What do you mean? I've read all the books on sexual addiction. I've heard the best sermons on Christian radio. I just need a little bit of accountability!"

It might surprise the reader to find out that the word "accountability" is not mentioned once in the Bible. The concept is in Scripture, but not in the weak way in which it is currently used today. Instead, the biblical concept is that of being discipled. I am not referring to receiving more information about Christianity. Listening to good sermons and reading interesting books can be helpful, but what the immature Christian needs most is for a mature saint to take him under his wing, so to speak, and bring godly instruction into his life. (This is what we do in the Pure Life Live-In Program.) The spiritual growth that is necessary for the man who is in the grip of sin will not come about by simply talking with other struggling men, nor will it come by acquiring more head knowledge on the subject. It only comes through true discipleship—Christ-centered discipleship.

Jesus had those occasions when He spoke to the multitudes, but He spent enormous amounts of time building spiritual character into the small group of men under His care. A man may hear sermons, but unless he is held accountable to respond to those words, he probably will not benefit from what was said. The man is lost in a crowd of listeners. He can ignore, disregard, even disagree with what he is hearing, and is never required to face the truth of what is being stated.

However, when a godly man dedicates himself to discipling the struggling Christian brother, something powerful happens.

Truth is imparted. Sin is dealt with head on. The mentor expects change. Most importantly, the man experiences firsthand someone who is walking in the light and confronting him. This is the biblical pattern for accountability. It seems that in the busy lifestyle Americans live, pastors no longer have the time to mentor men as they once did. Sin is running rampant in the Church because Christians can now live out their lives without any true accountability for their actions.

five

INSIDE THE MIND OF THE SEX ADDICT

THE TIME HAS COME for us to delve deeper into the mind of the sexual addict. To do this properly, we must examine once again the terrible yet accurate description of those who had been given over to lasciviousness presented to us in Romans chapter 1. In this section of Scripture, we are given eleven different aspects of the mind of the man in sexual sin. Before we discuss these in detail, let us take a quick glance at the list below.

1. vain in their imaginations; vs. 21
2. a darkened and foolish heart; vs. 21
3. thinking themselves to be wise, in reality foolish; vs. 22
4. trading the glory of God for an image; vs. 23
5. lusts of the heart; vs. 24
6. trading the truth of God for a lie; vs. 25
7. degrading passions; vs. 26
8. burning lust; vs. 27
9. a release of the knowledge of God; vs. 28
10. a depraved mind; vs. 28
11. inner man filled with all manner of wickedness; vss. 29-31

The corruption of the human mind does not necessarily happen in the exact order listed on the previous page; however, we will use the order Paul gave as a blueprint.

VAIN IMAGINATIONS

The imagination is one of the most fascinating and mysterious operations of the human mind. A person can be sitting in a prison cell, for instance, and take himself to any exotic location on the earth with his imagination. Physically he might be in a rat infested, dank, hole; but in his mind he can be sipping iced tea on a beach in Hawaii.

For the man given over to sexual sin, this imaginary life usually revolves around sex. In the world of sexual fantasy everything is always as he imagines it. The girl (or man) in the fantasy is extremely attractive. She acts exactly as he wants, and her only wish is to satisfy his every desire. The girl's features can be changed in an instant. One moment she is a tall blond. A few minutes later she becomes an exotic Oriental. Perhaps later she is a vivacious black girl. The variations are as numerous as the world's female population itself. Not only can the partner be changed instantly, so too, can the scenario. It may be the girl that he saw at the store that day "coming on to him." Later, it is his own personal harem. Again, the possibilities are endless.

In a man's world of imagination, everything is perfect. He does not have to deal with rejection. These dream girls all love him; none refuse to be with him. He never has to deal with impotence or nervousness either; everything goes smoothly. The girl is always flawless. There are no obnoxious odors, menstrual periods, diseases, or lack of interest. She does not act rudely, and she is not critical of him. She is not looking to take advantage of him or get his money. She will be willing to perform any desired sexual act because she lives to serve him. Finally, he does not need to worry about being caught by his wife or arrested by the authorities. In his perfect little dream world, nothing ever goes wrong.

What an ideal escape from the hardships of life! At any moment a man can be off in bed with the most beautiful women in the world. Why would he want to stay in reality where he is forced to deal with problems, difficulties, failures, and disappointments? One reason it is so easy to escape into one's imagination is because there are many painful consequences which accompany a life of sexual sin. The more pain a man must face because of his sin, the more he desires to escape reality by retreating into his secret little world.

Another aspect of the fantasy life is that SELF reigns supreme. In essence, everything revolves around the man's personal desires: i.e. what he wants, what he does not want, the way he likes it, the way he wants everything to go, and so on. When he returns to the world of reality, much to his dismay, he discovers that people are not concerned about him having everything his own way. Hence the dream world strengthens and fortifies a man's selfishness. The more he gives in to fantasy, the more selfish he becomes. As his self-centeredness increases he becomes further entrenched in the fantasy life where everything revolves around him. This creates numerous problems for him at home and in the workplace. Those around him suffer because of his growing self-centeredness. He shows little interest in loved ones, nor does he spend time with them as he should. When he *is* with them, his selfish nature can be so obnoxious and overbearing that they would prefer not to be around him.

Another devastating effect of the vain imagination is that it hinders God from being able to help him out of his dilemma with sexual addiction. As mentioned earlier, no one wants to step into the real world and deal with their problems and failures when they can choose to be locked safely away in a perfect world. As we will examine later, it is through the hardships of life that God disciplines a man into holiness. Even though correction is one of the sexual addict's greatest needs, the fantasy life makes the process of discipline seem absolutely unbearable. He is so accustomed to having his own way that the slightest crossing of his will seems overwhelming to him.

Bearing the load that comes with a wild, perverted imagination is an enormous burden. The sex addict does not realize the negative effect it has on his daily life. A fresh illustration of this comes to me from a scene I witnessed the other night. We had a wonderful, encouraging Thursday night meeting in the Pure Life chapel. After the meeting, two men, who had been assigned to straighten up the chapel, were stacking chairs. I was still seated on the platform, enjoying the lingering presence of God. One of them was about thirty and grossly overweight. The other was a physically fit young man of about twenty-two. The young man would grab a couple of chairs at a time and, in almost a sprint, energetically whisk them to where they belonged. However, the heavy-set man would pick up a chair with great effort and slowly make his way across the room with it, laboring every step of the way. Such is the case with the man who is bogged down with the weight of sexual sin. Even the smallest tasks that most people can routinely handle become extremely burdensome to him. His poor wife cannot comprehend why her husband is unable to spend a little time with their son. She does not understand this taxing load he is carrying around in life. All of his energy is being exhausted to maintain and to pursue his secret life. It is like a computer with eight megabytes of RAM trying to run a program which requires thirty-two megabytes. The inner strength and capability is simply not available.

Paul describes the imaginations of a man given over to sin as being "vain." They are as empty as the illusive mirages that deceive thirsty souls traveling through the desert, offering no benefit to a man's life. They are utterly worthless. In fact, they are worse. Not only are they devoid of any reality, but they also have the power to deplete a man's soul of anything that is of substance or value. The more a man gives himself over to a perverted thought life, the more his moral character rots from the inside out, leaving a great void inside. The term "light-weight" is often used to describe someone who lacks ability in a particular field of endeavor. And in much the same way, the man who continually succumbs to sexual sin becomes a spiritual "light-weight." Though he may possess a great deal of head knowledge concerning spiritual matters or have some extraordinary gift, there exists no spiritual substance *within* him. Merlin Carothers says this:

> There is something intriguing and mystifying about our ability to imagine things known and unknown. To God, that ability is sacred. He does not want it misused. And that is exactly why evil forces have an intense desire to see that ability misused. Our minds are the battleground; our imaginations are the trophy to be won.
>
> If we use our imaginative power to visualize anything that represents lust or impurity, we are in direct conflict with God's will. Men enjoy using the power of imagination to create a multitude of images that God has forbidden. For example, when a man sees a woman who is attractive to him, he can disrobe her in his mind, bit by bit, until she is completely undressed. He then can use his imagination to feel what it would be like to touch her body. He can continue this mental activity until he has experienced every possible sexual act. He has taken God's special, holy gift and consumed it upon the altar of lust...[1]

A DARKENED AND FOOLISH HEART

As the man continues to live a great part of his existence in the world of make-believe, lavishing upon himself every kind of pleasure, he soon discovers that fantasies about "normal" sexual activities become less appealing. Now he must search for something a little more perverse to hold his interest. The world of pornography, with all of its sordid stories of perversion, provide ample material from which he can choose from to satisfy his lustful desires. The depth and extent of deviancy in which he can delve into are limitless.

If one were to compare a person's inner workings to a computer, the heart would be the memory, the keyboard would be the senses that bring information into the computer, and the central processing unit would be the mind which completes all of the functions. The whole process begins when the man permits his mind to be flooded with perverted images and scenarios. Over time, the cumulative effects of this invasion take a toll on the man's heart. His memory banks are glutted with warped information. As a result, his infected heart, which is already wicked by nature, has now become even more diseased than in the beginning.

THE PRIDE OF INTELLECT

In the following verse Paul exposes the great delusion of the individuals who become immersed in evil, and yet consider themselves to be godly: "Professing to be wise, they became fools." It is interesting how this word *wise* (*sophos*) is used in other places in the New Testament: Jesus prayed, "I praise Thee, O Father, Lord of heaven and earth, that Thou didst hide these things from the wise and intelligent and didst reveal them to babes." (Matthew 11:25)

Paul reminded the Corinthian church:

> For it is written, "I will destroy the wisdom of the wise, and the cleverness of the clever I will set aside." Where is the wise man? Where is the scribe? Where is the debater of this age? Has not God made foolish the

wisdom of the world?... Because the foolishness of God is wiser than men, and the weakness of God is stronger than men. For consider your calling, brethren, that there were not many wise according to the flesh, not many mighty, not many noble; but God has chosen the foolish things of the world to shame the wise... (I Corinthians 1:19-20, 25-27)

Let no man deceive himself. If any man among you thinks that he is wise in this age, let him become foolish that he may become wise. For the wisdom of this world is foolishness before God. For it is written, "He is the One who catches the wise in their craftiness" and again, "The Lord knows the reasonings" of the wise, that they are useless. (I Corinthians 3:18-20)

There is a false wisdom that is outside of the knowledge of God which attracts people who are away from the Lord. It is called human intellectualism, and it is incubated by pride. As we will discuss later, pride and sexual sin are inextricably linked together. I mention it now because it plays such a major role in the process of mental degradation. Jesus thanked the Father that the truths of God were hidden from those who were wise in their own eyes. Only a humble heart can understand the true nature of God. Reading books, hearing sermons, and even studying the Bible for oneself will often only serve to increase a person's *mental* understanding of what God is like. However, unless he is in the Spirit in which the Word was given, he cannot truly know God. Unfortunately, many Christians, especially those in sexual sin, are mixed up about what it means to know God. They confuse information *about* Christianity with the heart knowledge of God which only comes to His humble, obedient servant. Hence, Paul writes, "Professing to be wise, they became fools," to explain that the more self-exalting people are in their thinking, the further away from God they become. This is perhaps the reason why an individual involved with something as evil as pornography can actually see himself as being godly.

THE FIRST EXCHANGE

When Paul said they "exchanged the glory of the incorruptible God for an image..." it seems he was making a direct reference to the temple in Jerusalem which, in Old Testament times, became the dwelling place of the glory of God. When Solomon dedicated the temple, we are told that "...when the priests came from the holy place, that the cloud filled the house of the LORD, so that the priests could not stand to minister because of the cloud, for the glory of the LORD filled the house of the LORD." (I Kings 8:10-11) What a glorious scene it must have been!

However, this all changed in New Testament times. The New Covenant teaches that the *inner man* is now the temple of God. In fact, Paul said, "Flee fornication. Every sin that a man doeth is without the body; but he that committeth fornication sinneth against his own body. What? know ye not that your body is the temple of the Holy Ghost which is in you, which ye have of God, and ye are not your own? For ye are bought with a price: therefore glorify God in your body, and in your spirit, which are God's." (I Corinthians 6:18-20 KJV) In other words, just as Solomon's temple was filled with God's *shekinah* glory, so too should one's inside world be a holy place where He is revered, worshipped and loved. It is what Jesus meant when He said, "You shall love the Lord your God with all your heart, and with all your soul, and with all your mind." (Matthew 22:37)

What happens when this temple becomes defiled with perverted thoughts and images? Paul says in Romans 1:23, "And changed the glory of the uncorruptible God into an image made like to corruptible man, and to birds, and fourfooted beasts, and creeping things," which alludes to something the Lord showed

Ezekiel. He was sitting in Babylon with the captives when the Lord whisked him away to Jerusalem, where many of the people of Israel were still living. This is the account Ezekiel gives when the Lord took him into the temple:

> "Go in, and behold the wicked abominations that they do here." So I went in and saw; and behold every form of creeping things, and abominable beasts, and all the idols of the house of Israel, portrayed upon the wall round about. And there stood before them seventy men of the ancients of the house of Israel, and in the midst of them stood Jaazaniah the son of Shaphan, with every man his censer in his hand; and a thick cloud of incense went up. Then said he unto me, "Son of man, hast thou seen what the ancients of the house of Israel do in the dark, every man in the chambers of his imagery? for they say, 'The LORD seeth us not; the LORD hath forsaken the earth.'" (Ezekiel 8:10-12 KJV)

The "chambers" of imagery which Ezekiel saw were simply ancient pornography. This is exactly what Paul was referring to when he said that men had exchanged God's glory for filthy images. When a Christian man introduces pornographic images into the temple of God there is an immediate, internal desecration that occurs. As much as some might attempt to minimize the effects that pornography has on a person's life (there are even some "Christian" psychologists who urge couples to enhance their marriage bed with it), the devastation it imposes on a person's inner life is immeasurable. This is why Paul reasoned with believers, "Do you not know that you are a temple of God, and that the Spirit of God dwells in you? If any man destroys the temple of God, God will destroy him, for the temple of God is holy, and that is what you are. Let no man deceive himself." (I Corinthians 3:16-18a)

LUSTS OF THE HEART

Lust and fantasy are both related to desire, which is the longing after something which appeals to a person. It is an expression of one's will—the part of one's inner self which dictates one's own inclinations in life. When someone says, "I will give $500 to the orphanage," he is expressing his determination to do what he *desires* to do; he *wants* to help that charity. Desire is birthed in a person's will. There is nothing necessarily wrong with yearning for something. Many personal longings are healthy and even pleasing to the Lord. For instance, the Psalmist said, "O LORD, Thou hast heard the desire of the humble; Thou wilt strengthen their heart, Thou wilt incline Thine ear." (Psalm 10:17) David said, "Delight yourself in the LORD; and He will give you the desires of your heart." (Psalm 37:4) Solomon said, "The desire of the righteous is only good..." (Proverbs 11:23) and "...the desire of the righteous will be granted." (Proverbs 10:24)

Desire is one of the drives that God instilled in human beings to help them to function in life. People's wants or desires are as diverse as the number of human beings on the planet. An individual's temperament, background, and environment all contribute to what he may pursue in life. Included in this list are the natural appetites of the human body, which can become warped and/or get out of control, as in the case of sexual addicts. Appetites become corrupted by sin.

Paul spoke of the "lusts of the heart." The Greek term here is *epithumia*, which means to long after something. Normally, it refers to craving something which is forbidden. Paul said that these lusts are deceitful (Ephesians 4:22), foolish and hurtful (I Timothy 6:9) and can reign over a person's body. (Romans 6:12) Peter said that they are unclean (II Peter 2:10) and war against the soul, (I Peter 2:11) and James said that they war against one's members (James 4:1) and entice to sin. (James 1:14) Jesus warned that to lust after a woman is to commit adultery with her in one's heart. (Matthew 5:28 Of this particular teaching of Jesus, Adam Clarke said the following:

> If voluntary and deliberate looks and desires make adulterers and adulteresses, how many persons are there whose whole life is one continued crime! whose eyes being full of adultery, they cannot cease from sin. (2 Peter 2:14) Many would abhor to commit one external act before the eyes of men, in a temple of stone; and yet they are not afraid to commit a multitude of such acts in the temple of their hearts, and in the sight of God![2]

Charles Spurgeon simply said, "What a King is ours, who stretches his scepter over the realm of our inward lusts!"[3]

Paul called them "lusts of the heart." We should take note of the fact that the lust comes from one's heart. Recently, I was speaking at a series of men's meetings in the Boston area on the subject of overcoming the power of lust. After one particular meeting, a curious, yet sincere young man came up to me with a look of bewilderment on his face. "Now, help me to understand this, Brother Gallagher," he said. "How is it that we get rid of the spirit of lust?" I knew right where he was headed. He, like many others, had been taught that lust came from demons which plagued the believer. Although demons do play a role in the bondage of habitual sexual sin, this young man's fundamental understanding was wrong. I asked him to open the Bible in his hand to James 1:14 and to read it to me. He read, "But each one is tempted when he is carried away and enticed by his own lust."

"Whose lust is it that he is enticed by?" I queried. As I asked the question, a look of utter amazement came across his face.

"It's my own lust, isn't it?" he asked in response to this new revelation.

I said to him, "Listen, the devil can dangle a carrot in front of your face, but there is something inside you that actually wants that carrot. You aren't lustful because some demon comes on you. You are lustful because you have within you a desire for what isn't right. Jesus said, 'For out of the heart come evil thoughts, murders, adulteries, fornications, thefts, false witness, slanders. These are the things which defile the man...' (Matthew 15:19-20) The devil can appeal to that lust, but he did not *create* it. It's already in us."

THE SECOND EXCHANGE

When Paul said they "exchanged the truth of God for a lie," he was referring to the willful substitution of an immutable truth for a specific falsehood. But this replacement is no small matter. It involves our fundamental belief about God. The whole essence of God's character is that He "is good and His mercies are forever." That biblical statement, which is repeated countless times throughout the entire Bible, sums up the knowledge of who God is.

Eve possessed the truth about God. She had been in His presence and certainly must have known that He was a good and loving Being. Surely during those wonderful encounters in the garden, she observed His sweet nature and His lowly character. Nevertheless, Satan came to her with an alternative perspective. He suggested the possibility that God had lied to her about the tree of the knowledge of good and evil. "He's holding out on you," was the insinuation. "He makes it look like knowing Him is everything there is to life, but it's a lie! You only know the good. There is a whole world of delicious evil that you haven't yet experienced. That's where real satisfaction comes from!"

As is usually the case with the devil, there is an element of truth in what he says. It is true, she had not experienced evil. It was also true, to a certain extent, that there is some satisfaction that comes from sin. The Bible refers to enjoying "...the pleasures of sin for a season..." (Hebrews 11:25) Sin is pleasurable, but only temporarily. The devil failed to mention that suffering, misery, and death are all unavoidable consequences of sin. Consequently, the one who is dedicated to the pursuit of sin has accepted the lie that a relationship with God is not sufficient enough to bring fulfillment. He is convinced that there must be something more to life. Naturally, since sin has taken him away from God, the joy which comes from that closeness is forgotten. Each time the devil dangles the carrot of some tantalizing pleasure in front of the man, he quickly loses any sense of reality of God he might still possess and plunges himself into the sea of sexual fulfillment.

The truth is that God is a good Father who desires only to do good to His children. However, their obedience plays a large part in His ability to fulfill this desire. The one who never repents, never comes into the truth about what God is really like. He never will experience the depth of fulfillment that is generated by a right relationship with Him. Instead, he sentences himself to endure the same merry-go-round over and over again: the promise of satisfaction, the act of sin, the emptiness of the experience, and its subsequent consequences. This is the exchange of the truth about God for a lie.

THE DISEASED SOUL

Our seventh characteristic cuts right to the core of a person's being. In verse 26, Paul speaks of "degrading passions." The Greek word for passions in this passage is *pathos*. The *Zodhiates Bible Dictionary* says the following: "These are lusts that dishonor those who indulge in them. *Pathos* is the soul's diseased condition out of which the various lusts spring."[4] *Vincent's Word Studies* sees this Greek term in the same way. When comparing *epithumia* (lust) with *pathos* (passions), it says that *pathos* "is the narrower and intenser word. *Epithumia* is the larger word, including the whole world of active lusts and desires, while the meaning of

85

pathos is passive, being the diseased condition out of which the lusts spring. *Epithumia* are evil longings; *pathos* ungovernable affections. Thus it appears that the divine punishment was the more severe, in that they were given over to a condition, and not merely to an evil desire."[5]

As the sexual addict continues to fill his mind with evil thinking, it begins to take its toll on his heart. It was, of course, the heart which produced the lust in the first place. Jesus said, "For from within, out of the heart of men, proceed the evil thoughts, fornications, thefts, murders, adulteries, deeds of coveting and wickedness, as well as deceit, sensuality, envy, slander, pride and foolishness. All these evil things proceed from within and defile the man." (Mark 7:21-23) Through the prophet Jeremiah the Lord said, "The heart is more deceitful than all else and is desperately sick; who can understand it?" (Jeremiah 17:9) Although the human heart has within it a propensity toward sin, it becomes increasingly more evil with the indulgence of sin. The more the person sins, the more corrupted his heart becomes. The more depraved his heart becomes, the greater the bondage of sin.

BURNING LUST

Those who have experienced the unquenchable flames of burning lust can understand why the fathers of the early church regarded the worst aspect of hell to be that a person is left to his own lusts with no possibility of satisfying them. To a small degree, this can be seen by holding a piece of meat just out of reach of a dog. His eyes concentrate only on the object in view. His mouth begins to salivate and his heartbeat increases. The sight and smell of the meat leads him into almost a trance-like state as he fixes his gaze upon it. This is a representation of the addict as he contemplates his routine. Solomon describes the hypnotic spell of sexual temptation: "With her many persuasions she entices him; with her flattering lips she seduces him. Suddenly he follows her, as an ox goes to the slaughter, or as one in fetters to the discipline of a fool, until an arrow pierces through his liver; as a bird hastens to the snare, so he does not know that it will cost him his life." (Proverbs 7:21-23)

The man driven by lust loses all sense of reality. He completely forgets the costs involved with sin and will often find himself doing things in this altered state of mind that he would never otherwise consider. He experiences this in two different ways.

First, he might perform degrading acts that would repulse or frighten him in a time of "sanity." I have had men confess to me of things they have done that actually made them sick to their stomachs afterwards. Some explained how their normal standards and morals flew right out the window as they entered that trance of lust. Men with a deep fear of arrest might solicit prostitutes while being driven by lust, while others expose themselves to women after their lust has been excited. Yet others, will molest their own children while in this state of mind. The list goes on.

Secondly, he finds his imagination running wild. I remember reading the story of a man who pulled up to a stoplight and exchanged glances with a pretty woman in the car next to him. The man's mind raced as he followed her around. Every time they would come up to another light, she would look over at him. Of course, in his state of mind, he imagined she was flirting with him. His fantasy came to a shocking end when she pulled up in front of a police station and ran inside. Suddenly, he realized that he had concocted the whole scenario in his own imagination.

The sex-crazed man becomes mesmerized by the object of his lust. It becomes a looming idol: something which takes on such a tremendous degree of importance that everything else in life must revolve around it. The idol has the power to keep the man in a constant state of unquenchable thirst. He will expend an enormous amount of time fantasizing about it. The drive to satisfy his desire will keep a peeping Tom at a window for hours or a "Don Juan" forever chasing women. The same theme persists: always chasing; never satisfied. The insatiability of lust is a commonality amongst sex addicts. "It is like a small flame that has been lit. As this fire is fed, it grows larger and larger. It demands more of our time and energy to be satisfied. Eventually, these appetites can become like a fire out of control—they become unquenchable."[6]

Sin is a demanding taskmaster. Fantasy has a way of requiring a person's fanatical allegiance, while giving little in return. One man, whose sexual routine included cross dressing, told of literally spending days going through dump sites looking for women's clothes to put on. It is absolutely insane how obsessive sexual bondage can be. The more the person fills his mind with this kind of thinking, the more intense his obsession will likely become. It is as Solomon said, "...the one who chases fantasies will have his fill of poverty." (Proverbs 28:19 NIV)

THE KNOWLEDGE OF GOD

As the person sinks deeper into the bile of depravity, he gradually loses his grip on the knowledge of God. Paul said, "they did not think it worthwhile to retain the knowledge of God..." This knowledge here simply means one's intimacy with Him. Obviously, a person cannot expect to be in league with the foul spirits of the demonic realm a good portion of his time and then afterwards think he will cuddle up into the Father's lap for some endearing moments of fellowship! Listen to what Paul has to say about this type of behavior:

> Do not be bound together with unbelievers; for what partnership have righteousness and lawlessness, or

what fellowship has light with darkness? Or what harmony has Christ with Belial, or what has a believer in common with an unbeliever? Or what agreement has the temple of God with idols? For we are the temple of the living God; just as God said, "I will dwell in them and walk among them; and I will be their God, and they shall be My people. Therefore, come out from their midst and be separate," says the Lord. "And do not touch what is unclean; and I will welcome you. And I will be a father to you, and you shall be sons and daughters to Me," says the Lord Almighty. Therefore, having these promises, beloved, let us cleanse ourselves from all defilement of flesh and spirit, perfecting holiness in the fear of God. (II Corinthians 6:14-7:1)

God is extremely lowly. He is so humble that if a person simply repents, He will come bounding toward him with gracious acceptance.* However, it should also be emphasized that the one who is backslidden must travel a long road back to a place of real intimacy with the Lord. It is a practical reality of straying away. A quote from *The Pulpit Commentary* best describes this:

> Oh, you who are forsaking Christ, if you be really his, you will have to come back; but no joyous journey will that be for you. No, indeed! It never has been, and never can be. Still blessed be the Lord, who forces you to make it, difficult and hard though it be. It is the hand which was nailed to the cross, and the heart which there was pierced for you, that now wields the scourge which compels you, in sorrow and in shame,

---

* I say this in relation to the fact that He is so quick to forgive and accept the straying sheep back into the fold.

to come back to him whom you left.[7]

THE REPROBATE MIND

There is a wonderful word in the New Testament that I would like to take a moment to mention here. The word is *dokimazo*. It comes from another Greek word which means "to be tested." *Dokimazo* carries with it the idea of a man whose character has been proven through the testings of life. To Timothy, Paul spoke of the requirements of a deacon, "And let these also first be tested (*dokimazo*); then let them serve as deacons if they are beyond reproach." (I Timothy 3:10) Peter used it in a different sense: "that the proof (*dokimazo*) of your faith, being more precious than gold which is perishable, even though tested (*dokimazo*) by fire, may be found to result in praise and glory and honor at the revelation of Jesus Christ." (I Peter 1:7) To be a man of *dokimazo* is to be a man of proven character.

In Romans chapter 1, Paul described men who were given over to a "reprobate mind." The word reprobate in the Greek is *adokimos*. The "a" in front of the word is a negative participle. It is used in the Greek just as we use the prefix "un-" (*un*holy, *un*loving, *un*godly, etc.). Thus, in this sense, it means that God has thrown up His hands, so to speak, and given them over to be men *without character* who are likely to say, do, act, and pursue anything or anyone under the sun in their burning lust.

THE CUP IS FULL

As we reach the end of the first chapter of Romans, words describing those fully committed to a lifestyle of ungodliness seem to gush out of Paul's broken heart: "...unrighteousness, wickedness, greed, evil; full of envy, murder, strife, deceit, malice; they are gossips, slanderers, haters of God, insolent, arrogant, boastful, inventors of evil, disobedient to parents,

without understanding, untrustworthy, unloving, unmerciful..."
When reading through this list of sin, it is very tempting to pick
out a few that do not apply and minimize the ones which do. Paul
is simply showing what the man becomes once he has given
himself over to a sordid, licentious lifestyle. He says that they are
filled with these ungodly characteristics—twenty-one different
aspects of the inside world of a man in sexual sin.

Paul is not implying here that they have a small problem and
a few personality quirks of which God will one day deliver them.
NO! They are *filled* with unrighteousness, wickedness, greed and
evil. This is the hideous reality of sexual addiction.

six

THE PROCESS OF SIN

THE ACT OF SEXUAL SIN for the addict is not one simple deed, but rather a complex series of actions. Typically, the man is simply engaged in his normal activities of life—working, running errands, watching television, and so on—when the thought of sexual sin comes into his mind. He ponders the idea for some time until it becomes strong enough to motivate him into action. He then engages in a sequence of events which becomes his particular routine resulting in acting out his sin. Compelled through these successive steps by a driving lust, he eventually accomplishes the erotic experience which has captivated him since the initial temptation. Once the entire episode has been completed, he must now face the consequences of what he has done. The book of James reveals this process from a spiritual perspective:

> Let no one say when he is tempted, "I am being tempted by God"; for God cannot be tempted by evil, and He Himself does not tempt anyone. But each one is tempted when he is carried away and enticed by his own lust. Then when lust has conceived, it gives birth to sin; and when sin is accomplished, it brings forth death.

Do not be deceived, my beloved brethren. (James 1:13-16)

The Pulpit Commentary says the following about this text:

Temptation originates within the heart of the sinner himself. It is in vain for him to blame his Maker. Sin is no part of our original constitution, and it is not to be excused on the plea of an unfavorable environment. A man sins only when he is "enticed" by the bait, and "drawn away" by the hook of "his own lust." That is, the impelling power which seduces towards evil is the corrupt nature within us. The world and the devil only tempt effectually when they stir up the filthy pool of depraved personal desire. "Lust" includes, besides the appetites of the body, the evil dispositions of the mind, such as pride, malice, envy, vanity, love of ease, etc. Any appeal made from without to these vile principles and affections can be successful only with the consent of the will. Every man is personally responsible for his sin; for each man's sin takes its rise in "his own lust."...

Lust is throughout this passage personified in allegorical fashion as a harlot, ever striving, like the harlot Folly of Pro. ix. 13-18, to allure and captivate the will. First, she draws the man "who goes right on his way" out of the path of sound principle and wholesome pleasure; and then she entices him into her embrace with the siren strain, "Stolen waters are sweet." Lust may be said to "conceive," when it obtains the consent of the will, or disarms its opposition. The man who dallies with temptation, instead of meeting it with instant and prayerful resistance, will be sure eventually to succumb to it. From the guilty union of lust with the will, a living sin is born. The embryo corruption becomes developed into a deed of positive transgression. And this is not all. Sin, the progeny of lust, itself grows up from the infancy of mere choice to the adult life of settled habit; and "when it is full-grown," it in turn becomes, as the result of union with the will, the mother of death. It was so with the sin of our first parents in Paradise. It was so with the sin of Achan (Josh. 7:21); he saw, coveted, took, and died. It is so with the sin of licentiousness, which has suggested the figure of this passage; the physical corruption which the practice of sensuality entails is just a sacrament of spiritual death. Death is the fruit of all sin. Sin kills peace; it kills hope; it kills usefulness; it kills the conscience; it kills the soul. The harlot-house of lust and sin becomes the vestibule of perdition.[1]

Thomas A Kempis gives his viewpoint:

First there cometh into mind a bare thought of evil, then a strong imagination thereof, afterwards delight, and evil motion, and then consent. And so little by little our wicked enemy getteth complete entrance, for that he is not resisted at the beginning.[2]

The *Jamieson, Fausset, Brown Commentary* adds:

Every man, when tempted, is so through being drawn away of... his own lust. The cause of sin is in ourselves. Even Satan's suggestions do not endanger us before they are made our own. Each one has his own peculiar (so the Greek) lust, arising from his own temperament and habit.[3]

TEMPTATION

Temptation always precedes the process of sin. Thoughts

are either placed in a person's mind by one of Satan's emissaries or simply appear as a longing of the flesh. Regardless, the mere existence of temptation itself does not constitute sin.

In Homer's *Odyssey*, one reads of the adventures of a Greek legend by the name of Ulysses. During one of his adventures he encounters the "sirens" whose seductive songs invoked stark madness that would eventually result in the death of any who heard them. As Ulysses' boat prepared to cross by the coast of the "sirens," he stopped up his men's ears with wax so they could not hear the deadly song, while he listened tied securely to the mast. Only the ropes could restrain the madness that came over him. This illustrates the sexual addict being tempted. As that captivating thought starts looming, often the only way to resist it is to be "tied securely to a mast."

Solomon said, "For the lips of an adulteress drip honey, and smoother than oil is her speech." (Proverbs 5:3) This phrase describes how the devil presents temptation. Honey represents promised fulfillment. The temptation seems irresistible because it is laced with the deception that the act of sin will bring about tremendous pleasure and satisfaction. The truth is it has been a long time since the sex addict has experienced any real pleasure in his sin. Nonetheless, the tantalizing thought is presented, all is forgotten and the act of sexual sin looks absolutely intoxicating and therefore irresistible.

The smooth oil represents the craftiness of the enemy. He knows when we are at our weakest moment. He does not mind waiting for days or even weeks if it means a greater defeat for the Christian. Paul twice speaks of the "the schemes of the devil." (Ephesians 6:10, II Corinthians 2:11) The demonic forces of hell have been carrying out their "guerrilla warfare" quite diligently for a long time. Fully camouflaged and extremely calculating, they launch the perfect illusion, timing each consecutive attack "to steal, and kill, and destroy" (John 10:10) God's property.

Once Satan has managed to get a fish hook in the sexual

addict, at his leisure, all he needs to do is to give a gentle tug on the line to get the man going. It often comes in the form of remembering past pleasurable experiences. Frank Worthen comments:

> FLASHBACKS: Very few sexual encounters in the gay life-style could be considered great. Almost always, there is an element of wishing it could have been better. Often we'd feel used, short changed and degraded after such an encounter. Satan, however, has a way of throwing flashbacks of previous sexual experiences at us. In the memories he presents, all negative connotations are written out. We remember only the positive.
>
> He also tempts us through our natural tendency to make associations. We're all triggered by certain music, smells, sounds and visual images. These evoke distinct, vivid memories of past experiences.[4]

Ronald A. Jenson talks about the "triggers" that often lead a person into sin:

> A trigger is any event or emotion which evokes an inevitable response. Planning thinks about both the triggers and the usual result they bring in you. What are your triggers?... If you can identify the thing which leads up to your difficult time, you can prepare for and outmaneuver defeat and failure.[5]

I found in my life that there were four circumstances that usually proved disastrous for me if they all happened at the same time. The first, of course, was the actual temptation. Again, demons used perfect timing to implant their thoughts. They usually did not bother to tempt me unless they could synchronize it with the other three needed elements: the physical build-up, money, and opportunity.

The physical build-up I would experience, if I had not had sex in several days, greatly increased my desire to act out. As my hormones built up, I would become immensely sensitized to sexual stimuli.

It was also vital that I had plenty of money to spend on my sin. Regardless of what the sexual activity was, it usually cost money. I could easily spend ten dollars in quarters at the movie arcade located in any adult bookstore. Of course, going to prostitutes or massage parlors would be much more expensive.

Lastly, I had to be given the opportunity. If my wife was at work or if I had an excuse to be gone, I had the chance to commit my favorite routine.

Warning: any wife who is going to help her husband through the process of overcoming this habit will have to closely monitor a number of things, the first being his money. As soon as I was serious about obtaining the victory over sexual sin, my wife and I agreed that I was not to have more than five dollars in my pocket at a time. I was not allowed to have a credit card or an ATM card. This one safety valve was an extremely important part of the victory which ensued. The man who means business will not hedge on this issue. Secondly, she must be attuned to her husband's problem and keep a close watch over his actions. If he suddenly stands up and announces that he needs to go shopping, she should question him about his exact intentions. The wife who is deceived a few times quickly learns to become suspicious about any odd behavior. Once again, a man who wants to be set free will appreciate and welcome such devotion from his spouse.

Naturally, one of the areas that may be out of her reach is his job. However, if he works at a factory, office, or store, and simply cannot leave his job, she can rest assured that he is less likely to get into trouble while at work. She will know exactly what time to expect him home from work every night. If he says that he has to work overtime, she will dutifully examine his pay check.

There are many men who are in job situations conducive to falling into sin. Take Sam, for instance. He was an outside salesman for a reputable firm selling vinyl windows to various home improvement stores. He had a regular route of stores that he visited each month. He asked me for advice concerning his habit of frequenting massage parlors during the day. I told him that he needed to find a different job. Hearing this, he looked at me with an expression of utter shock and quickly responded, "I love my job. I make good money for my family. This job is *perfect* for me!"

"I don't doubt that your job is perfect," I responded. "The enemy is quite adept at providing jobs that are perfect for his evil designs. Sam, if victory over sin doesn't mean any more to you than giving up a job, you might as well resign yourself to a lifestyle of failure. You will never change," I informed him. Unfortunately, to my knowledge, Sam is still making good money at his job and continues to visit massage parlors. He preferred his job over getting the victory.

Larry was another man who faced a similar "fork in the road." He owned a business which required that he maintain a web site. He routinely checked the news and his stock portfolio on the internet. He looked forward to going on-line everyday at noon and just before closing to check his stocks and the news. Larry also was in the habit of browsing various pornographic sites as well. Though he wanted to quit, every time he thought of giving up the internet, he would quickly dismiss it because he "needed it for his job." The truth was that he did not want to give up his daily ritual, so to speak, of getting on "the web." He had the same disappointed look on his face as Sam did when I suggested that he give up the internet. "But I need it for my job," he insisted.

As we talked, I did some probing and the real issue came to light. "I guess I'm just holding onto my routine of going on-line to see the news and stocks. But what do I do about my web site?

We have to maintain it," Larry admitted. This problem was a little more legitimate. We talked further and I discovered the man who was responsible at his company to maintain the website was a Christian. We brought Jim into Larry's office and explained the problem to him. It was very humbling for Larry to confess to an employee, but he truly wanted help. They disconnected Larry's computer from their web server, took the software off his computer, and put a new password on Jim's computer so Larry could never gain access to view pornography from his office. He forfeited his daily routine on the web, but this simple solution was all it took for him to find the freedom that had been eluding him for some time.

Larry was willing to do whatever it took. His attitude is an example of what Jesus meant when He said, "And if your right eye makes you stumble, tear it out, and throw it from you... And if your right hand makes you stumble, cut it off, and throw it from you; for it is better for you that one of the parts of your body perish, than for your whole body to go into hell." (Matthew 5:29-30)

THE IDOL OF FANTASY

The initial step into sin is allowing the thought of temptation to fester. It is extremely difficult to thwart the processes of thought once entertained. James said that a person is tempted "when he is carried away and enticed by his own lust..." This illustrates a man's lust actually picking him up and carrying him to a place where he cannot defend himself and *then* enticing him. It is almost as if his carnal desires momentarily take control of his mind and carry him away to some dream world where he is then utterly defenseless. Once there, he is swallowed up in the evil imaginations of his own sick heart.

This is not something that he does not *want* to do. On the contrary, it is exactly what he does *want* to do. The New International Version translates it, "but each one is tempted when by his *own* evil desire he is dragged away and enticed." It is not only the object of the temptation that he covets, but the actual temptation itself! He wants to fill his mind with that tantalizing temptation! It is no wonder that he has such a difficult time exercising self-restraint. Just as a person savors every spoonful of delicious pudding, the sexual addict savors every thought of the ultimate sexual encounter. The longer he allows himself to fantasize, the more likely he will act it out. He is, in essence, erecting an idol of fantasy. The longer he entertains the fantasy the larger the idol grows. At this point he is being enticed.

These thoughts are difficult to control because the person sees only the instant gratification. The fantasy of the impending experience overshadows past vows to discontinue such behavior. All that lies in sight is the "beauty" of the anticipated act. He completely forgets about God and loved ones. His past attempts to quit are now lost in the sea of forgetfulness. It appears that he just cannot help himself. As the lust builds in his mind, his behavior becomes reckless. Things he never imagined doing under normal circumstances now become "great expectations." He is starting to enter into a trance, becoming like the dog mesmerized by a piece of meat held just out of his reach. His heart begins to race, his breathing becomes short, and his palms begin to sweat. He is actually becoming intoxicated with desire. The cycle of addiction is now in motion and he has reached the "point of no return." Dietrich Bonhoeffer best describes this struggle:

> At this moment God is quite unreal to us, he loses all reality, and only desire for the creature is real; the only reality is the devil. Satan does not here fill us with hatred of God, but with forgetfulness of God. And now his falsehood is added to this proof of strength. The lust thus aroused envelopes the mind and will of man in deepest darkness. The powers of clear dis-

crimination and of decision are taken from us.[6]

PHYSICALLY MOVING TOWARD SIN

The next step is taken when the body actually gets up and moves. The person may fool himself into thinking he will just cruise the area where the "action" is and not do anything, but he almost always does. I can remember thinking in my own mind, "I'll just drive by where the hookers are, just to see what they look like." Another way I would be deceived was by telling myself that I would only look at a magazine. The problem was, once I started looking at the magazine, I would enter into that mind-altered state where everything becomes sexual and nothing is forbidden. After looking through the magazines, I wanted to see the movies. As soon as I began watching the movies, I wanted the real thing. A person viewing pornography becomes warped in his decision making. Sin is never satisfied. One sin leads to another sin. One bad decision leads to another bad decision. Perhaps this is why the prophet Micah warned, "Woe to those who scheme iniquity, who work out evil on their beds! When morning comes, they do it, for it is in the power of their hands." (Micah 2:1)

THE POINT OF NO RETURN

Once the body is in motion, rationalization takes over. "Oh well, it's too late to stop now. I might as well get it over with!" This is "the point of no return." Now unrestrained and uninhibited by fear, guilt or the possibility of danger, the addict is fully convinced that this is the only reasonable route in which he can take. Solomon would describe him as a man with, "An heart that deviseth wicked imaginations, feet that be swift in running to mischief." (Proverbs 6:18 KJV) Thus, the addict becomes totally committed to acting out his fantasy. The tidal waves of lust will carry him far out into the ocean of perversion where he so longs to be. Although he had intended only to drive by the prostitutes, massage parlors, or whatever his particular source of temptation might have been, once he experienced the sights and sounds of the "red-light district," the pull of sin overwhelmed him.

THE VARIOUS ROUTINES

Now different behaviors come into play. Each addict has his own fantasy—his own routine. Actually, this is where they find the real excitement. Note: The addict's routine begins immediately when he moves toward his sin. Just as an alcoholic fondly thinks of his friends at the bar, the excitement of the music, playing pool, flirting with girls and the "fun" of a night out drinking; the addict thinks of the many things that comprise his sexual routine. He hurries to the place where this can be achieved and, since orgasm cannot continue indefinitely, the addict must make the buildup last. Some have made this period last for more than twenty-four hours at times, not wanting the thrill and exhilaration to ever end. This routine varies from addict to addict. For some, it is going from movie to movie in an arcade, consumed with a lust for variety. For others it might be cruising, looking for prostitutes—male or female. For the rapist it will be hunting down a victim. The peeping Tom will look for a likely window. The flasher will search for a potential viewer. While they are all different, they share one thing in common: lust has been conceived in the heart of each one, and each one is now on a personal mission to satisfy himself to the best of his ability.

THE ACT OF SIN

Sin. The actual act. It is often a terrible disappointment after a prolonged period during which the fulfillment of the fantasy was anticipated. Nevertheless, it is the object of desire on which the person has fixed his mind. Once he has entered into the trance and begun the routine, it is highly unlikely that he can stop himself from following through with some kind of sexual act. I can remember thinking objectively as I left the movie arcade for a massage parlor. I knew that the experience was not going to be that great, and yet, it seemed that I could not stop myself from finishing the act. I had started the machinery rolling and only the sex act was going to be enough to *justify* concluding it. Thus, once the sex addict has invested his time and energy into his fantasy, it will require something special to culminate the entire process. Some men are able to limit their sexual sin to viewing pornography, but even for them, something special will need to be achieved for them to finish what they themselves have set in motion.

DEATH

Finally, when the act of sin has been committed, it brings forth death: death of self-respect and death of feelings. It will also bring despair, anger, helplessness, hopelessness, guilt, condemnation, and vows never to do it again. It is a horrible price that Satan and his demons exact upon those deceived. First, they lead him by the nose into sin; then once committed, they condemn and attack him for being weak and despicable. The shame grows deeper and deeper.

Once the sexual act is over and the lust has drained from his body, the person can begin to see the sin more clearly for what it is. The empty promises of the fantasy are nowhere to be found; all that remains is the horrible penalty for his sin. During the temptation he was oblivious to the consequences of his choices. Now, they are in full view. As Solomon laid out the presentation of sin, he described in riveting detail the consequences of giving in to sexual temptation. He brings it all to life in the following passage:

> For the lips of an adulteress drip honey, and smoother than oil is her speech; but in the end she is bitter as wormwood, sharp as a two-edged sword. Her feet go down to death, her steps lay hold of Sheol... Now then, my sons, listen to me, and do not depart from the words of my mouth. Keep your way far from her, and do not go near the door of her house, lest you give your vigor to others, and your years to the cruel one; lest strangers be filled with your strength, and your hard-earned goods go to the house of an alien; and you groan at your latter end, when your flesh and your body are consumed; and you say, "How I have hated instruction! And my heart spurned reproof! And I have not listened to the voice of my teachers, nor inclined my ear to my instructors!" (Proverbs 5:3-13)

On two different occasions, Solomon used the Hebrew word *aharit*. In verse four he says "in the end..." In verse eleven it is expressed "at your latter end." *Aharit* comes from the Hebrew word *ahar*, which means to linger. What Solomon has shown, is that the sin does not just disappear once it has been indulged. The effects of it may linger for a long time. We have already mentioned the death that is experienced following each act of sin. In addition to these, there are also the long-term consequences of a lifetime of giving over to sexual sin.

Adam Clarke comments on this passage:

> The mourning here spoken of is of the most excessive kind: the word *naham* is often applied to the growling of a lion, and the hoarse incessant murmuring of the

sea. In the line of my duty, I have been often called to attend the death-bed of such persons, where groans and shrieks were incessant through the ejaculating pains in their bones and flesh. Whoever has witnessed a closing scene like this will at once perceive with what force and propriety the wise man speaks. And how have I hated instruction, and despised the voice of my teachers! is the unavailing cry in that terrific time. Reader, whosoever thou art, lay these things to heart.[7]

Time and again I have often witnessed the anguish of a man when he is forced to finally take responsibility for his past actions. Needless to say, the longer it is avoided, the worse the heartache will be.

RESOLUTIONS AND REPENTANCE

As the addict enters the beginning stage of remorse, he will often make certain promises to God vowing never to repeat the same sin again: "Lord, I swear I won't do this ever again!" As his eyes are opened to the reality of the horrible emptiness and nature of his sin, he readily makes such a vow; for, it is at this moment that he truly sees sin for what it really is.

However, the problem with making such a resolution is that it stems from the man's own strength and determination to resist and overcome an evil. This sort of "promise-keeping" will never endure future temptations in the same area. It is for this exact reason that the sex addict has attempted countless times before to break the habit, yet to no avail.

The man desperately needs repentance. True repentance comes when a man's heart has changed its outlook on sin. A man will only quit his sinful, destructive behavior when he has truly repented of it in his heart. As he moves closer to the heart of God, he begins to develop a "godly sorrow" over his sin.

Overcoming Temptation

As the person grows stronger in his Christian walk and closer to God, he begins to see the whole act of sin, including the consequences, rather than just the reward. This is the principal reason I have been successful in overcoming my own personal temptations. As I drew near to the Lord when I began coming out of the bondage, I was able to see the effects of my sin and rebellion more clearly. Rather than concentrating on the "delicious" experience, I was able to realistically see that past experiences usually were only mediocre, at best. Instead of focusing my thoughts on how much fun it might be, I saw clearly the consequences that awaited me: the *aharit*. I would recall the guilt-ridden days of shame, disgust, and condemnation. Worst of all, I remembered being isolated from the Lord.

I overcame temptation because I refused to allow myself to dwell on sexual thoughts. When a fantasy entered my mind, I would make the conscious decision not to entertain it. The person who affords himself the luxury of savoring a fantasy is setting himself up for a huge fall. The time to deal with temptation is when it *first* appears. The longer the thought lingers, the more difficult it is to resist.

Fleeing Temptation

Having examined the entire process of sin, let us now return to the beginning and study a little more closely how to escape the snares of sexual temptation. The Bible gives one way to deal with these allurements: RUN! Paul admonished Timothy to "flee from youthful lusts." In Genesis 39 we see the story of a man of God who had to deal with sexual temptation.

And it came about after these events that his master's wife looked with desire at Joseph, and she said, "Lie with me." But he refused and said to his master's wife, "Behold, with me here, my master does not concern himself with anything in the house, and he has put all that he owns in my charge. There is no one greater in this house than I, and he has withheld nothing from me except you, because you are his wife. How then could I do this great evil, and sin against God?"

And it came about as she spoke to Joseph day after day, that he did not listen to her to lie beside her, or be with her. Now it happened one day that he went into the house to do his work, and none of the men of the household was there inside. And she caught him by his garment, saying, "Lie with me!" And he left his garment in her hand and fled, and went outside. (Genesis 39:7-12)

Notice, if you will, the difference in the way these two people handled what was, undoubtedly, a mutual attraction. It is probable that Potiphar's wife was a beautiful woman. Perhaps she was one of the leading ladies in society. She must have dressed in the finest of silks and wore the costliest of perfumes. Next to the unpolished slave girls that Joseph was accustomed to, she must have seemed incredibly glamorous.

It is interesting to note that she did not take an interest in Joseph until *after* he had been exalted by her husband. Before he was promoted to his high position, she probably did not even notice him. Now, these two were around each other every day. Potiphar's wife must have come to respect Joseph for the way he efficiently handled his duties. After he had been raised up, she "looked with desire at Joseph."

This happens with some women when they see a man of God exalted. There is something about a powerful presence behind the pulpit they want to capture. Many women begin to fantasize about how they might seduce the man of God. Surely most any well-known evangelist could attest to women trying to entrap and seduce them. Once a woman goes after a man in this way she will often do anything to accomplish her devilish mission. In her mind she thinks if she could conquer him sexually, she would somehow "capture" that power or that charisma which emanates from his personality.

This is what Potiphar's wife attempted. She observed the boldness and confidence in Joseph and wanted to possess it in some way. She did not realize that these notable qualities were in him because he was a godly man. She was driven by her own carnal desires, and as she watched him work around the house day after day, the lustful thoughts began to lodge in her mind. She could have dismissed them, but she chose to dwell on them. Perhaps, before she even knew it, she blurted out one day, "Lie with me." Shocked that this slave turned her down, she was faced with an even greater challenge. The account says that Joseph tried to reason with her as to why he could not do this. But she would have none of it. Every day she flirted with him, which most likely bordered on what is commonly referred to today as being "sexual harassment." Nevertheless, Joseph, a man of honor and integrity, continued to steadfastly resist her unlawful advances toward him. Finally, when she could bear it no longer, and her lusts became an obsession, she threw herself at him and almost begged him, "Lie with me!" When Joseph ran out, she came to the painful, humiliating realization that she could never have him sexually and so she had him thrown in jail.

Joseph must have had some struggle with temptation as he looked upon this radiant, refined Egyptian beauty who greatly availed herself to him. But, he handled this mutual attraction differently; he made "no provision for the flesh." He dismissed the idea immediately and refused to even consider it. When she finally threw herself on him, he knew the secret to getting out of temptation. He ran! This is the best way to handle a temptation; run the other way!

A WAY OF ESCAPE

One important aspect of dealing with temptation is that there is *always* a way out. Paul said, "No temptation has overtaken you but such as is common to man; and God is faithful, who will not allow you to be tempted beyond what you are able, but with the temptation will provide the way of escape also, that you may be able to endure it." (I Corinthians 10:13)

When I struggled with temptation, I actually doubted the Bible because this verse seemed so untrue to me. I hated it when preachers used this verse. "They don't understand what it's like," I would say to myself. However, I would like to share a couple of thoughts on this verse. First, there is no longer any doubt in my mind about the truth of this statement (and every other statement in the Bible!). Looking on those temptations in retrospect, I can now see that God always *did* provide a way of escape. Because I was so entangled in my sin, and in such a habit of giving in to temptation, I was not tuned in to the guidance of the Holy Spirit. I either did not see the way of escape or chose to ignore it. I was so accustomed to losing these battles that I made up my mind that I simply could not win, so why try? I had become so conditioned to giving in to temptation that I convinced myself I could not overcome it. Moreover, I was so enthralled by my sin, that I did not *want* to find a way of escape. But the truth of the matter is, an escape was always available.

Paul said that God would "not allow you to be tempted beyond what you are able..." An illustration of the word "able" is the line that is drawn on the side of a ship. As the ship is loaded with cargo and sinks into the water, it approaches the point at which the "flimsaw line" parallels the water level, indicating that the ship has been loaded to capacity. When the loaded ship sinks to where that line is under water, they know the ship has been overloaded. We are never tempted beyond our "flimsaw line." We are never loaded with more temptation or testing than we can bear. God never allows our temptations to go beyond that line. He always provides for us a way of escape!

Thus, we must learn how to be sensitive to the escape route He provides. We can only learn His methods by studying His ways. This is the reason it is so important that we know where to go to find help. If we haphazardly seek out just any source for answers, we will likely be misguided and led further astray.

PART TWO

THE RIGHT COURSE

seven

THE ROOT ISSUES

PEOPLE STRUGGLING with habitual sexual sin often have a desire to get to "the root issues." Because of the humanistic efforts of certain "schools of thought" (i.e. psychology), many have been led to believe that such root causes are buried deep within an individual's childhood and therefore must be dug up and examined thoroughly. This whole concept of seeking solutions to present problems by exploring the past was first formulated by Sigmund Freud.* The theories he formulated helped to shape the modern field of psychology. Some of his concepts about the "emotional" problems people contend with were helpful; however, most were simply bizarre. Ultimately, the major therapy he conceived to help people, psychoanalysis, relied upon the patient's memories of childhood experiences as the key to unlocking their present problems. The

---

* Carl Jung, a contemporary of Freud, was the father of the modern "inner healing" movement. Jung, who claimed that "spirit guides" led him to his conclusions, believed that tranformation of troubled individuals would occur as they established a dialogue between their conscious and unconscious mind. Certain Christian psychologists later brought "Jesus" into this dialogue, insisting that the patient imagine Him helping in the midst of childhood traumas. There is, of course, no biblical support for such notions and, as Dave Hunt clearly revealed in *The Seduction of Christianity*, such practices are spiritually dangerous.

idea was that the memory of traumatic early encounters would cause the patient to somehow experience a psychological break-through, resulting in a new ability to cope with the daily stresses of life. This theory, which is no longer adhered to in the psychological community, nonetheless, still played a key role in the formulation of many of the theories of psychotherapy which abound today.

While it is undeniably true that the environment a child is reared in has a tremendous impact on the direction of his life and development, there is absolutely no evidence to suggest that simply remembering those incidents either affects or changes the present. If anything, this sort of therapy only encourages the counselee to blame others, rather than take personal ownership of his decisions and actions.

Dealing With the Present

The Bible clearly teaches the Christian who is struggling with sinful habits to deal with the "here-and-now," instead of at-tempting to resolve problems by focusing on past memories. Referring to the pursuit of spiritual perfection, Paul said, "Breth-ren, I do not regard myself as having laid hold of it yet; but one thing I do: forgetting what lies behind and reaching forward to what lies ahead, I press on toward the goal for the prize of the upward call of God in Christ Jesus." (Philippians 3:13-14) There is absolutely no biblical support for dredging up traumatic experi-ences of one's childhood. Although in counseling there may be an occasional need to address something that occurred in childhood, one should not look to the past as the key to dealing with the present.

The Bible teaches the struggling believer to deal with his sinful nature. Can you imagine God saying, "You shall not murder... unless of course you were abused as a child, then it is understandable." How ridiculous! Yet, in the news, as well as on today's talk shows, many people make excuses and rationalize their mistakes and sinful lifestyles by pointing an "all-accusing" finger at their relatives or others from their past. The truth is, before a person can ever hope to overcome habitual sin, he must first be willing to take responsibility for his *own* actions. This means dealing with one's present behavior without excuses. What has happened in the past cannot be changed. Consequently, those who are going to be victorious over sin must learn to forget what lies in the past and focus their attention on the present.

The following story shows us how David responded when he came face-to-face with his great moral failure.

> Then it happened in the spring, at the time when kings go out to battle, that David sent Joab... But David stayed at Jerusalem. Now when evening came David arose from his bed and walked around on the roof of the king's house, and from the roof he saw a woman bathing; and the woman was very beautiful in appearance... And David sent messengers and took her, and when she came to him, he lay with her...
>
> Then the LORD sent Nathan to David. And he came to him, and said... "You have struck down Uriah the Hittite with the sword, have taken his wife to be your wife... Indeed you did it secretly, but I will do this thing before all Israel, and under the sun." Then David said to Nathan, "I have sinned against the LORD." (II Samuel 11-12)

The first step toward victory over life-dominating habit is understanding that you are in your present circumstances because of the choices *you* have made for yourself. David took full responsibility when confronted about his sin with Bathsheba. He did not offer the pitiful excuses that can often be heard today: "I was going through a difficult period in my life." "It was the devil that set the whole thing up. God knows that I am a man with natural passions. What does He think a man would do under such circumstances?" "My wife has been distant with me lately. No wonder I fell to the temptation!" David knew he was wrong. He made a conscious decision to do it—no one else. When God punished him for his sin, he did not stand up and shake his fist at God. Instead, he understood and humbly accepted the punishment for his actions.

BLAMING PARENTS

Some of us, including myself, did not get a very fair start in life. I spent many years blaming others for my predicament. Although I was surrounded by negative influences at home, I chose to pursue the path of immorality. Blaming parents for our sin has always been a problem. Read what God said to His people through the prophet Ezekiel:

> Then the word of the LORD came to me saying, "What do you mean by using this proverb concerning the land of Israel saying, 'The fathers eat the sour grapes, But the children's teeth are set on edge'? "As I live," declares the Lord GOD, "you are surely not going to use this proverb in Israel anymore. Behold, all souls are Mine; the soul of the father as well as the soul of the son is Mine... The person who sins will die. The son will not bear the punishment for the father's iniquity, nor will the father bear the punishment for the son's iniquity; the righteousness of the righteous will be upon himself, and the wickedness of the wicked will be upon himself." (Ezekiel 18:1-4, 20)

God addressed this issue because His people were blaming their parents for their actions. They were using the transgressions of their fathers as an excuse to commit their own sins. God even banned them from using this phrase. They were not to exploit another's sin as a means of justifying their own actions.

However, there are people who have legitimately been wronged in life. These people are the most prone to use the abuse they have suffered as an excuse to stay in sin. Julie was such a person. She had been raised by an abusive step-father who began molesting her at a young age. As a teenager she rebelled and began having sex with practically anybody who wanted her. She continued with this reckless behavior even after becoming born again.

Though her childhood is a heartbreaking story, Julie will be destined to continue living a life of degradation until she decides to take responsibility for her own sin: right now in the present. By holding on to deep bitterness toward her step-father, and using his abuse as an excuse to stay in sin, she is paralyzed from experiencing the freedom God wants her to have. Unfortunately, there are those around her who think that her sin is justifiable because of her past sufferings. She is a victim who needs to accept God's love, not a sinner who must repent. Julie enjoys her sin and is happy to have counselors who will reinforce the idea that she is not responsible for her actions. Sometimes we must confront a person's sin head-on for his or her own benefit. Humanistic mercy says that we should treat Julie as a victim. God's mercy says that she is responsible for her actions as an adult, and unless she repents, she will remain separated from Him, stuck on a hopeless merry-go-round of sin, pain, and degradation. Misguided human sympathy only makes the situation worse.

This humanistic approach in dealing with sin reminds me of a story my aunt once told me. When I was a young boy I developed a bad case of German measles. The doctor told my mother that she must scrub my eyes out everyday or risk my getting an infection that could cause blindness. We were visiting my aunt's home at this time. One day my mother pinned me down and tried to clean out my eyes, but when I started screaming and kicking in protest she stopped. Upon seeing this, my aunt grabbed me up and "mercilessly" scrubbed my eyes! Now I ask you, which one was expressing godly mercy for me at that moment? It was my aunt.

Sometimes we, too, need to be handled firmly with God's Word for our own benefit. No one would deny that Julie has been a victim of an evil, corrupt step-father. Indeed, what was done to her was a horrible thing. But if she does not begin accepting responsibility for her present actions, she will never know real freedom from the pain of her past.

BLAMING THE MATE

While some blame their parents for their present problems, others blame their spouses. One of the "cop-outs" I have heard many times is, "I am unfaithful to my wife because she doesn't meet my needs." The man who commits something as evil as adultery because his wife fails to satisfy his sexual demands is actually worse off in his heart than the adulterer who is simply out of control with his sex life. It is one thing for a man to have an addiction which continues to spiral out of control, even to the point of committing adultery, but to make a premeditated and calculated decision to have sex with another person because his wife is not as obsessed with sex as he is, shows an extremely cold and selfish nature.

In actuality, the man who attempts to blame his wife's lack of interest in sex as the reason for his adultery, is not being honest with himself. He simply *wants* to do it. The man who truly loves his wife would never think of such a thing. Adultery would not be something he would even consider much less attempt. A godly man would immediately examine his own life in order to discover why he is receiving such a response from his wife. Then he would attempt to understand what he could do to better meet her needs. The man who claims that he is being short-changed is usually neglecting his wife's needs. In his extreme selfishness he does not love his wife as he should, otherwise, she would be more prone to respond to his advances. Most often the primary problem is not with the wife, but with the husband.

BLAMING GOD

As incredible as it may seem, many men try to blame God. Some actually get angry at Him because He "let them get this way," or because He will not immediately set them free upon their demand. Needless to say, they are walking on thin ice! It is not God's fault when people choose to walk in sin. He has graciously done everything He can to make salvation and liberty available to us. James says that God never tempts man (James 1:13). Paul says let God be true and every man a liar (Romans 3:4). Our beginnings may not seem fair, but we still cannot blame God. Afterall, He never makes any wrong decisions for us.

This is a very important step for some of you reading this book. Many of you will tend to skip over this section disregarding what is being considered here. We *must* take responsibility for our sin. We must tell God that we have sinned against Him and against others. This should not be done as some secret formula to receiving forgiveness, but with a heart-felt sorrow over the wrongfulness of our actions—leading to true repentance.

THE REAL ROOTS

When looking for the roots of sexual addiction we do not need to look any further than our own natures. Jeremiah said, "The heart is deceitful above all things, and desperately wicked: who can know it?" (Jeremiah 17:9 KJV) David said, "Behold, I was brought forth in iniquity, and in sin my mother conceived me." (Psalm 51:5) Solomon remarked, "Foolishness is bound up in the heart of a child..." (Proverbs 22:15) Paul claimed that we have all sinned and fallen short of the glory of God (Romans 3:23) while John said that "if we say we have no sin we deceive ourselves." (I John 1:8) And finally, Jesus declared, "But the things that proceed out of the mouth come from the heart, and those defile the man. For out of the heart come evil thoughts, murders, adulteries, fornications, thefts, false witness, slanders. These are the things which defile the man..." (Matthew 15:18-20)

The root of habitual sexual sin stems from the heart, not the past. One of the great fundamental teachings of the Christian faith is the doctrine of the depravity of man. While man was made in the image of a holy God, his nature became corrupted when he fell into sin in the Garden of Eden. Since that time, there has been no one righteous, "no not one." (Romans 3:10) We are depraved beings who crave that which is appealing to our carnal natures. It is *natural* to desire that which is sinful and unlawful. While most people do not act upon their thoughts, I think we would all stand amazed if we knew the thoughts that pass through the minds of "decent" folks.

The reality of this once struck me while my wife and I were in San Antonio, Texas. We were waiting for our friend while she ran into the local hall of justice. As we were sitting in her car casually talking, two well-dressed young ladies walked by. It was evident that they were office workers on their lunch break, going for a relaxing stroll. As they approached, I was impressed with what nice people they seemed to be. I had really been struggling with the thought of "good" people being sent to hell by a loving God. Not long before this I had questioned God, "Lord, how can you send decent people to hell?" It had been one of those nagging questions that did not sit right with me. As these two young ladies walked by the car we were in, one of them blurted out a profanity. At that instant the Lord made real to me that even those who might be considered as "decent" by human standards are not so in the eyes of a holy God.

The truth is that even people considered "good" are not really so. They are *not* inherently good as Carl Rogers would have us believe. We, as a fallen race of people, have a natural propensity toward sin and rebellion against our Creator. It is this innate attraction for lawlessness that habitual sexual sin stems from. Though not everyone struggles with the *same* sin, every individual has sin that comes naturally. As Paul so aptly quoted from the Old Testament:

> As it is written: "There is no one righteous, not even one; there is no one who understands, no one who seeks God. All have turned away, they have together become worthless; there is no one who does good, not even one. Their throats are open graves; their tongues practice deceit. The poison of vipers is on their lips. Their mouths are full of cursing and bitterness. Their feet are swift to shed blood; ruin and misery mark their ways, and the way of peace they do not know. There is no fear of God before their eyes." (Romans 3:10-18)

DEALING WITH THE ROOTS

From the time we are old enough to understand we are being bombarded with the message "Your life is what you choose to make it." Our parents tell us that we need to strive toward accomplishments; and in school we are taught to be proud of our work. From pre-kindergarten to high school our teachers are constantly boosting our "self-esteem." Team sports and extracurricular activities thrive on *esprit de corps*. School Spirit is used as an excuse to verbally degrade and make fun of other schools, often times under the supposed ·

innocence of "rivalry." We are encouraged to believe in ourselves and make the most of every opportunity, even at the expense of another's reputation or feelings. The "I owe it to myself" mentality has escorted Americans along the broad pathway of selfishness. "Looking out for number one" has become America's main objective.

What does all of this have to do with sexual addiction? The answer is simple. What is outlined in the previous section is a direct outgrowth of two roots of sexual addiction: Pride and Self-Centered Living. Much of our lives have been dictated by these two base motives. It is time to come to grips with what truly lies beneath the addict's lack of control. In a nutshell, he is proud beyond measure and has chosen to give himself practically anything he wants or desires. Since human beings do indeed have a sinful nature, one might expect everyone's life to be full of mayhem. However, a person's life is out of control to the extent which he or she is self-centered and prideful.

Dealing with sexual addiction in the Christian's life can be compared to dealing with bedsores of those suffering with leukemia. You can treat these painful lesions with the latest ointments, creams, and bandages, but until you cure the leukemia, the patient will stay bedridden and continue to suffer with such irritation.

In the same way, sexual addiction is a by-product of a self-centered lifestyle. The person is addicted to illicit sex *because* he is consumed with SELF. You can "treat" this problem for the rest of your life, but until the selfish nature is dealt with, it will always remain. This is the reason Pure Life Ministries puts an emphasis on dealing with *all* the aspects of a believer's spiritual life. As the believer matures as a Christian, he will become increasingly more interested in the lives of others. The less *self*-centered he becomes, the less important *self*-gratification will be in his life.

THE DEATH PROCESS

Once a person is born again, God immediately begins a process of renewal in his life—changing him into a "new creation." (II Corinthians 5:17 NIV) However, his response or willingness to allow God to reshape him into the likeness of His Son, Jesus Christ, is vitally important if he hopes to mature in the Lord and walk in daily victory over his sin. There are Christians who at first decide not to grow. There are also those who grow slowly, while others mature more quickly. Whatever the case may be, God is trying to change us from the old, carnal nature into a new, Christ-like person. He methodically strips away all the characteristics of self. The less of me that is present, the more room there is for the Personhood of Jesus to shine through. As we learn to die to self, we become increasingly more Christ-like.

God may use many kinds of experiences in our lives to bring about this transformation. We are all familiar with Romans 8:28 and often use it whenever things go badly. However, most of us take this verse out of context. It is the next verse that is the key. "And we know that God causes all things to work together for good to those who love God, to those who are called according to *His purpose*. For whom He foreknew, He also predestined to become *conformed to the image of His Son,* that He might be the first-born among many brethren;" The key words in this section of Scripture are "His purpose." What is God's purpose for His children? To "become conformed to the image of His Son." Hence, all things (i.e. circumstances, trials, adversity, suffering, loss, and etc.) are instrumental in bringing about this divine inward change. God desires to mold us into "replicas" of Jesus to be dispersed throughout the earth as His vessels of mercy. Our part in this process is to learn to "die to self" so that God can have free reign to make us more like Jesus Christ, who "laid down His life for us." (I John 3:16)

DENYING SELF

What all sexual addicts share in common is a lack of self-control. They have been unable to control their sexual urges. They have never learned how to "deny" themselves. In fact, they have obsessively pursued pleasure to the point that they have uncaringly sacrificed their walk with God, their marriages, and their families in the process. Fulfilling their every desire has been their number one priority. However, Jesus said, "If anyone wishes to come after Me, let him deny himself, and take up his cross daily, and follow Me. For whoever wishes to save his life shall lose it, but whoever loses his life for My sake, he is the one who will save it." (Luke 9:23-24)

Overcoming habits of sexual sin requires more than simply exercising self-control, otherwise it would not be called an addiction. The person fighting such a battle must learn to say "no" when temptations arise. Yet, there is still more.

The person walking in victory is one who has learned to "deny self." This must become a way of life. Indeed, Jesus requires this of *all* who profess to be followers of His. Denying self means that we must lay aside what *we* desire to do in every area of life, and choose rather to do God's will. Such obedience is gradually worked into the man who willingly submits to God's discipline, allowing Him to govern and rule his life.

I have found that most people who are addicted to one particular thing also fail to exercise control in other areas of their lives. For instance, overeating is very common among sexual addicts. Others run up credit card bills with complete disregard to the inevitable consequences. Still others may indulge in sports, entertainment, or any number of frivolous pursuits. Often this occurs because the underlying problem is not sexual addiction, but rather the lack of control, restraint, and discipline that comes from a life of self-gratification. One of the keys to overcoming an addiction is to learn restraint in *every* area of life;

not just the area of the addiction. As the person learns moderation in every area of life, he will find that the temptation to indulge in sexual sin will be weakened. Pursuing other forms of pleasure only serves to strengthen the addiction because gratifying oneself simply reinforces self-centeredness.

Taking up one's cross, as Jesus commanded in Luke 9:23, means putting an end to the old nature—the self life. Calvary represents death to the old way of living. As Paul said, "Therefore, if anyone is in Christ, he is a new creation; the old has gone, the new has come!" (II Corinthians 5:17 NIV) Something should be drastically different in the person who has come to Christ. There should be a fundamental and noticeable change in the person's nature. The Cross of Calvary represents the end of an old era and the ushering in of a new. I think A.W. Tozer best relates this:

> The old cross is a symbol of death. It stands for the abrupt, violent end of a human being. The man in Roman times who took up his cross and started down the road had already said good-bye to his friends. He was not coming back. He was going out to have it ended. The cross made no compromise, modified nothing, spared nothing; it slew all of the man, completely and for good. It did not try to keep on good terms with its victim. It struck cruel and hard, and when it had finished its work, the man was no more.[1]

PRIDE—THE CANCER OF THE SOUL

The other root of sexual sin is pride. Solomon said, "Pride goes before destruction and a haughty spirit before a fall." (Proverbs 16:18) It seems that the more prideful a person is, the more difficult overcoming sexual sin becomes. Pride is simply being filled with self and a sense of one's own importance. This attitude must be seriously dealt with if a person hopes to overcome self and his consequent sexual sin. C.H. Spurgeon said:

> Pride is so natural to fallen man that it springs up in his heart like weeds in a watered garden, or rushes by a flowing brook. It is an all pervading sin, and smothers all things like dust in the roads, or flour in the mill. Its every touch is evil. You may hunt down this fox, and think you have destroyed it, and lo! your very exultation is pride. None have more pride than those who dream that they have none. Pride is a sin with a thousand lives; it seems impossible to kill it.[2]

C.S. Lewis noted:

> The more pride one has, the more one dislikes the pride in others. In fact, if you want to find out how proud you are—the easiest way is to ask yourself, 'How much do I dislike it when other people snub me, or refuse to take any notice of me, or patronize me, or show off?' The point is that each person's pride is in competition with every one else's pride. Pride is competitive by nature.[3]

William Gurnall, the great Puritan writer of the seventeenth century, gave a chilling description of pride:

> Pride was the sin that turned Satan, a blessed angel, into a cursed devil. Satan knows better than anyone the damning power of pride. Is it any wonder, then, that he so often uses it to poison the saints? His design is made easier in that man's heart shows a natural fondness for it. Pride, like liquor, is intoxicating. A swallow or two usually leaves a man worthless to God.[4]

Now that a definition of pride has been firmly established, we will examine how pride is manifested in our lives. This will aid in overcoming its hold.

A HAUGHTY SPIRIT

When one thinks of the word haughty, an image of a wealthy snob quickly comes to mind. However, the Bible uses the term to describe any attitude of "being better than others." One need not be rich to be filled with haughtiness. Seeing oneself as smarter, prettier, stronger or more capable than others are all aspects of arrogance. Although this kind of mentality is encouraged in our culture, there is no room for it in the kingdom of God. The Psalmist said, "...No one who has a haughty look and an arrogant heart will I endure. For though the LORD is exalted, yet He regards the lowly; but the haughty He knows from afar." (Psalm 101:5; 138:6)

Consider the reality of those statements. If we, as Christians, have arrogance in our lives, we *cannot come close to God*. He will not even endure us! The more highly we think of ourselves, the farther we distance ourselves from God. The believer who persists in his arrogance is in a frightfully dangerous position.

This reminds me of a man we had in the live-in program one time. I hate to say it quite so forcefully, but this man reeked with arrogance! You could almost feel the tension when he walked into a room. It was obvious from the first day he arrived that he saw himself exalted above everyone else in every area of life. How could we help him with such an attitude? He was unwilling to humble himself and left within two weeks of arriving.

SELF-PROTECTIVE PRIDE

An individual with self-protective pride has a very difficult time being vulnerable to others. He is extremely defensive and easily offended. This person has fortified himself with an elaborate system of walls and defense mechanisms, in an attempt to keep himself from vulnerability. Because the person with self-protective pride is generally a sensitive person by nature, often the slightest offense will drive him to "save" himself from further harm. Hence, the walls of his personal fortress thicken and become even more impenetrable to any additional "intruders."

James said, "God is opposed to the proud but gives grace to the humble." (James 4:6) The person who struggles with such a protective nature must learn to put his trust in God and understand that being humiliated (which is the worst-case scenario and rarely happens) is not something horrible, but something God will use for his own good. Thomas A Kempis said, "It is good that we be sometimes contradicted, and that there be an evil or a lessening conceit had of us; and this, although we do and intend well. These things help often to the attaining of humility."[5]

The person with protective walls must let down his guard and realize that it is okay to be seen as something less than perfect. In fact, it is a freeing experience that will help him to become a warmer and more loving person. As he learns to make himself more vulnerable to other people, he will find that his towering and protective walls will come tumbling down. Those walls represent a fear of man that will be replaced with a greater concern for others. As the aged apostle of love expressed: "There is no fear in love; but perfect love casts out fear, because fear involves punishment, and the one who fears is not perfected in love." (I John 4:18)

Josh had a great deal of self-protective pride. From the time he was a child, he had always been overly-sensitive to the correction of authority figures or to the sarcastic jokes of classmates. When he came to Pure Life for help, he had enormous walls built up around himself. He would not allow himself to be vulnerable at any time. As he continued through the Live-In Program, this changed. "What really helped me was when I would see the staff humble themselves in front of the men, repenting of something they might have done that wasn't quite right," Josh said. "I came to trust them when I saw that they too were willing to admit their failures." Gradually, Josh learned to express the love of Christ to those around him.

UNAPPROACHABLE PRIDE

The person with unapproachable pride cannot be corrected, reproved, or confronted on any matter. He is noticeably tense whenever he is confronted about areas in his life which need corrected. Solomon said, "He who corrects a scoffer gets dishonor for himself, and he who reproves a wicked man gets insults for himself. Do not reprove a scoffer, lest he hate you, reprove a wise man, and he will love you." (Proverbs 9:7-8)

A proud and foolish person will not receive reproof. This is unfortunate because effective biblical counseling, which tends to be confrontational, is essential to the growth process of any Christian desiring to overcome sin in his or her life. The person with "unapproachable pride" must learn to view correction as beneficial, rather than as an attack that he must vigorously defend. He must be willing to listen to the counsel of others and allow himself to be reproved by them when necessary.

KNOW-IT-ALL PRIDE

The person with know-it-all pride is usually very talented, gifted, and knowledgeable. He tends to think that he can do anything, and in many ways, he often can! He has a great deal of distrust in the abilities of others because of his super-inflated view of himself—his incorrigible ego. He views himself as the man with all the answers because he loves to think highly of himself. But in reality, he has deceived himself into believing that other people have nothing to teach him. He contemptuously discredits the abilities of others because of his arrogance. Paul said, "Let no man deceive himself. If any man among you thinks that he is wise in this age, let him become foolish that he may become wise. For the wisdom of this world is foolishness before God..." (I Corinthians 3:18-19)

Consequently, the person with "know-it-all pride" needs to learn to humbly ask advice from others. Burt's life changed when he began doing this. A strong leader by nature, he had always gotten himself into positions of leadership. Indeed, he was quite talented in many areas of life. However, Burt was also extremely prideful about his own abilities. The Apostle Paul said, "Knowledge makes arrogant, but love edifies." (I Corinthians 8:1b) Eventually Burt began to see the ugly selfishness of his attitude and the lack of love he had for those around him. Fortunately, at our suggestion, he began asking other people advice about doing things that he was quite capable of doing for himself. This little exercise helped him tremendously. Although he practically had to tie his tongue in a knot as the other person began teaching him, little by little, he became more humble.

SELF-EXALTING PRIDE

An individual dominated by self-exalting pride feels the need to be the center of attention. Not only does he thrive on everyone noticing him, but he usually has the natural personality that attracts people. He is generally very gregarious and fun-loving. Not only does he enjoy the attention he receives, but people love giving it to him!

Solomon said, "Let another praise you and not your own mouth; a stranger, and not your own lips." (Proverbs 27:2) The person struggling with this kind of pride needs to learn to develop a quiet meekness. Rather than always promoting himself and making sure that everyone notices his good deeds, he must learn to quietly work for the Lord and allow Him to do the promoting. James admonishes us: "Humble yourselves in the presence of the Lord, and He will exalt you." (James 4:10)

UNSUBMISSIVE PRIDE

Those who struggle with unsubmissive pride are rebellious to authority. This person is also confident in his abilities (as characteristic of someone in know-it-all pride) and thinks *he* should be the one in leadership. He arrogantly places himself at the same level of those God has placed over him. He may make brazen statements like, "I hear from God, not man."

Since the 1960's, rebellion has run rampant in America. Rather than accept orders from a superior at work or at church, society teaches us to continually question authority. How different is God's perspective on authority. "Obey your leaders and submit to them;" Hebrews 13:17 says, "for they keep watch over your souls, as those who will give an account."

This rebellious spirit is also pervasive in the Church today. We need to humbly accept our position under the leaders God has set over us. If God has placed us under the care and authority of a pastor, we should submit ourselves to his leadership as unto God.

SPIRITUAL PRIDE

Lastly, anyone with a "holier-than-thou" mentality is in the opposite mind-set of those Jesus described as being "poor in spirit." The one with spiritual pride imagines himself to be a spiritual giant. God detests self-righteousness and spiritual pride. Jesus was angry with the Pharisees because of their false piety—their outward facade of holiness. They were no more sinful than others around them, but they *acted* as if they were premier role models of sanctity. However, Jesus had the following to say about them: "Woe to you, scribes and Pharisees, hypocrites! For you are like white-washed tombs which on the outside appear beautiful, but inside they are full of dead men's bones and all uncleanness. Even so you too outwardly appear righteous to men, but inwardly you are full of hypocrisy and lawlessness." (Matthew 23:27-28)

Many in the Church today act the same way. Some sit smugly in the pews judging everyone around them to see if they measure up to "their standards." Others are the "super-spiritual types" who are always hearing a so-called "word" from God, though their Christian walk is often characterized by instability, compromise, or even outright disobedience. Hence, they are spiritually arrogant, considering themselves to be at a level of maturity at which they have not yet arrived. It is for this reason that I strongly believe that Christians in sexual sin should not be in leadership, as it will only serve to promote their egos.

Paul said, "For through the grace given to me I say to every man among you not to think more highly of himself than he ought to think; but to think so as to have sound judgment, as God has allotted to each a measure of faith... Be of the same mind toward one another; do not be haughty in mind, but associate with the lowly. Do not be wise in your own estimation." (Romans 12:3, 16)

THE WAY OUT IS DOWN

Genuine humility is a fruit of the Spirit that comes from true brokenness—the breaking down process of self. The more of the old nature that remains in a believer, the less room there is for Christ or His attributes. Martin Luther said, "God created the world out of nothing, and so long as we are nothing, He can make something out of us."[6] Andrew Murray said, "This is the true self-denial to which our Savior calls us—the acknowledgment that self has nothing good in it except as an empty vessel which God must fill. It is simply *the sense of entire nothingness, which comes when we see how truly God is all, and in which we make way for God to be all.*"[7] (Emphasis in original)

It is not a matter of having high self-esteem or low self-esteem. Anyone who matures as a believer will eventually come to the place where *self*-esteem is replaced with *Christ's* esteem. A man does not combat the low opinion he may have of himself by trying to pump himself up. The only real answer for someone struggling with (so called) "low self esteem," is to humble himself and allow the Lord to infuse a sense of assurance and fulfillment that comes to any child of God who is walking in obedience to Him. Drawing nearer to the Lord results in a corresponding decrease in self-awareness, which is vital to achieving lowliness of mind through the guidance of the Holy Spirit.

One of the themes of the New Testament is servanthood. Oh, how foreign the concept of servanthood is in the Church today! It is not lowliness that most desire, but loftiness! Striving for honor is such a part of our human nature that it seems practically unavoidable. Even the disciples, during the very eve of our Savior's crucifixion, argued amongst themselves about who was the greatest. Jesus answered them and said, "Let him who is the greatest among you become the servant." (Luke 22:26) After saying this, He got on His hands and knees and washed their feet. The Lord was showing them, through this act of total servitude and selflessness, how to be a servant. He said, "You call me Teacher and Lord; and you are right, for so I am. If I then, the Lord and the Teacher, washed your feet, you also should do as I did to you. Truly, truly I say to you, a slave is not greater than his master; if you know these things, you are blessed if you do them." (John 13:13-15)

Washing feet is not popular in the Church today. I know, we should not get legalistic and think that we should have to get on our hands and knees and wash each other's feet... then again, maybe it would not be such a bad idea after-all! If our lowly Savior did it, surely we can humble ourselves and do the same. I can remember the first time I got on my knees and washed the feet of the men in the live-in program. My flesh recoiled in horror at the idea of it! I knew that the Holy Spirit was gently nudging me, so I forced myself to do it. And do you know what? It was a liberating experience! I was amazed at how good it felt to lay aside my carefully guarded image. What people thought of me was suddenly very unimportant. Such an act of serving will do so very much for the person who is filled with self, pride, and the sin which accompanies the two.

Becoming a servant is a mind-set that a person must develop. It involves a lifestyle of putting others before oneself. Pride and self-centeredness are so intertwined in the fabric of our beings that it is virtually impossible to deal with one without dealing with the other. Until a person learns to put others before himself, he will never truly be free from the desire to gratify his selfish flesh. Humbling oneself by acts of servitude is one of the greatest tools God has given us to overcome the self life. Self-centeredness is the foundation that sexual addiction thrives upon. Living in an awareness of the needs of others and having a servant's heart will absolutely undermine the self-centered life and counteract the powerful temptation of lust for more of that which is forbidden.

eight

FREEDOM COMES SLOWLY FOR A REASON

> Therefore we do not lose heart, but though our outer man
> is decaying, yet our inner man is being renewed day by day. For
> momentary, light affliction is producing for us an eternal weight
> of glory far beyond all comparison. (II Corinthians 4:16-17)

GOD TRANSFORMS A MAN in two distinct ways:
either through a miracle, which occurs instantaneously
or through a process of change over an extended
period of time. Many drug addicts who persisted in their habits
for years, have been set free instantly upon coming to the Lord.
God does not always choose to deal with them in this manner,
although I have heard of many cases in which He has done so.

However, the Lord almost always deals with those in sexual
sin through a gradual, well-organized process of transforming
the man into a new creation. In all my years of counseling men
who struggle with sexual sin, I could count on one hand those
who were instantly delivered.

Just as it has usually taken a man years to entangle himself
into such a spiritual mess, it will take some time for him to work
his way out of it. In today's "microwave" society, in which
people get cured of their ailments quickly, we have become
accustomed to expecting immediate results for everything we

desire. As a result, people often get impatient with God's timetable. As we will explore in this chapter, you will see there are good reasons why change does not happen quickly.

One of the things we must realize is that if God were to instantly set us free, it would then be much easier for us to return to old habits. However, when a person has to fight and struggle to break the powerful grip of sin, he will appreciate the freedom he eventually experiences. I remember when I first quit smoking, after I came to the Lord. Kathy and I set a date to quit and prepared ourselves for a great battle. We planned to spend the day hiking, hoping to alleviate some of the tremendous amount of stress we expected. When the day finally came, it was almost a disappointment. There was no battle. It was too easy! I was working at the jail a few weeks later when I found myself in a stressful situation. Another deputy was smoking a cigarette, and I was tempted to have one too. I remember thinking that quitting smoking was easy, so why not? I started smoking again, but the next time I quit I had to work for it!

All of the pain my wife and I have endured has had a real effect on me. It has enabled me to see the consequences of my sin more clearly. During those times of battling the temptations of sexual sin, I became determined to resist them, partly because of the price I had already paid. I simply did not want to have to pay such a price again; I knew the end result all too well.

RELIANCE ON GOD

Also, during the painstaking, reshaping process, God is teaching the man to totally rely on Him. I will never forget the Scripture that God gave me as I was agonizing my way through this process. It was something Paul related as he struggled. "And He has said to me, 'My grace is sufficient for you, for power is perfected in weakness.' Most gladly, therefore, I will rather boast about my weaknesses, that the power of Christ may dwell in me." (II Corinthians 12:9) Although, at the time, I could not understand how this could apply to my situation, I knew it was from God and had no choice but to patiently wait on Him to set me free. During this period of total powerlessness and weakness, I had to completely lean on Him. As a deputy I was trained to deal with any situation that presented itself. Now, I could no longer trust in myself to handle my problems on or off the job. God showed me that I could not overcome without Him; He had to do it and I had to wait on Him.

God is a master craftsman and actually *uses* a man's sin to eventually draw him closer to Himself. The consequences of a man's sin are often instrumental in driving him to his knees so that he will desperately cry out to the Lord for help. Being utterly powerless over sin makes a man dependent upon God. If he could quit his sin in himself why would he then need the Lord? Consequently, God uses circumstances to teach the man to fully rely on Him and to convince him of the truth the Psalmist wrote, "...deliverance by man is in vain." (Psalm 60:11)

GOD'S TIMING

One should also realize that God deals with man in His own timing. He knows when each person is prepared for the next step in the journey to freedom. The person dealing with sexual sin can often see no further than that seemingly insurmountable sin in his life. He wants to be freed of his sin and the suffering associated with it. Yet God sees the man's heart and his entire future. He knows there are many deeply-rooted issues which must be exposed and subsequently dealt with. God is often more concerned about exposing and expelling the underlying issues of the heart than He is about the outward sin with which the person struggles. Since the man is looking to Him for help, the Lord is able to use this critical period of his life to uncover other areas which are aiding and abetting his unremitting addiction to sex.

Oblivious to the fact that God has even greater plans for his life, the man bound up in habitual sin is inclined to be preoccupied simply with being set free. Delivering him out of the clutches of his sexual sin is only part of what the Lord desires to do in his life, though. For instance, the lack of love the man shows for those around him might seem to be a secondary issue, but it is a matter of extreme importance to the Lord. Yes, He wants to see the man delivered, but He is also concerned about the character of that man once he has been "loosed" from his sin. Will his selfishness simply be spent on being a work-a-holic? Will he live out the rest of his life with no concern for the lost who are going to hell around him? Will he continue to be self-centered with his family? Will those at work have to continually endure his temper? As the writer of Hebrews exhorts us: "...let us lay aside *every* weight, and the sin which doth so easily beset us..." (Hebrews 12:1 KJV) As was discussed in the last chapter, the underlying problem of sexual addiction is self-centeredness. God desires to use this season in the man's life to work on his selfish and prideful nature. The man in sin often sees no further than the immediate freedom he desires, but the Lord looks at the long term results.

As the man goes through the process of restoration, God tries to birth and cultivate the fruit of the Spirit. He expects that man to possess a great godly love for others. The Lord wants to see his life filled with true peace and joy which can only come from the Spirit. He teaches the man the enormous value of being patient with other people. During this period of time, He also builds up his faith, instilling goodness and changing his insensitive character into one of gentleness. And yes, He even develops the divine self-control which can withstand the temptations of the enemy.

However, a life transformed from one of corruption and utter uselessness to one of fruitfulness and purpose, is not spared the experience of pain. Deliverance from sexual addiction also involves personal loss. A true overcomer must part with certain relationships, places, and things that were intimately associated with his sinful lifestyle. This is extremely difficult and often traumatic to the sex addict who, for many years, has looked to his sin for comfort, pleasure, and as an escape from the real world. The man invariably finds himself grieving the loss of, not just the pleasure of the sin, but also the other elements which accompanied the lifestyle of that sin. The truth is, the idolatry of sexual sin has stolen God's rightful place in the man's life, causing him to turn to his "idol" as a reason for life and to always run to it for comfort. It has become a sanctuary from the pain of reality. *He has worshipped at its altar for many years.*

Learning to Fight

There is an aspect to Christianity described in the Book of Revelation that must be mentioned here. In chapters 2 and 3, John is instructed to write letters to seven churches which were located in the province of Asia. These seven letters cover all of the general struggles churches have encountered through the centuries. Most expositors agree that these letters represent the different kinds of churches that have existed over time. One phrase is repeated at the end of each letter: "To him who overcomes..." Seven different aspects of eternal life are then promised for each overcoming church.

The Greek word which we translate as "overcomes" is *nikao*, which means to conquer or subdue. It comes from the root word *nike*, meaning victory. Thus, we learn that Christians are meant to conquer or subdue something. Some synonyms for the word conquer are surmount, prevail against, subjugate, master and overpower. These terms describe the kind of life the believer is expected to live and experience.

Throughout his Christian journey, the believer will constantly be faced with obstacles to living a holy life. As I will discuss later, most of these hindrances lie within his own flesh. Others are placed in his path by the spirit of this world. Whatever the source of opposition, he is expected to overcome these snares. Paul spoke of "fighting the good fight," (I Timothy 1:18; 6:12) "waging war," (Romans 7:23) "weapons of our warfare," (II Corinthians 10:4) "our struggle" (Ephesians 6:12) and being a "soldier in active service." (II Timothy 2:4) Peter said we should "abstain from fleshly lusts, which wage war against the soul." (I Peter 2:11) James stated that it is "your pleasures that wage war in your members." (James 4:1) There is no question that the believer must learn to battle against his own carnal desires and temptations presented by the enemy.

The Old Testament illustration of this is found in the book of Judges. According to Scripture, God actually allowed wicked, demon-worshipping nations to remain in Palestine. The reason: "Now these are the nations which the LORD left, to test Israel by them (that is, all who had not experienced any of the wars of Canaan; only in order that the generations of the sons of Israel might be taught war, those who had not experienced it formerly)." (Judges 3:1-2)

The land of ancient Palestine was full of fertility cults. The Israelites were forced to battle against the people who offered them the very thing that they wanted. Throughout the history of the nation of Israel, the people vacillated back and forth between the worship of Jehovah and the worship of idols. God could have simply rained fire down from heaven upon all of those idolators, but instead, He told His people to drive them out. This type of mortal combat in the natural epitomizes the battles which are fought in the spiritual realm by the New Testament believer whose weapons "... are not carnal, but mighty through God to the pulling down of strong holds." (II Corinthians 10:4 KJV)

Consequently, the Christian sex addict must wage war against the enemies of his soul, "Casting down imaginations, and every high thing that exalteth itself against the knowledge of

God, and bringing into captivity every thought to the obedience of Christ." (II Corinthians 10:5 KJV) He must strive to abandon the dichotomous love-hate relationship with his sin. His flesh loves it and wants it to remain, though he understands the evil of it and longs for God to set him free. He cries out to the Lord and then, a day or two later, is right back in the middle of his sin. Rather than giving him an instantaneous deliverance or a desired "quick-fix," the Lord wants him to learn how to battle against it. Why? In order that he learn to hate evil as the Lord does. As any good soldier, the man who overcomes must endure, and yet, stay in the fight to the very end, depending solely on the Lord's help. Eventually, he will truly develop a righteous indignation (i.e. hatred) for his sin and the evils which war against his soul.

HOW LONG WILL IT TAKE?

An individual dealing with sexual addiction needs to understand that it takes time to overcome. Defeating this addiction will begin only when he accepts the fact that he needs to change his unmanageable sex life. How long it will take depends on two things I will discuss in this section.

The first is the depth of his involvement with sexual sin. Has the person been doing it for years? Has he been in denial over his problem? Has he been refusing to face responsibility for his actions? How deep has he gone into depravity? If there is proof that a deeply-rooted addiction exists, the time it will take to loosen the powerful hold that sin has had on him will be lengthy. In such cases, the addiction has grown so large and has become so deeply ingrained into his very being, that it has become a large part of who he is as a person. It is understandable how frightening it may be for him to relinquish something he identifies as part of his nature.

If his problem has gone no farther than pornography and/or masturbation, then he is fortunate, indeed. Overcoming the habit of masturbation is much easier than conquering a deep-seated addiction such as homosexuality, for instance. The further the person has gone down "The Spiral of Degradation," the more difficult will be his climb out. Thus, the more extensive the perversion, the greater the battle will be as God seeks to restore him to sanity.

The other factor is the person's determination to find freedom at any cost. Personally, I would rather work with someone who has long-standing problems but is honest with himself and is determined to endure whatever he must so that he may come into real victory. Sometimes the man with the worst addiction is the one who finds the greatest freedom. Understanding his need, he knows he *must* find his way to God no matter what.

On the other hand, I have dealt with those whose problems are not that severe and yet they never seem to make headway. Some simply put little or no effort into finding victory. Others make victory the center of their lives but look to the wrong places. Take Ben, for instance. Although his level of addiction was not extreme, and though he put much effort into quitting, he has had little result. He determined in his mind that the biblical approach was too simplistic and decided to follow the secularized, twelve-step route. I tried to persuade him that only God could set him free and that he would need to depend on Him alone, but he ignored my advice. He started a twelve-step group in his city and is apparently in the same condition now that he was in four years ago. In the meantime, those who have thrown themselves on the mercy of the Lord, have had wonderful results!

OVERCOMING THE MOUNTAIN

Climbing the steep, rugged mountain to freedom will take time but perseverance, coupled with determination to obtain freedom at any cost, will pay off! It may take time, but it is God's desire to set him free.

Some experience liberty as soon as they have a structured way out. This happened for Lance. He heard me when I appeared on my first radio show in Sacramento. It was as if he could have walked away from his sin at any time prior to this, but he just needed to be reassured. He came to our very first meeting and never looked back to his old lifestyle. Lance had the spiritual maturity to overcome and only needed to be instilled with the hope that he could.

However, others require more time, but as they battle through, the periods of sexual purity will become longer and longer. This was the case in my life. I have not met many men during my years of ministry who were more obsessed and out of control with sexual activity than I was. I had gotten to where I was utterly given over to sexual gratification. My battle out of that pit was not an easy struggle. Nevertheless, I was determined to be set free. At first, the addiction seemed like a treacherous mountain climb. As I look back on the process I went through, I now realize that the steps outlined in this book were a stairway leading directly up the side of that mountain.

Yes, an enormous pinnacle loomed high above me. Of course, it was much too high for me to simply jump over. Without a doubt, the more I looked at it, the more impossible it seemed to scale. How did I do it then? I simply took one step at a time. Each day I awoke and purposed to do my best. If I missed the mark, it simply meant that I slipped back a few steps. Before long, I was back to that place on the stairway headed in the upward direction. All I needed to do was keep my eyes on the foothold ahead of me, forgetting how high that mountain was, and continue my ascent, upward bound.

It was not long before I was able to look back and see that I had come a long way. Although I might have still slipped occasionally, I was closer to the Lord than I had ever been and the slips were less frequent. Yes, I had made considerable progress. Somehow, when I considered how far I had come, the distance I had ahead of me no longer seemed like an impossibility. I began to have hope.

Eventually, after I relentlessly continued my pursuit of higher elevations and daily adhering to the steps outlined later in this book, my saying "no" to temptation became easier and more automatic in some instances. "No, I don't really *want* to go to the bookstore today!" My personal victories were now outnumbering defeats.

Once, I went several months, only to find myself back into my sin again. I had learned to live without illicit sex but had gotten caught on a particularly "weak" day and succumbed to temptation. What followed were a few weeks of major struggling. It proved to be my last fling, however. When I turned away that time, it was for good. Although I would still have occasional struggles after that, the sin had lost its hold on me.

I had climbed up the side of that mountain and did not even know it. It took several months of living a pure life to realize that sexual addiction no longer had a hold on me. I had been so focused on the steps in front of me, that I had forgotten to look at the top of the mountain. It was no longer there! It was behind me!

I wonder what would have happened without the steps outlined in this book. I probably would have remained at the bottom, looking up in dismay. I would have been wishing I could be over the top of that mountain, but not knowing quite how to do it. Oh, I would have made an occasional attempt to scale up the side; but without clear direction, it would have simply been a futile endeavor. I would have wandered aimlessly along the side of the hill, not knowing which way to go, and not having anything to cling to. I could have always made a run up the side, full of determination and great effort. Nevertheless, I would soon tire and fall back down the hill, more exhausted and discouraged than ever. I can testify that the only way over that mountain is simply to climb painstakingly upward, a few feet at a time, one day at a time—always going forward, keeping your eyes on God, and doing your best each day. Unless God chooses to perform some other miracle, this is the only way to get over that mountain.

DEALING WITH GUILT

Again, overcoming an enormous mountain like habitual sexual sin usually does not occur quickly. As the man is in the struggle to overcome, he will have to accept the fact that he may occasionally slip. I said accept it, but do not use it as an excuse to willfully give over to your sin! Each time you give over to sin, you pull yourself further away from God. You will endure additional pain and anguish to make up for lost ground. Please realize and understand that there is a price to pay for failure. This is needful, though. Every failure will only intensify your hatred of your sin. If and when you do fail, it is important not to panic and give up. Nothing thrills the enemy more than to tempt someone into sin and then buffet him with condemnation and guilt.

However, the proper balance must be maintained. If a person does not experience any sense of guilt, he will never feel compelled to change. On the other hand, if he becomes overwhelmed with guilt, he will simply lose hope and throw up his hands in defeat. Guilt is a feeling put into our consciences for a good reason. Without experiencing feelings of guilt when we do wrong, we would never be convicted and thus, never know the difference between right and wrong. Guiltiness over sin is a natural response to it.

But God has made provision for our "missing the mark." All we need do is confess the wrongness of our actions to God, asking Him to forgive us, and it is immediately forgotten forever.

The Bible says: "If we confess our sins, He is faithful and righteous to forgive us our sins and to cleanse us from all unrighteousness." (I John 1:9) "As far as the east is from the west, so far has He removed our transgressions from us." (Psalm 103:12) "There is therefore now no condemnation for those who are in Christ Jesus." (Romans 8:1)

As we go through this process of coming into freedom, let us keep our eyes on the Lord, not on the sin. If we are always focused on how badly we are doing or our past sinful behavior, we will never sense any victory. As we will discover later in the book, God's grace has the power to take us through this process and to bring us out the other side free of the hold of sin.

nine

HOW MUCH DO YOU CARE?

"Yet even now," declares the LORD,"Return to Me with
all your heart, and with fasting, weeping, and mourning; and
rend your heart and not your garments." Now return to the
LORD your God, for He is gracious and compassionate, slow
to anger, abounding in lovingkindness, and relenting of evil.
(Joel 2:12-13)

HOW BADLY DO YOU WANT to be changed? Are
you desperate enough to do whatever it takes to be
loosed from the ties that bind? Much of the remainder
of this book will offer practical steps and techniques that you
may utilize as you begin your life as an overcoming Christian.
True freedom will not come if you do not heed to the steps
provided. It is as simple as that.

In the Scripture above, the Lord is compelling His people
through the prophet Joel to turn to Him with all their hearts. He
knew that half-hearted commitments were not enough. If your
problem at all resembles what mine was like, you have, no doubt,
been lukewarm or even rebellious for years. I was torn between
wanting to be a happily married Christian man and still wanting
to be a "swinging single." Even after my conversion to Christ,
which was a very real experience, I continued to resist doing

those things necessary to bring about my deliverance from sexual sin.

Of course, you have a tremendous advantage over me. I learned these steps the hard way. If I had had the specific guidelines outlined in this book, the length of time it took to overcome my sinful ways of living would have been shortened dramatically. I did not know if I would ever change! I knew of no one with the same problem who had succeeded in overcoming it. But, you do! This alone should provide a great deal of hope and encouragement to you. You *can* be set free from your bondage. I am not saying that it will be easy, but you can change if you are willing to follow the steps outlined in this book. Worthen discusses change:

> *Do we really want change?* When we reach the point where we realize that our own efforts are getting us nowhere, we accept the conclusion that we can't change ourselves. The next question to ask is, "Do we really want our lives to be different?" God usually does very little in our lives until we get honest with Him. He knows if we're asking Him for deliverance when we really don't want it. Often, we have an investment in our problems. We've spent years becoming comfortably adjusted to our situation. Keeping our sin has its benefits: we get a certain amount of sympathy, it allows us to escape responsibilities and it provides a form of excitement. Often we'd rather rearrange our thinking to accommodate our sin than tackle a seemingly impossible problem. If change isn't happening in our lives, we may need to admit that we really don't want it.
>
> *Motives for change.* While some of us don't want to change, others truly desire it. Yet, we still fall into the success/failure pattern. Sometimes the underlying issue is our motives. We may want to be free from

homosexuality only because of the stigma attached to our sin. It embarrasses us to view ourselves as being someone who doesn't "have it all together." We'd like to have a problem-free life so we can take pride in ourselves and have the respect of others... It's true that God uses the humiliation, the inconvenience and the distasteful consequences of sin in our lives to bring us to repentance. However, a lasting freedom from sin comes when our motives are pure: when we don't want to grieve God's Holy Spirit. Our desire for a full, rich relationship with the Lord is the motivation which clears the way for real change.[1]

You have probably been agonizing spiritually for months now, complaining bitterly to God about your tormented life. As mentioned before, you cannot blame God for the poor choices you have made. However, He will change you if that is what you sincerely desire. If you really want Him to... it all depends upon your willingness to allow Him to straighten out your crooked path. You may have blamed others for your problems for years, but now it is time to get tough, pull yourself up by the bootstraps, and be determined to beat this thing with the strength and power of God! No one else can do it for you.

What comes to my mind is the picture of a boxer who is being pummeled in the corner by the other fighter, when suddenly, he has had enough and comes out swinging! This must also happen to you. You must shake off that complacency and come out swinging! Is this not what the Lord was saying through the prophet Joel: Turn, fast, weep, mourn and rend? These are action words which describe someone determined to get what he needs from the Lord. Winning this battle will require this kind of serious commitment. How can one know that he will truly find freedom from sexual sin by doing these things? The divine "If-Then Principle," as I call it, promises that he will.

THE IF-THEN PRINCIPLE

Throughout the Bible, God has made a multitude of promises to His people. Many of these promises, however, depend upon the believer doing something first. Although not all of them actually have the words "if-then" contained in them, they all have a conditional nature which is understood. Read each of the following verses as if God were talking directly to you:

If my people, which are called by my name, shall humble themselves, and pray, and seek my face, and turn from their wicked ways; then will I hear from heaven, and will forgive their sin, and will heal their land. (II Chronicles 7:14)

Delight yourself in the LORD; and He will give you the desires of your heart. Commit your way to the LORD, trust also in Him, and He will do it. (Psalm 37:4-5)

Trust in the LORD with all your heart, and do not lean on your own understanding. In all your ways acknowledge Him, and He will make your paths straight. (Proverbs 3:5-6)

Rejoice in the Lord always; again I will say, rejoice! Let your forbearing spirit be known to all men. The Lord is near. Be anxious for nothing, but in everything by prayer and supplication with thanksgiving let your requests be made known to God. And the peace of God, which surpasses all comprehension, shall guard your hearts and your minds in Christ Jesus. (Philippians 4:4-7)

There is a common theme through all of these promise

verses. *If* we *do* something, i.e. repent, trust, delight, pray, and so on, *then* God will do something for us. Sexual addiction is not going to be overcome by sitting back and waiting for God to throw a thunderbolt. The determined man must initiate the fight himself.

Did God decide you were to be saved and suddenly make you a Christian? Perhaps you were not aware of it. Perhaps all you saw was that He started bringing conviction into your heart through the Holy Spirit. He graciously orchestrated circumstances so that you would turn to Him. The key is that at some point you had to take a purposeful step toward Him. Having done that, He met you at the altar where He joyfully received you as His own.

This same principle applies to overcoming sin. We must take the first step. I can remember the rut my wife was once in as she worked in a sweatshop for $4.00 an hour. She hated that job and for good reason! It was a very dismal place to work. She wanted out of there badly, but could not seem to get hired anywhere else. One day, God revealed to me the reason why. She had a bad attitude about the place. She would often go in to work late, do a lousy job while she was there, and frequently find some excuse to leave early. I told her that God was never going to move her from that job until she changed her attitude. She knew that it was true and determined within herself to be the best employee that business had. She began going to work on time and putting out more work than ever before. Within a week, a large insurance company that she had applied at months before, hired her! She learned a valuable lesson from this experience. She could have continued to complain and be ungrateful, but she chose to do what the Lord would have her to do, regardless of the circumstances. God honored that commitment and blessed her greatly. As you look at your circumstances, you must decide if you are going to continue on the easy path, or travel the road the Lord has paved for you. It will not be easy but the "If-Then Principle" promises that He will honor your first step and will help you through this struggle.

CRYING OUT TO GOD

It is important to understand that God loves His people tremendously and is in a passion to help them. When someone gets to the point of desperately wanting the Lord to remove the sin in his life, he will start crying out to Him for His help, which is never far away. God guarantees freedom to His children, but it is their responsibility to meet the conditions. The "If-Then Principle" helps struggling saints to recognize that if they will cry out for His help without ceasing, He will respond to their appeals. Persistence in prayer was established by God as the means to receive His help. To further explain this truth, Jesus gave the following two stories which demonstrate the benefit of being bold:

> And He said to them, "Suppose one of you shall have a friend, and shall go to him at midnight, and say to him, 'Friend, lend me three loaves; for a friend of mine has come to me from a journey, and I have nothing to set before him'; and from inside he shall answer and say, 'Do not bother me; the door has already been shut and my children and I are in bed; I cannot get up and give you anything.' I tell you, even though he will not get up and give him anything because he is his friend, yet because of his persistence he will get up and give him as much as he needs. (Luke 11:5-8)

> Now He was telling them a parable to show that at all times they ought to pray and not to lose heart, saying, "There was in a certain city a judge who did not fear God, and did not respect man. "And there

was a widow in that city, and she kept coming to him, saying, 'Give me legal protection from my opponent.' And for a while he was unwilling; but afterward he said to himself, 'Even though I do not fear God nor respect man, yet because this widow bothers me, I will give her legal protection, lest by continually coming she wear me out.'" And the Lord said, "Hear what the unrighteous judge said; now shall not God bring about justice for His elect, who cry to Him day and night, and will He delay long over them? (Luke 18:1-7)

No one understands to the fullest all that is involved in answered prayer or being set free from bondage. However, we do know that the Lord has given us important principles here that we can depend on to help us. If you doubt that God really listens to the cries of His children, examine these passages that boast of His mercy:

Then we cried to the LORD, the God of our fathers, and the LORD heard our voice and saw our affliction and our toil and our oppression; and the LORD brought us out of Egypt with a mighty hand and an outstretched arm and with great terror and with signs and wonders; (Deuteronomy 26:7-8)

And when the sons of Israel cried to the LORD, the LORD raised up a deliverer for the sons of Israel to deliver them, Othniel the son of Kenaz, Caleb's younger brother. (Judges 3:9)

But when the sons of Israel cried to the LORD, the LORD raised up a deliverer for them, Ehud the son of Gera, the Benjamite, a left-handed man... (Judges 3:15)

> And the sons of Israel cried to the LORD... And the
> LORD routed Sisera and all his chariots and all his army,
> with the edge of the sword before Barak; and Sisera
> alighted from his chariot and fled away on foot.
> (Judges 4:3, 15)

> Now it came about when the sons of Israel cried to
> the LORD on account of Midian, that the LORD sent
> a prophet to the sons of Israel... (Judges 6:7-8)

These passages are just a few accounts of God's response to
the cries of His people. Time and time again the nation of Israel
would get themselves into trouble because of their disobedience. Yet, whenever they cried out to God for His help, He
would rescue them. Your situation might be much the same as
that of Israel. It is because of your disobedience that you are in
the predicament you find yourself in, and yet there is a merciful
God who hears the cries of His children.

I once thought that all of the trips I made to the altar crying
out for God's help were a waste of time. Then as I re-examined
those isolated incidents, I came to realize that those trips to the
altar were instrumental in bringing about my deliverance! If you
really want to be set free from the bondage of sexual sin, cry out
to God daily. Do it today! Do it now! Your cries will be heard!

After David committed the sin of adultery with Bathsheba,
he humbled himself and prayed the following prayer:

> Be gracious to me, O God, according to Thy loving-
> kindness; according to the greatness of Thy compassion
> blot out my transgressions. Wash me thoroughly from
> my iniquity, and cleanse me from my sin. For I know my
> transgressions, and my sin is ever before me. Against
> Thee, Thee only, I have sinned, and done what is evil in
> Thy sight, so that Thou art justified when Thou dost

speak, and blameless when Thou dost judge.

Behold, I was brought forth in iniquity, and in sin my mother conceived me. Behold, Thou dost desire truth in the innermost being, and in the hidden part Thou wilt make me know wisdom.

Purify me with hyssop, and I shall be clean; wash me, and I shall be whiter than snow. Make me to hear joy and gladness, let the bones which Thou hast broken rejoice. Hide Thy face from my sins, and blot out all my iniquities.

Create in me a clean heart, O God, and renew a steadfast spirit within me. Do not cast me away from Thy presence, and do not take Thy Holy Spirit from me. Restore to me the joy of Thy salvation, and sustain me with a willing spirit.... The sacrifices of God are a broken spirit; a broken and a contrite heart, O God, Thou wilt not despise. (Psalm 51:1-17)

If you start crying out to God in the same spirit, you will see Him begin to work in your life. You must come to Him with a broken and contrite spirit, having reached "the end of your rope," no longer doing things your way, but humbly crying out to the Lord for His help. Again, God hears the cries of His children.

To illustrate how God answers our prayers, I want to tell you a true story which occurred about seven years ago. There were two men in a church who, unbeknownst to either of them, were both struggling with sexual addiction. Chuck found out about Pure Life Ministries and immediately began the process to enter the live-in program. Gene, the other man, was the youth pastor of the same church. The senior pastor had just discovered that Gene had had a sexual relationship with one of the teenaged boys. A friend gave Gene an earlier copy of this book, which he read in one sitting. Gene's life was crumbling around him. In his state of desperation, he rashly told the Lord that if He wanted him to get help through Pure Life Ministries then He should have Steve Gallagher call that day. His challenge to God was not an attempt to test the Lord or lay down conditions. It was simply the urgent plea of a man who did not know what else to do.

Gene was totally unaware that Chuck had sent in an application to the live-in program which I was reviewing that *very* morning. For some unexplainable reason, rather than putting down his home telephone number on the application, he wrote in the number of the church. I will never forget what happened that morning when I called. "Coincidently," the secretary was out sick that day, so when the phone rang, Gene was the one who answered it.

"Good morning, this is Victory Christian Center. May I help you?" Even though Gene was greatly distraught inside, he was forcing himself to go through the motions at work.

"Yes, may I speak to Chuck Green?" I asked.

"Chuck is a member of the church here, but he doesn't work here. I can take a message for him, though. Who shall I say called?"

"Yes, my name is Steve Gallagher." When I said those words I heard the telephone drop. "Hello. Are you there?" It was a full two minutes before Gene responded to my questions.

"Are you the Steve Gallagher who wrote *Sexual Idolatry*?" he asked incredulously.

"Why yes, I am." After hearing that, Gene went on to explain to me the whole story. Within two days he was in the live-in program. Over the next six months Gene's life was transformed, and eventually he was restored to the ministry. God surely hears the cries of His children!

THE PRAYER OF FAITH

There is one more aspect to the cry for help which is very

important. The prayer of faith plays a major role in the addict's ultimate deliverance. In spite of what some teach, faith is not something that is simply mustered up through the denial of reality (i.e. The sick person who acts as though the sickness is not there, etc.). The center of the Christian faith is Christ, and our faith is inextricably tied to who He is. What a person believes about the Lord determines everything in his life as a believer. Thus, for the most part, our ability to believe the Lord for victory is directly determined by our level of trust in Him. This trust is based in one's knowledge of His character. God is ever at work attempting to instill a sense of His trustworthiness to His children. Those who come into a closer, more intimate relationship with the Lord find Him to be a sweet, loving Person. The following is an excerpt from my book *Living In Victory*:

I have a good friend named Jerry who has four kids. He is a godly man with what seems to be an infinite amount of patience. When one of his kids misbehaves, he calmly and lovingly explains to them why they are about to be punished and then proceeds to dispense the required spanking. Typically, the kids see him as being a kind and loving father. If one of them needs something, they are not afraid to ask him. In fact, if it is something that they know to be a legitimate need, they ask with much confidence (perhaps too much sometimes!). Why do they have such confidence in him to grant their request? Jerry has proven his love and his kindness to them consistently over the years. They trust him because they know his character.

Isn't this exactly what Jesus teaches us in the Sermon on the Mount? He said, "Ask, and it shall be given to you; seek, and you shall find; knock, and it shall be opened to you. For everyone who asks receives, and he who seeks finds, and to him who knocks it shall be opened. Or what man is there among you, when his son shall ask him for a loaf, will give him a stone? Or if he shall ask for a fish, he will not give him a snake, will he? If you then, being evil, know how to give good gifts to your children, how much more shall your Father who is in heaven give what is good to those who ask Him!" (Matthew 7:7-11)

The basis for believing prayer isn't that we are able to grit our teeth and somehow conjure up sufficient faith to stifle all doubting thoughts. The foundation for believing God is our recognition of His goodness and His willingness to abundantly meet our needs.

The Greek word for believe is *pistos. Vine's Expository Dictionary* defines it as, "to believe, also to be persuaded of, and hence, to place confidence in, to trust, signifies, in this sense of the word, reliance upon, not mere credence."[6]

Another dictionary takes it even further when it considers the reason for the trust: "To persuade, particularly to move or affect by kind words or motives... To bring over to kind feelings, to conciliate... to pacify or quiet an accusing conscience... To win over, gain the favor of or make a friend of (someone)."[7]

These descriptions of the word believe remind me of the movie *Driving Miss Daisy*. In this movie, a Jewish woman in Georgia hires a black man as a chauffeur during the '50s. Deeply distrustful of all, cantankerous, and arrogant, the woman treats everybody around her with disdain. The black man, a devout Christian, continually humbles himself to her throughout their long relationship. At the end, as they have both grown old together, she lets her walls down for all to see her love and admiration for him. He won her heart by his humility and kindness.

This is a real picture of the way the Lord gets us to believe in Him. Year after year, He goes under us, helps us, encourages us, and blesses us. Eventually, the heart melts and He has won another to Himself. Only the hardest heart could resist such amazing love. For this reason, we must guard our hearts from straying away from Him.[2]

One of the terrible and frightening aspects of sin is the unbelief that it fosters. The more deeply entrenched the sin, the greater the darkness of unbelief. Many men who come to the Pure Life Ministries Live-In Program are very cynical. Part of the problem, of course, is that they have heard countless empty promises touted by those trying to draw followers to their particular system of recovery. We are not overly concerned when a man arrives with a skeptical attitude because we know that within a month or so he will see the reality of God, which will provoke a great deal of hope within him. There are always those who will not believe the best about God. They are like the wicked servant Jesus spoke of who attempted to justify his laziness by redirecting the blame at God: "'Master, I knew you to be a hard man...'" (Matthew 25:24) Many choose to believe God is harsh in order to somehow justify their disobedience. As was the case with the servant who hid his talent, excuses will not alter the course of reality on the day of reckoning.

The fact is, the Lord greatly desires to help the struggling believer and is available to provide the necessary power to overcome if the man will only humble himself and ask. The believing prayer says, "Lord, I realize that it is my fault that I am in this predicament. I come to Your throne looking for mercy. My request is not based on any merit of my own, but upon Your great heart. I believe what the Bible says about You. You are a God of mercy and compassion, and I believe that You will help me out of this mess because of what You are like." This is the prayer which the Lord will be quick to answer.

PART THREE

INFLUENCES

ten

THE SINFUL FLESH

Now the deeds of the flesh are evident, which are:
immorality, impurity, sensuality, idolatry... (Galatians 5:19-20)

IN THE NEXT THREE CHAPTERS, we will examine the
three forces which work tirelessly to compel us toward sin.
They are the flesh, the world, and the enemy.

Let us first explore "the flesh," which is the only influence
of the three generated from within us. The Bible primarily
utilizes this term as a designation of mankind. Genesis 6:12 is
one example: "And God looked on the earth, and behold, it was
corrupt; for all flesh had corrupted their way upon the earth."
Man's primary composition is flesh and so the term is used
representatively of man throughout the Scriptures. Even in the
spiritual sense, a person is confined to his fleshly body with the
soul and spirit residing within it simultaneously. Where the
man's body is, he is. Whatever happens to the body, befalls the
man. His soul accompanies his body. It is the body of a man
which we see and interact with.

Human beings were created with certain innate drives,
impulses, and appetites such as hunger, thirst, and even the
desire for sex. If maintained within the proper limits for which

they were created, they are all beneficial and extremely vital to the maintenance of human life itself. However, "the desire(s) of the flesh," as Paul coined them, are not limited to the basic urges described. There are many things the "flesh" man desires. These impulses prompt man to seek out the things which will provide comfort, physical satisfaction and pleasure. Since the flesh desires only that which brings it gratification, the "desire(s) of the flesh" are inherently selfish by nature. Consequently, indulgence in any one of them tends to promote a tremendous level of self-centeredness within the person.

Sin is another factor to be considered. The physical nature of man is not concerned with pleasing God. It is only interested in comfort, pleasure, and the preservation of self. Therefore, the man who has not had an encounter with God lives his life completely under the auspices of his demanding flesh. The desires of the flesh drive the person to do things which are in total opposition to the nature and kingdom of God. Sin, any behavior forbidden by God, acts as the ruling influence within the man's being. Indeed, every human being is born with a corrupted nature bent toward sin. As mentioned in the seventh chapter, we are all born with a fallen nature polluted by sin. It is "the inward principle of evil which possesses our nature, and lies back of the will, beyond the reach of our power..."[1]

Living under the dominion of a sinful nature establishes habits which eventually form a lifestyle. Deep ruts are dug into the person's life. He becomes comfortable responding to his inner longings. By the time he becomes a believer, the passions of the flesh have already ruled his life for many years. These deeply entrenched habits have been constantly reinforced and strengthened by the old nature which has become accustomed to having its own way. When the desire for sexual behavior wells up within him, he gives into the craving without a second thought. Again, the foundational purpose for life, even for the most decent non-believer, revolves around pleasure, gratification, and self-preservation.

When a person is born again, suddenly a new influence is introduced into his being. It is the Spirit of God which now resides within him. Whereas before, most decisions of life were made with the intention of satisfying his natural desires, now the person is imparted with a whole new value system. Though a new morality has been infused into the person, the physical longings of the flesh are still relentless in exerting their influence. Thus, we find Paul agonizing over the age-old struggle of believers, "For the flesh sets its desire against the Spirit, and the Spirit against the flesh; for these are in opposition to one another, so that you may not do the things that you please." (Galatians 5:17) There is now a war that takes place within the person that was non-existent before. There was no battle previously because the flesh enjoyed total freedom in its influence.

DUAL NATURES

It is significant to note that Jesus described the conversion experience as being "born again." In fact, much of the New Testament describes a process of growth whereby those who are "babes in Christ" gradually reach spiritual maturity. Unfortunately, many Christians remain immature for a time. However, those who do grow find the old carnal nature slowly fading as a new nature emerges.

Man is a tri-part being: flesh, soul, and spirit. The flesh longs for satisfaction at any cost. It always seeks that which is sensual and satisfying. It is unconcerned with God, family, friends, or anyone else. It wants only its lusts and desires to be fully satisfied.

The spirit is a vacuum within a person's being which is filled with the Spirit of Christ upon conversion. It craves the things of God and yearns for spiritual fulfillment. It only wants to do what is pleasing to God. It is from here that we get the pangs of guilt when we are disobedient to the Lord.

Finally, the soul (mind), is made up of the emotions, will, and intellect. When a person is first born again, the flesh is a powerful, muscular force. Comparatively, the spirit is an underfed weakling! However, as the Christian begins to mature spiritually, the spirit man becomes stronger and more able to subdue the flesh man as God intended.

Inside the soul is where the war rages between the flesh and the Spirit. Although it is our intellect and emotions that battle, it is the will that ultimately makes the final decision. God gave every person a free will to choose between right and wrong. Every moment we must decide which side we will feed. Just as the flesh grows stronger when we feed it with sensuous living, our spirit grows stronger when it is nourished with the things of God.

Which will you feed the most? Will you feed your carnal man, building him stronger and stronger? Or will you strengthen your spiritual man who Paul says is "being renewed?" The remainder of this book will teach you how to methodically build your spiritual man. As he is nurtured, strengthened, and renewed, the old, carnal man will gradually weaken and wither. This is one of the most important secrets to breaking free from sexual bondage.

Everything about Christianity directly opposes the flesh and its desires. The old, carnal nature desires a life revolving around pleasure. Christianity contradicts such a hedonistic lifestyle. The flesh desires to see itself vaunted and puffed up. Christianity withstands pride. The old nature wants to use the "wisdom of the world." Christianity preaches against human reasoning. Everything the flesh wants, is contrary to the Spirit.

Paul claims that we have "put on the new nature." (Colossians 3:10 RSV) This new nature must be nourished daily by the Word of God through the power of the Holy Spirit. Perhaps you have heard the illustration about the Eskimo walking down the street with two huskies. A man asked him which dog was the strongest. The Eskimo replied, "The one I feed the most."

I admit that in my own strength I am absolutely powerless over sexual addiction. I am convinced of my weakness because I have failed countless times in the past when temptations overwhelmed me. However, as my mind was renewed each day, my spirit man was strengthened. To my surprise, I discovered that I do indeed have two very distinct natures within me. Now I choose to feed the new nature which I want to dictate the course of my life.

THE WAR WITHIN

The struggling Christian who still feels weak spiritually reminds me of a movie I saw many years ago. The hero was a narcotics detective who was kidnapped and injected with heroin. You could see the determination written on his face. He wanted to escape, but his body just would not cooperate. He mustered up all his strength and struggled to make it to the door, but every time he tried to get up, he would fall right on his face. The spiritually weak are much the same. The influences of the world, the flesh, and the devil seem so overwhelming that each time the person tries to do right, he finds himself failing again and again. Paul described this war that goes on within every true believer in Romans chapter 7:

> I don't understand myself at all, for I really want to do what is right, but I can't. I do what I don't what to— what I hate. I know perfectly well that what I am doing is wrong, and my bad conscience proves that I agree with these laws I am breaking. But I can't help myself, because I'm no longer doing it. It is sin inside me that is

stronger than I am that makes me do these evil things.

I know I am rotten through and through so far as my old sinful nature is concerned. No matter which way I turn I can't make myself do right. I want to but I can't. When I want to do good, I don't, and when I try not to do wrong, I do it anyway. Now if I am doing what I don't want to, it is plain where the trouble is: sin still has me in its evil grasp.

It seems to be a fact of life that when I want to do what is right, I inevitably do what is wrong. I love to do God's will so far as my new nature is concerned; but there is something else deep within me, in my lower nature, that is at war with my mind and wins the fight and makes me a slave to the sin that is still within me. In my mind I want to be God's willing servant but instead I find myself still enslaved to sin.

So you see how it is: my new life tells me to do right, but the old nature that is still inside me loves to sin. Oh what a terrible predicament I am in! Who will free me from my slavery to this deadly lower nature? Thank God! It has been done by Jesus Christ our Lord. He has set me free. (Romans 7:15-25 Living Bible)

The Physical Drive

There is nothing wrong with sex as long as it is confined to intimacy between a man and his wife. God wants married couples, whom He has enjoined, to enjoy each other—thus, He made it a pleasurable experience (see chapter seventeen). However, confusion and perversion emerge when people deviate from the purpose for which God ordained.

The desire for sex is one of the basic, physical drives of the human being. It is among hunger, thirst, and sleep as the most important natural impulses. God instilled these desires in us so that we would do the things required to exist and survive as individual people and as a species. If we did not have hunger, how often would we eat? If we did not experience thirst, how often would we drink? If we did not grow sleepy, when would our bodies get rest? If God had not put a wholesome desire within us to have sex, how would we reproduce?

As with all of these drives, when someone abuses the purpose for sex, it becomes doubly hard to get it back under control. A person who has become addicted to alcohol or drugs has a tremendous battle in order to break free. His freedom from their gruesome pull not only depends upon his surrendering his life to Jesus Christ but also upon his willingness to modify certain aspects of his lifestyle. It is imperative that he changes his friends and the places he goes. Old acquaintances and neighborhoods may trigger another relapse and sabotage any progress he has already made. However, for the one who is addicted to food or sex, such modifications will only benefit him to a certain degree. He will always be around food and people at some point in his life and be forced to deal with an inbred desire for food or sex—these desires are virtually impossible to avoid. An alcoholic could go through his entire life without ever handling another drink, but sex addicts must learn to their appetites. This is an extremely difficult thing to do; hence, it is not easy for the addict to escape the bondage of sexual sin. In addition to the incessant cries and ruthless demands of his flesh for more, he has the world constantly telling him that he can have more any time, any place, and with whomever he so desires. Worthen says:

> The flesh always wants what is easiest to obtain. It is never interested in anything requiring pain or effort. It always wants to go back to what was comfortable... Our flesh prefers to groan and throw up the white flag. We need to remember, flesh is on the other side! Flesh is happy to respond to any invitation to sin. The flesh will

also criticize our defense with messages such as: "You're fighting the very thing you desire most!"[2]

PHYSICAL BUILDUP

Another thing that must be considered when talking about the sexual drive in a man is the physical buildup he experiences when he has been abstinent for some time. Men have two egg-shaped sperm-producing organs that are called testicles. When sexual response is inhibited, they gradually fill to capacity with sperm. As this happens, men become very easily aroused by the slightest sexual stimuli.

I often have singles come to me asking how to get the victory over a habit of masturbation. Their dilemma is serious and legitimate because of the physical buildup that occurs. They do not have the luxury of releasing this reservoir of semen that produces such strong sexual urges. Yet, in another way, it is easier for them than the married man struggling with bondage. Single guys often think that married men should not have any further problems with sexual sin. What they fail to understand is that married men cannot simply quit having sex; they have to learn to *control* it. The thoughts of fantasy a married man dwells on while making love to his wife are just as sinful as the thoughts of fantasy that a single man thinks about while masturbating. A man does not get delivered of lust by getting married. He has to control his thought life after marriage just as he did when he was single. The thrill of a new wife will last for a while, but those tantalizing fantasies will return to haunt him until he has truly conquered them spiritually.

In a sense, the single man truly does have it easier; he can starve his flesh. Although the physical desire is there, he can become so accustomed to the lack of sexual activity that eventually the "habit" of sex is broken. It seems that the most difficult period of time a man faces is five to ten days after the last ejaculation. When that hormonal level first starts peaking, it is as though *everything* has a sexual connotation! This lasts for a few days but then begins to dissipate. It is almost as though the man becomes *asexual.* The overwhelming desire for sex seems to dwindle and reaches a more manageable level.

Many single young men have been so bound to the habit of masturbation that they have seldom gone ten days without a release. Overcoming masturbation is by no means an impossible task as many presume. For the person who wants to be free, God has made a way of escape. The question is: Do you really want to be set free? As I said before, God is not going to take a habit from you that you want to hold on to. Oh, I know that your flesh craves it, but do you sincerely want the victory?

CATERING TO THE FLESH

I remember the satirical sheet a police sergeant once wrote. It was called something like: "How To Raise A Common Criminal." It listed approximately fifteen suggestions as to how to raise your child to become a criminal. Some of the things I can remember are: give in every time he demands something, don't disagree with him, don't punish him, don't teach him respect for other people, and so on. I think you get the picture. With that in mind, I would like to share what I would call, *Ten Steps To Carnal Living:*

1. Spend as much time watching secular television as possible. You owe it to yourself!
2. Eat sweets as often as you possibly can and give in to every craving for food immediately.
3. Worry about loving yourself more, and God and others less.
4. Fill your life with fun things and avoid adversity at all cost.

5. Be a taker, not a giver; after all, you already pay taxes!
6. Never do anything that anyone would construe as fanaticism; you do have an image to uphold!
7. You need not worry about having daily devotions; you do not have time!
8. When you are confronted with sin in your life, go directly into delusion.
9. Anytime you have a problem, always refer to a psychology book; psychologists know much more about life than God.
10. Give in to every sexual urge; after all, God created them in you.

The preceding was written in fun, of course, but it helps us to see how easily we can continually build the flesh up at the expense of our spiritual life. Each time we please the flesh, whether it be something seemingly harmless or something that is downright sinful, we are strengthening the flesh. Therefore, we are increasing its hold on our lives through continual reinforcement.

THE POWER OF HABIT

Many people encounter difficulty overcoming the power of the flesh because they have spent many years developing specific patterns of life which are hard to modify. A lifestyle is made up of various habits. Abandoning a life catered to the flesh in order to obtain one controlled by the Spirit requires changing certain routines. Nelson E. Hinman discusses the "Power of Habit:"

But I say the power of habit is rooted in the deepest recesses of our minds, well below the areas of quick recall... All of our skills are developed by good practiced habits. It gets down into our subconscious mind and controls us. As long as you drive your car having to think about everything you do, you are a dangerous driver. But by "practicing" your driving, it becomes *habit*. Once you establish the of driving, you become a very good driver. How do you do this? By practice. How about typewriting? Some people can walk up to a typewriter, having never even touched one before and in a remarkably short period of time can be touch typing. How? By practice...

The thing we don't realize is that by the same way we can develop bad habits. Baseball players sometimes develop bad habits. That is what coaches are for; they spot a player who is developing a bad habit and they work with them until they eliminate it. You can understand that but the thing you probably do not stop to think about is that by this same identical process we develop emotional habits; both good and bad...

We can understand this a little more clearly if we talk about anger. Anger is a learned response. I know, for I had a problem with anger for over twenty years... I got that way by habitual response. I learned to do it. The more I practiced at it the better I got at it. Well, I had to learn how to reverse it...

We can train our minds to act any way we want them to act, up to a given point. But there is a thing in the Bible called "sin" that interrupts the best you can do. However, it is not placed beyond your control because God has given us a book of directions and instructions on how to deal with those things.[3]

Sexual addicts have developed habits of responding sexually to outside stimuli. Over the years they have learned to react to certain situations with lust or fantasy. When I would drive down the street and see a pretty girl walking, I would leer at her. This eventually became a habit. When I used to go to bed with my wife, I often fantasized about other women. When I felt the urge for illicit sex, I was accustomed to yielding without a fight. I needed to learn to break these awful habits and exercise self-control. How? By practice!

Practice Makes Perfect

Paul and Peter both understood the importance of establishing proper habits through practice.

Now the deeds of the flesh are evident, which are: immorality, impurity, sensuality, idolatry, sorcery, enmities, strife, jealousy, outbursts of anger, disputes, dissensions, factions, envying, drunkenness, carousing, and things like these, of which I forewarn you just as I have forewarned you that those who *practice* such things shall not inherit the kingdom of God. (Galatians 5:19-21)

Finally, brethren, whatever is true, whatever is honorable, whatever is right, whatever is pure, whatever is lovely, whatever is of good repute, if there is any excellence and if anything worthy of praise, let your mind dwell on these things. The things you have learned and received and heard and seen in me, *practice* these things; and the God of peace shall be with you. (Philippians 4:8-9)

For by these He has granted to us His precious and magnificent promises, in order that by them you might become partakers of the divine nature, having escaped the corruption that is in the world by lust.

Now for this very reason also, applying all diligence, in your faith supply moral excellence, and in your moral excellence, knowledge; and in your knowledge, self-control, and in your self-control, perseverance, and in your perseverance, godliness; and in your godliness, brotherly kindness, and in your brotherly kindness, love...

Therefore, brethren, be all the more diligent to make certain about His calling and choosing you; for as long as you *practice* these things, you will never stumble. (II Peter 1:4-10)

We can see in these sections of Scripture that we have a choice about what we *practice*. If we practice (or sow) ungodliness, then we will desire (or reap) ungodliness. By the same token, if we practice godliness, then we will desire a greater godliness. Feelings always follow behavior. The proper habits need to be established into our minds, and as they are, we will *desire* to continue in them. Jay Adams discusses the need to establish new habits:

> Counselors must recognize that too many Christians give up. They want the change too soon. What they really want is change without the daily struggle. Sometimes they give up when they are on the very threshold of success. They stop before receiving. It usually takes at least three weeks of proper daily effort for one to feel comfortable in performing a new practice. And it takes about three more weeks to make the practice part of oneself. Yet, many Christians do not continue even for three days. If they do not receive instant success, they get discouraged. They want what they want now, and if they don't get it now, they quit...
>
> We have seen, therefore, that breaking a habit is a two-sided enterprise that requires regular, structured, endurance in putting off and putting on. Dehabituation is more than that; it also involves rehabituation. When a counselee turns his back upon his old ways, at the same

time he must turn to face God's new ones.[4]

The primary enemy we will face is our own fallen nature. It is our flesh that longs for gratification. It is within these recesses that sin abides. Although we are under an attack from without, if we can win the war within, the outside enemies will fall before us.

eleven

SEPARATING FROM THE WORLD

Enter by the narrow gate; for the gate is wide, and the way
is broad that leads to destruction, and many are those who enter
by it. (Matthew 7:13)

IT IS EASY TO UNDERSTAND WHY people in this day
and age have a misconception about sex. Everywhere you
turn, you find the promotion and exploitation of sex. Hollywood is committed to portraying the hero as the master seducer.
Movies are overrun with beautiful, scantily clad (or nude)
starlets. Advertisers blatantly use sex to sell their products.
Fashion designers do their utmost to make sure that young
women show off as much flesh as possible. Company parties
hire male or female strippers for entertainment. Homosexuality
is unashamedly flaunted and advocated. People openly live
together in sin. Needless to say, the moral fabric of our society
is being unraveled right before our eyes.

Society teaches young people that sex is not only accepted,
but expected. Take the life of an average twelve-year old boy. He
gets up in the morning and goes to school. In health class he is
taught sex education that refuses to take a moral stand against
pre-marital sex or even homosexuality. Often, while with his

schoolmates, he overhears the popular, and often precocious, boys talk about their sexual escapades. On the way home from school, he stops in the local convenience store and sees magazine covers behind the counter or on the stands with nude women plastered on the front of them. At home he listens to the popular groups on the radio sing about sex. After dinner he watches a movie on television in which the characters are engaged in various sexual scenarios. The hero is almost always a womanizer—the "Casanova" type. Then there are the commercials that showcase beautiful women in bathing suits to sell anything from sports magazines to automobiles. With such overwhelming exposure as this, why should anyone be surprised that a young teenager turns into a sex addict?

A permissive society, such as ours, makes the road to sexual addiction very smooth. Just as our culture makes it easy for a person to slide down the path deeper and deeper into bondage, it also makes it equally difficult for the person, who so desires, to escape it. Everywhere he turns, he is constantly confronted with and reminded of what he is trying to avoid. Erwin Lutzer gives his viewpoint of society's reasoning: "For those who believe in free love, sex is primarily a physical experience. When you're hungry you eat, when you're tired you sleep, and when you're turned on, you have sex. Such reasoning may sound right, but it's off the target by a mile."[1] Lester Sumrall says that "The carnal world would have us believe that pleasure is the only purpose of sex. Some prudish Christians think that pleasure has nothing to do with sex. Both are wrong."[2]

Consequently, when a person grows up in a society that presents this hedonistic message, which is basically: "If it feels good, just do it," it is very hard for his mind to dismiss the untruth of it. If he becomes born again, he must suddenly live by new standards. But because western civilization is simply addicted to immorality, it is especially difficult for the new Christian struggling with sexual addiction.

SEPARATING OURSELVES

Paul, as he was trying to encourage the believers who lived in the immoral climate of Corinth, said the following:

> Do not be bound together with unbelievers; for what partnership have righteousness and lawlessness, or what fellowship has light with darkness? Or what harmony has Christ with Belial, or what has a believer in common with an unbeliever? Or what agreement has the temple of God with idols? For we are the temple of the living God; just as God said, "I will dwell in them and walk among them; and I will be their God, and they shall be My people. Therefore, come out from their midst and be separate," says the Lord. "And do not touch what is unclean; and I will welcome you. And I will be a father to you, and you shall be sons and daughters to Me," says the Lord Almighty. (II Corinthians 6:14-18)

God has called us to *separate* ourselves from the world. How could we ever hope to cleanse our minds from the filth of the past if we continue to wallow in the world's sensuous thinking? A. W. Tozer explained it this way: "Men think of the world, not as a battleground but as a playground. We are not here to fight, we are here to frolic. We are not in a foreign land, we are at home. We are not getting ready to live, we are already living, and the best we can do is rid ourselves of our inhibitions and our frustrations and live this life to the full."[3]

THE ENEMY'S PLAN TO DEMORALIZE

In 1986, when the Iron Curtain was still intact, I listened to an ex-KGB propaganda agent speak at a local college. He had defected some time before and discussed the methods that he and other Soviet agents had used to overthrow governments. He defined a four-step process utilized to turn free countries into closed, communist nations. They were:

1. Demoralize,
2. Destabilize,
3. Revolt,
4. Close and Normalize.

The first objective was to propagate their message to the people and then seek to disrupt the flow of the government by causing unrest. Next, there would be an outright revolt. Finally, they would seal off the borders and seek to turn it into a "normal" communist state. This dear Soviet man did not realize that these principles are demonic in origin.

It is the strategy of the first step that I wish to examine. The agent said that it takes up to twenty years of repeatedly and systematically circulating a message to the people of that country that communism is good. Of course, this message is initially rejected. However, as the message continues in front of the people for a long period of time, they gradually become desensitized and shift from what was once a "middle-of-the-road" political stance, to what is now considered "far-left." The frightening part is that they do not even realize that they have shifted politically. They believe they are still positioned securely in the middle of the road. This is what has occurred in the United States. We have been bombarded by the leftist message for so long that what has become the accepted middle of the road is now far to the left of what it once was. We are no longer concerned about being overthrown by communism, but social-istic principles are currently the foundation of our educational system.

While the United States is far to the left politically of where it was previously, so too are we far to the left morally. Forty years ago a couple living together in sin would have been run out of town, a homosexual would not have dared to flaunt his lifestyle, and pornography was a picture of a woman nude from the waist up. We have truly been demoralized. Tim LaHaye tells of this process in his timely book, *The Battle for the Mind:*

> During the last 200 years, humanism (man's wisdom) has captivated the thinking of the Western world. After conquering Europe's colleges and universities, it spread to America, where it has developed a stranglehold on all public education. Recognizing as they did the strategic nature of both education and the communications field in waging their battle for the minds of mankind, the humanists gradually moved in, until they virtually controlled both. Almost every major magazine, newspaper, TV network, secular book publisher, and movie producer is a committed humanist, surrounding himself with editors and newscasters who share his philosophy and seldom permit anything to be presented that contradicts humanism, unless forced to by community pressure.[4]

Although he is commenting on only one aspect of the overall demonic attack, one can still see how the spirit of this world has successfully desensitized our nation morally and with respect to God.

THE PASSIVITY OF THE AMERICAN CHURCH

Peter said, "Be sober, be vigilant; because your adversary the devil, as a roaring lion, walketh about, seeking whom he may devour." (I Peter 5:8 KJV) In this brief passage of Scripture, Peter stresses the importance of carefully guarding our minds against the "wiles of the devil." Be sober and vigilant. These words create an image of a soldier standing on guard duty, expecting to be attacked by enemy forces at any moment—completely alert. There is no time for slumber. He must vigilantly keep watch lest the enemy slips in unawares. How can the enemy do this? Let us take a look at the opposite of vigilance, which is passivity. Webster defines passive as: "Not active, but acted upon; affected by outside force or agency. Receiving or enduring without resistance or emotional reaction; submissive."[5]

This is what has taken place in the majority of the Christian population in America today. We have become so enslaved to maintaining a life of comfort that we are spiritually lethargic. Rather than aggressively tearing down the strongholds of the enemy and waging a war for the souls of our loved ones, we have allowed the enemy to rape, rob, and exploit us. Instead of affecting the world around us for the cause of Christ, we have allowed this world's system to influence us. Consequently, we are spiritually unfit for war; we have become spiritually fat and lazy. Paul said, "Suffer hardship with me, as a good soldier of Christ Jesus. No soldier in active service entangles himself in the affairs of everyday life, so that he may please the one who enlisted him as a soldier." (II Timothy 2:3-4)

The Christian struggling with sexual sin must acquire a new attitude about what Christian living is all about. Our purpose in life is not to greedily fulfill every desire; we are here to serve the One who has called us. We are not to be gluttons for pleasure, but rather soldiers willing to suffer hardship for the sake of Christ. Rather than being immersed in the sensuous living of the world, we should be separated from it. In one poignant statement loaded with meaning for each of our lives, Paul tells us not to "be conformed to this world, but be transformed by the renewing of your mind, that you may prove what the will of God is, that which is good and acceptable and perfect." (Romans 12:2) As we saw earlier, God's will is for His children to be transformed into the likeness of His Son. (Romans 8:29) How does this transformation occur? It happens by a renewal of the mind. The mentality of the world must be put off and replaced with the mind of Christ. As Paul said, "You were taught, with regard to your former way of life, to put off your old self, which is being corrupted by its deceitful desires; to be made new in the attitude of your minds; and to put on the new self, created to be like God in true righteousness and holiness." (Ephesians 4:22-24 NIV)

Being a Christian means to be alive and active. It could be compared to fish. A live and healthy fish is constantly swimming against the current of the river. The easy thing for him to do would be to float along, but he has a natural inclination to fight the current. A dead or sickly fish, on the other hand, puts up little or no struggle. He just floats downstream with all of the other debris and weak ones. Does this at all describe your spiritual life?

A Demonic Conspiracy

The primary way the average Christian opens himself up to the enemy's attack is through the media; the most powerful form of media in today's society is the television. David Wilkerson explains:

> Satan is succeeding through television in a way not possible by any other kind of demonic invasion. Through that speaking idol, he can accomplish in this generation what he accomplished in Eden... But the sodomites are in now—in our homes. And we are now the blinded ones. Homosexual writers, actors, and producers flaunt their evil right before our eyes; and admit it or not, you and all in your home are under a demonic sodomite attack.[6]

It almost seems as though there is a demonic conspiracy in

America to control and utterly possess the minds of Christians. Since a great number of people watch television, most have come to assume that it is right. In fact, television has become such an integral part of the American Christian's life that the person who does not include it into his life is considered odd or fanatical—*by Christians!* Actually, family togetherness in many homes is centered around "the tube." God warned the people of Israel against this thinking: "You shall not follow a multitude in doing evil..." (Exodus 23:2) Just because it seems everyone watches television does not mean that it is right, nor does it mean that we will not be held accountable for our own choices.

The Effects of Television

Many saints believe they are capable of watching television without being affected by it. It may seem to a person that he has complete control over what he accepts when he watches television, but that is not the case. Television is geared toward mind control and successfully brainwashes viewers each day. That is the reason advertisers are so willing to pay millions of dollars for a few seconds of advertising time. Dr. Jenson explains the effects of television on the Christian:

> Satan uses the world's system obviously and boldly. He works through our schools, universities, and governments, but most overtly through the media. And the most powerful tool of the media is television. It should be obvious to us today that Satan is using television in a mighty way. We are surrounded by strategic warfare that is calculated to immobilize Christians...
>
> Children basically learn from the time of infancy by seeing, and their emotions are directly connected to these "images" even before they can talk. And adults are not really different. A film or television program often

moves directly past our thinking, rational minds to our emotions, apart from any rational, spiritual evaluation....

Harvard University concluded a project which included a comprehensive study on television's role on the sexual education of children. Their study revealed that 70% of all allusions to intercourse on television involve unmarried couples or prostitutes. Much of television's erotic activity involves violence against women, which is reflected in statistics which show that 50% of all women in this country have been victims of rape, incest, or battery...

You might say that this does not affect you or your children because you are a committed Christian. That is just not true. Satan is subtle—he develops attitudes slowly. This is not a crusade against television. I am just saying that we are experiencing warfare against our minds. The point is that television has desensitized Christians to sin and pain while filling our minds with artificial emotion and unreality. For many children, the test of reality is whether or not they have seen it on television. If they have not, then it is not real...

This subtle brainwashing goes on day after day. The need for solitude and quietness was never greater than it is now.

Satan uses the world's system to stimulate our sin.[8]

The next time you watch television, pay attention to what the commercials say. Notice that they are telling you what to do, as you sit there passively allowing them to do so. "Buy this if you want to be macho." "Buy this if you want your house to be the nicest on the block." "Buy this if you want to be accepted by your peers." "Buy this if you want to enjoy yourself." Mind control. It is scary to even think about how much power television has. The believer who watches a fun-loving Budweiser commercial might not run right out and buy a six-pack of beer, but how does its message affect his need for inner sobriety? What is the cumulative effect of seeing sexy women night after night on TV? How is he affected when he accumulates countless hours watching situation comedies which mock everything which is decent?

Television can be compared to hypnosis, a tool that is used to put a person in a passive state to accept subconsciously what he would not accept under normal consciousness. Television is a lethal weapon that the enemy is using to desensitize, demoralize, and eventually destroy the minds of people.

Frank Mankiewicz and Joel Swerdlow courageously wrote a book called, *Remote Control—Television and the Manipulation of American Life*. In this secular work they detailed what television has done to this nation. The following segment deals specifically with homosexuality:

> Under heavy pressure from organized gay activists, television has for the most part, though, been instrumental over the past decade in helping homosexuals "come out of the closet," individually and collectively. We can find dramas, explicit and sensitive, on the subject, as well as a generally dignified treatment elsewhere:... Anita Bryant... became not a heroine—as she would have, twenty years ago on network television —but the butt of jokes and hostility on the networks.[9]

Even these writers, who probably do not even know Christ, recognize what this powerful media form is doing to shape the minds of the American public. Throughout their book, they provide irrefutable evidence as to how our minds are manipulated through this "innocent" source of enjoyment.

Donald Wildmon is also aware of the way it is being used against believers:

Television is the most pervasive and persuasive medium we have. At times it is larger than life. It is our only true national medium. Network television is the greatest educator we have. It tells us, in its programming, what is right and wrong, what is acceptable and unacceptable, whom to believe and not to believe, whom to trust and not trust, and whom we should desire to emulate...

It is teaching that adultery is an acceptable and approved lifestyle. It is teaching that violence is a legitimate way to achieve one's goals or to resolve conflict. It is teaching that profanity is the language of the respectable. But these are only surface messages. The real message is deeper.

It is teaching that hardly anyone goes to church, that very few people in our society are Christian or live by Christian principles. How? By simply censoring Christian characters, Christian values, and Christian culture from the programs. It is teaching that people who claim to be Christian are hypocrites, cheats, liars, or worse. It does so by characterization.[10]

How would you feel if someone put you in front of several thousand people and started ridiculing your belief in God? That is exactly what television is doing. Its producers are laughing at and mocking us. Have we become so calloused that we are still willing to align ourselves with the world system which hates the things of God? It is tragic that Christians are so well versed in the most popular situation comedies, the funniest commercials, the "hottest" dramas, and yet spend such little, precious time quietly before God, studying and meditating on Scripture and interceding for the lost.

Unfortunately, people are quite addicted to television. The question is often raised about what one would do to escape boredom without the TV, as if that somehow justifies the spiritual cost it exacts. I, too, thought this way when I first entered into "life after television." The evening hours seemed to go at a snail's pace those first few weeks. It was not long before those empty hours became filled with meaningful times with my wife and enjoyable times of real fellowship with other believers. It is never easy to break a habit the flesh has become accustomed to, but the grace of God is available for those who are determined to cut themselves off from the influences of this world system.

For many, the decision they make on this particular issue will determine their degree of struggling in the future. Those unwilling to cut themselves off from the spirit of this world will find that they have very little strength to take the other necessary steps to overcome the hold of sexual sin on their lives.

twelve

BATTLES IN THE SPIRITUAL REALM

THE PERSON WHO IS DETERMINED to overcome sexual addiction must prepare himself to battle through and combat his old nature which still longs for the pleasure of sexual sin. Not only does his flesh desire it, but a habit of indulgence has been well established. Throughout a believer's daily life, he discovers that our culture promotes a resounding message that unlawful sex is a good and desirable thing that provides endless possibilities to satisfy every fantasy imaginable. As if all of this were not enough, the struggling Christian must realize and accept the fact that there is a highly organized army of powerful beings who are dedicated to thwart his attainment of freedom.

It is very important for the one who struggles to have a proper understanding of his real enemies in this spiritual battle. There are those who believe that the entire difficulty in overcoming habitual sin is only a result of spiritual warfare, thereby minimizing the role of the flesh and the world. I recall a conversation I once had with a minister about sexual lust. I had briefly told him of my work with sexual addicts. "When I deal with someone in sexual sin," he replied tersely, "I just cast the demon out and I'm done with it!"

"Yes, I understand that demons can affect people in some ways, but until a person learns to deal with his own flesh, casting a legion of devils out of him will not solve his problem," I responded.

Many who operate in the area of deliverance greatly over-emphasize the role demons play in habitual sin. They seem to be looking for an easy answer, or perhaps they are simply enthralled with the idea of ordering demons around.

At the opposite end of the spectrum are those who claim that all of a person's problems can be attributed only to himself. This is equally as wrong. The idea of there being demonic forces at work in this world is a concept that they prefer not to think about. Their perspective of the spiritual realm tends to be extremely vague and shallow. They would never refute what the Bible says about the enemy, but they are inclined to limit demonic activity to witch doctors in some dark village in Africa.

The truth is that there is a sophisticated army of beings who operate under the auspices of the devil himself. Most scholars believe that Satan was one of the twelve original archangels created by God. He is not simply an "evil force" or an "evil influence" as some believe. He is an angelic being who, like humans, is limited to time and space. However, unlike man, he is a spiritual being who is not confined to the limits of physical matter.

His army is composed of demons of various sizes, strengths, abilities, and functions. (See Luke 11:14; Matthew 12:22; I John 4:6) They range from princes of countries, (Daniel 10:13) down to lowly soldiers. (Luke 8:30) Paul gives an indication of this intricate hierarchy in the Book of Ephesians, "For our struggle is not against flesh and blood, but against the rulers, against the powers, against the world forces of this darkness, against the spiritual forces of wickedness in the heavenly places." (Ephesians 6:12)

Like any military outfit, it seems as though there are generals,

captains, and soldiers—or at least some equivalent thereof—
and that demons have been specially assigned to harass and
attack individuals. This is mostly conjecture of course, but
apparently the designated demon will be selected on the basis of
that person's particular area of struggle. To the one who struggles
with depression, a devil of dark gloom would be appointed. For
those who battle a hot temper, a spirit of rage or murder would
be given the task; and for an exaggerated sex drive, an enemy of
lust would be commissioned. It is likely that these demons have
the ability to create spiritual atmospheres which are conducive
to an individual's struggle. The renowned Dr. Merrill F. Unger,
a professor of Old Testament Studies at Dallas Theological
Seminary for twenty years, says the following about demonic
activity in his book *Demons In The World Today*:

> In demon influence, evil spirits exert power over a
> person short of actual possession. Such influence may
> vary from mild harassment to extreme subjection when
> body and mind become dominated and held in slavery
> by spirit agents. Christians, as well as non-Christians, can
> be so influenced. They may be oppressed, vexed, de-
> pressed, hindered, and bound by demons.[1]

UNDER GOD'S UMBRELLA

Regardless of their specialty, demons are limited in their
sphere of influence and license to harass or torment a believer.
As a child of God, one should always be mindful of the fact that
Satan and his cohorts can do no more than what is allowed by
the Lord and His spiritual laws.

There are certain laws which govern the physical realm
dictating how humans must conduct the activities of their daily
lives. Light a match under a dry sheet of paper, and it will burn
because certain components have been introduced together

which result in fire. Drop a bowling ball out of a window, and it will fall until something stops its progress. These are examples of cause-and-effect laws, and there are many which we must deal with in the physical realm everyday. Much of what we do in life is dictated by various physical rules of nature.

By the same token, there are spiritual laws which govern the invisible realm around us. Paul described one of these in the Book of Galatians. "Do not be deceived, God is not mocked; for whatever a man sows, this he will also reap. For the one who sows to his own flesh shall from the flesh reap corruption, but the one who sows to the Spirit shall from the Spirit reap eternal life." (Galatians 6:7-8) This spiritual law states that if a person commits one act, he must endure the consequences which will follow. Jesus gives another example of a rule of the kingdom of God, "And whoever exalts himself shall be humbled; and whoever humbles himself shall be exalted." (Matthew 23:12) It does not matter if someone approves or disapproves of these laws, nor does it matter if they are regarded. These are cause-and-effect rules of the kingdom of God that cannot be escaped.

There also seems to be spiritual laws regarding the involvement of demonic forces in the lives of believers. When a Christian rebels against God's kingdom by committing a willful act of sin, he is aligning himself with the enemy. The apostle John said, "the one who practices sin is of the devil..." (I John 3:8) The primary point of this statement is, simply, that the person who *habitually* transgresses God's laws is in league with Satan—the great rebel himself. However, there is a secondary truth which can be drawn from this statement. As a person commits acts of sin he is opening himself up to a greater degree of influence by the enemy. For instance, if a Christian man goes into a pornographic bookstore, he has willfully made himself vulnerable to the devilish thoughts that will plague him for weeks to come. Once the man has "opened himself up" to pornography, devils have the "legal right" to continually attack and torment him with those pornographic images.

Another example is anger. When a person's will is crossed, there is a huge temptation to rise up out of a humble spirit and get mad. Anger is an emotion of the flesh which generally emerges out of pride. Some have "bad tempers," meaning they habitually allow themselves to be dominated by anger. It is wrong for a follower of the lowly Jesus to get mad at someone, but when that person lets that anger control him to the point of rage, he has given place to a devil. Paul said, "Be angry, and yet do not sin; do not let the sun go down on your anger, and do not give the devil an opportunity." (Ephesians 4:26-27) or as it is expressed in the NIV, "...do not give the devil a foothold." Anger, like lust, is a carnal impulse which the enemy seeks to intensify in a person's life. Dr. Unger states:

> Demon influence may occur in different degrees of severity and in a variety of forms, both in Christians and non-Christians. In its less severe forms, demon attack comes from without through pressure, suggestion, and temptation. When such pressure, suggestion, and temptation are yielded to, the result is always an increased degree of demon influence. Although the human race fell in Adam and became a prey to Satan and demons, the forces of darkness have always been severely restricted. They can enslave and oppress fallen man only to the degree he willingly violates the eternal moral law of God and exposes himself to evil.[2]

Those who foolishly open the door to sexual sin can expect the enemy to take full advantage of the opportunity to bring the person into a greater place of bondage. Merlin Carothers, well known for his popular teachings on praise, tells of demonic influence on the thought life:

But any thought connected with illicit sex is like a monster waiting to take over. It can be kept hidden for many years, but at the right moment it emerges. In fact this evil force is often willing to wait for the right moment to manifest itself. It wants to damage the greatest number of people possible. Does this frighten you?

Let me assure you that I'm not talking about evil spirits possessing Christians. There exists in this world an evil force whose desire is to destroy everything God wants to build, however. That force, Satan, is far more clever than the average Christian believes. Satan leads his people to live in open rebellion against God, but he is content to work secretly in the inward parts of Christians. His strategy is to entice us to want things that God has forbidden. Once the desire is created, Satan keeps fortifying that desire. He repeatedly brings it to our attention until it outweighs our desire to be obedient to God...

It is never safe to step into Satan's territory. He goes about seeking whom he may devour. He selects his own time to accomplish his own purposes. We never know what he will do. I've had men tell me that they lived with immoral thoughts and desires for twenty-five years before they yielded to immoral acts. Time is irrelevant to Satan. If you believe that he is a reality, and that he has spiritual power, it will profit you greatly to stay out of his territory! He, too, has a plan for you and it very likely will be fulfilled if you allow any part of your life to be under his control. He is especially interested in what's on your mind.[3]

The attacks of devils are not limited to the guilty, though. The innocent are sometimes assaulted. However, no attack can occur upon a believer without the consent of God. Take, for instance, the time Jesus told Peter, "Simon, Simon, behold, Satan has demanded permission to sift you like wheat; but I have prayed for you, that your faith may not fail..." (Luke 22:31-32) Once the person belongs to God, the enemy can demand all he wants, but he must have permission before he can attack. Believers have been purchased from the devil by the blood of Jesus.

A profound picture of this is shown to us in the first chapter of the Book of Job. In this section of Scripture the reader is given a fascinating glimpse into the unseen regions of the spiritual realm where great temptations are devised. Job is described as a man who "was blameless, upright, fearing God, and turning away from evil." It goes on to say that he lived in such a state of righteousness that whenever his sons would get together for a feast, he would offer up a special sacrifice to God, thinking "perhaps my sons have sinned and cursed God in their hearts."

After establishing the godly character of Job, the scene shifts to the throne room of the Almighty where Satan slithers in amongst the other angels. Beaming with a certain parental pride, God says, "Have you considered My servant Job? For there is no one like him on the earth, a blameless and upright man, fearing God and turning away from evil."

To this the devil rasps, "Does Job fear God for nothing? Hast Thou not made a hedge about him and his house and all that he has, on every side? Thou hast blessed the work of his hands, and his possessions have increased in the land. But put forth Thy hand now and touch all that he has; he will surely curse Thee to Thy face." So unbeknownst to this upright man on earth, a dare uttered in an entirely different realm is about to result in Job's whole life being shaken upside-down.

One of the reasons this story was put into Scripture was to show believers that our Heavenly Father has established boundaries that the enemy cannot cross without His permission.*

---

* For a study into God's sovereign designs in allowing trials and temptations, see *Living In Victory*.

MASTERS AT TEMPTATION

Demonic beings have been tempting, harassing and attacking believers since the inception of mankind. They use unsaved humans to act out the deeds of hatred, arrogance, and perversion which are all part of their evil natures. This is the eternity that the unsaved can expect.

Those who are on the pathway of following God are dealt with somewhat differently. As mentioned before, demons are restricted in their level of influence. I will use the Marines who were involved in espionage in Moscow in the eighties, as an illustration. The only thing these embassy guards had to worry about was letting themselves get duped into telling secrets. The Russians had certain boundaries they must work in. They could not use torture to force the Marines to pass along military information. They could not threaten their lives or even yell at them. The only possible way they could obtain secrets was through the process of seduction. That is precisely what they did. The Russians used a beautiful woman as their ploy to entice a Marine into revealing secrets. This Marine did not place his country above himself. He may have been willing to die for his country on a battlefield, but he was unwilling to die to his own desires. He lost the biggest battle he would ever face. It was not a battle involving bullets; it was a battle with temptation.

In the same way, when the enemy determines to plot the downfall of a believer, he can only work within the boundaries set forth by God. As Paul pointed out, "No temptation has overtaken you but such as is common to man; and God is faithful, who will not allow you to be tempted beyond what you are able, but with the temptation will provide the way of escape also, that you may be able to endure it." (I Corinthians 10:13) The veteran apostle does not promise a life free of temptations, but rather that God will keep them within His limits and always provide a way of escape in order that the believer may continue to stand.

The scene we witnessed in the book of Job is typical of what occurs when a fallen spirit desires to sift one of God's children. Take, for instance, the story we examined earlier of Joseph and Potiphar's wife. We are only given the earthly picture of what occurred, but what happened in the spiritual realm preceding this incident? I can easily imagine the serpent once again slithering into the throne room of God. "Does Joseph fear God for nothing? Hast Thou not made a hedge about him and his house and all that he has, on every side? Thou hast blessed the work of his hands, and his possessions have increased in the land. But allow me to tempt him with this beautiful woman, and he will turn his back on You. But if for some reason he doesn't, allow me to have him thrown into prison, and he will surely curse Thee to Thy face." I suspect a similar conversation did in fact occur prior to the great temptation Joseph faced that day. Consequently, the temptation an individual faces, regardless of what it may be, must *first* be cleared by the Lord.

SCHEMERS AGAINST CHRISTIANS

There is no end to the craftiness of the enemy. They have been in the business of luring people into sin and rebellion against God for six thousand years. I can testify that the enemy has tried many times to lure me back into his domain of darkness. One such incident occurred not long after I began walking in victory. I was selling real estate at the time, and I received a phone call from a lady who asked me to show her one of the houses that our company had listed for sale. I agreed and took the keys to the house to meet her there.

I pulled into the driveway and proceeded to wait for her. As I sat there, I was overwhelmed with urges to go inside the house, "just to look around." I made the mistake of going inside. Once inside, there was an unshakeable desire to look for pornography.

I could not believe that I was actually searching diligently through each room for erotic magazines. Sure enough, I found a big stack of them in a back room. I picked one up and glanced at it, but threw it down in disgust and hurried out of the house. The lady who called me never did show up. The enemy had set me up, but fortunately it did not go any further than a quick glance.

Devils will also attempt to counter good deeds with an attack. Not long after having shared my testimony on *The Oprah Winfrey Show* in 1988, I found myself under a powerful attack while travelling. I was on my way back to Sacramento (my home at that time) from Phoenix, where I had been ministering. I had not seen my wife in over a week which made it a particularly vulnerable time for me. As I made my way through the desert of Arizona, I found myself driving at the same speed as a girl in an adjacent lane. I would pass her, and then she would pass me. I doubt if she was trying to flirt with me, but I found myself toying with the idea of it. When I came to my senses and realized what I was doing, I sped away from her. Nonetheless, this incident was just enough to get my mind thinking in the wrong direction.

As I continued making my way north toward Bakersfield, I started yearning for a pornography shop. I had long since overcome my addiction to pornography, but nevertheless, the temptation was absolutely incredible. It seemed as though my car was filled with a thick cloud of sexual lust. I was determined that when I reached town, I would find a porn shop to visit. I finally reached Bakersfield; yet, when I saw the downtown exit, I managed to continue on the freeway. The instant I passed that off-ramp, the cloud of lust disappeared! Looking back, I can now see that it was a demonic attack. Never under estimate the power and the devices of the enemy. The Bible confirms this:

> ...in order that no advantage be taken of us by Satan;
> for we are not ignorant of his schemes. (II Corinthians 2:11)

But I am afraid, lest as the serpent deceived Eve by his craftiness, your minds should be led astray from the simplicity and purity of devotion to Christ. (II Corinthians 11:3)

And no wonder, for even Satan disguises himself as an angel of light. Therefore it is not surprising if his servants also disguise themselves as servants of righteousness; whose end shall be according to their deeds. (II Corinthians 11:14-15)

Be of sober spirit, be on the alert. Your adversary, the devil, prowls about like a roaring lion, seeking someone to devour. (I Peter 5:8)

Make no mistake, demons will do anything they can to get the believer to fall in order to draw him away from the Lord. They are brilliant strategists who have probably been following the man since he was born. They are knowledgeable of his weaknesses and know exactly how to entice him into their snares.

PULLING DOWN STRONGHOLDS

When a person gives in to sexual sin repeatedly over a period of time, a foothold is established by the enemy within that person's being. If that sin continues to a point that it is uncontrollable, it becomes a stronghold of the enemy.* A devil of perversion has set up a fortress within the soulish realm of the man. The longer the sin continues, the more fortified the presence becomes.

---

* No, I do not believe Christians can be demon possessed. Believers are the property of God, not Satan. However, it seems apparent that repeated sin enables the enemy to fortify the strength of their ability to tempt the addict into that particular sin.

I have made a few visits to the Golan Heights at various times over the years. One can easily understand why Israel has been reluctant to surrender this small area to the Syrians. Enemy forces had taken their time to become firmly entrenched in the side of the hills overlooking the Sea of Galilee. For many years they had bombarded the Israeli settlements below. When war broke out in 1967 between Israel and the Arab nations surrounding her, it took fierce fighting to dislodge the Syrian presence above the lake. Buried under tons of concrete, their artillery must have seemed invincible to the Jews.

This is what the saint feels like who must face the intimidating prospect of dislodging an enemy buried deep within his being. Although this may seem quite overwhelming, Paul assures us that it is not the case: "For though we walk in the flesh, we do not war after the flesh: (For the weapons of our warfare are not carnal, but mighty through God to the pulling down of strong holds;) Casting down imaginations, and every high thing that exalteth itself against the knowledge of God, and bringing into captivity every thought to the obedience of Christ." (II Corinthians 10:3-5 KJV)

Much of the remainder of this book will teach principles required to oust the enemy. There is no real need to discuss it at length now. We simply mention it here so that you can better understand the battle which lies ahead. However, it would be good to note what Paul said about the place which fantasy plays in establishing and maintaining a stronghold. The enemy will maintain his position only to the extent that the believer continues to entertain sexual fantasies. Paul tells us to cast those imaginations down. It may take time before the man has a pure thought life, but it is vital that he begins to exercise mental discipline now. Peter said, "Therefore, gird your minds for action, keep sober in spirit, fix your hope completely on the grace to be brought to you at the revelation of Jesus Christ. As obedient children, do not be conformed to the former lusts which were yours in your ignorance, but like the Holy One who called you, be holy yourselves also in all your behavior; because it is written, 'you shall be holy, for I am holy.'" (I Peter 1:13-16)

GENERATIONAL CURSES

There are many teachers who have developed an elaborate system of "deliverance" based on one verse in the Old Testament. As He gave Moses the Ten Commandments, the Lord said, "You shall not worship them or serve them (speaking of idols); for I, the LORD your God, am a jealous God, visiting the iniquity of the fathers on the children, on the third and the fourth generations of those who hate Me." (Exodus 20:5) According to these teachers, if a person is in habitual sin he must "break the generational curse," which will thereby sever the legal ground the enemy has had on his life.

I am always extremely concerned when people confidently teach concepts that are not strongly supported in Scripture. While this notion may have a certain appeal to those who overemphasize demonic involvement in the Christian's life, the scriptural support is simply not there. I do believe that there is something evil which can be handed down from a father who is bound in sin to his son. I have heard stories, on more than one occasion, of a son who grew up without his father in the home and later discovered that his dad was also a sex addict. Often one hears about a son struggling with depression just as his father did or perhaps an alcoholic whose dad drank heavily. This could be accounted for in a couple of different ways. It could be that the same "lust" which his father had to contend with was inherited by him. (See James 1:14) The other possibility is that we simply do not understand how the devils who oppress the father can attack the son as well.

Whatever the case may be, reciting some "prayer-formula" to "break the curse" is not only a practice without any scriptural support, but it does absolutely no good. Furthermore, as we have already discussed in Chapter Seven, the Lord forbids the shifting of blame for our actions upon our parents. "The son will not bear the punishment for the father's iniquity, nor will the father bear the punishment for the son's iniquity; the righteousness of the righteous will be upon himself, and the wickedness of the wicked will be upon himself." (Ezekiel 18:20) The whole notion that one must simply make some statement to overcome (or even partially overcome) sexual addiction/bondage is sheer fantasy and an example of the many, pathetic "band-aid answers" being provided for those looking to escape personal responsibility for their own sinful actions. If there is a generational curse, it will be broken as a person experiences true repentance. When the sin stops, its effects stop with it.

THE SCHEMES OF THE DEVIL

Victory is a vague concept to those who have become accustomed to losing spiritual battles. They have mostly known only defeat. There seems to be no power to resist seducing spirits with their seemingly irresistible temptations. However, the power is available for the child of God to withstand the adversary. Paul ministered a long time in the city of Ephesus where much of the church congregation there consisted of former devil worshippers. These were people who had to face the enemy in an extremely wicked environment. From his prison cell in Rome, the old warrior wrote the epistle which has come to be known as Ephesians. In it he gave the following treatise on spiritual warfare:

> Finally, be strong in the Lord, and in the strength of
> His might. Put on the full armor of God, that you may
> be able to stand firm against the schemes of the devil.
> For our struggle is not against flesh and blood, but

against the rulers, against the powers, against the world forces of this darkness, against the spiritual forces of wickedness in the heavenly places. Therefore, take up the full armor of God, that you may be able to resist in the evil day, and having done everything, to stand firm. Stand firm therefore, having girded your loins with truth, and having put on the breastplate of righteousness, and having shod your feet with the preparation of the gospel of peace; in addition to all, taking up the shield of faith with which you will be able to extinguish all the flaming missiles of the evil one. And take the helmet of salvation, and the sword of the Spirit, which is the word of God. With all prayer and petition pray at all times in the Spirit, and with this in view, be on the alert with all perseverance and petition for all the saints. (Ephesians 6:10-18)

The first thing Paul established was the source of all believers' power to fight the enemy. The Amplified Bible brings out the full meaning of what he was expressing in verse ten. "... be empowered through your union with Him; draw your strength from Him—that strength which His [boundless] might provides." Paul was touching here on a subject of enormous importance: spiritual battles are not fought with one's own strength or abilities. I know it sounds ridiculous to express it in such a simple way, but we need to be reminded that spiritual warfare is indeed spiritual! As Paul said in the passage in II Corinthians, "For though we walk in the flesh, we do not war after the flesh." To the degree the battle is fought in the spirit realm, is the degree that warfare will be effective. For believers, the source of their spiritual power is the Holy Spirit.

This leads us to another important truth regarding the power of God. He will only demonstrate His power in our lives to the extent that we are weak in ourselves. Our weakness creates a true dependence upon God. In the last three chapters of Paul's second epistle to the church at Corinth, he used the word weakness thirteen times,—in several instances to describe himself. He was trying to teach the Corinthians that spiritual power is different from personal power. His critics had said that "his personal presence is unimpressive, and his speech contemptible." (II Corinthians 10:10) Paul did not deny this, but simply responded by quoting Jeremiah, "He who boasts, let him boast in the Lord."

In the eleventh chapter of II Corinthians, Paul recorded all the suffering he had undergone through preaching the gospel: beatings, whippings, stonings, shipwrecks, constant dangers, hunger, and thirst. God permitted these afflictions in order to keep Paul weak and dependent upon Him. In the twelfth chapter, Paul tells how God had to further weaken him through "a thorn in the flesh" so that he could continue to pour out His power through Paul's life. God said to him, "My grace is sufficient for you, for power is perfected in weakness." To this Paul responded, "Most gladly, therefore, I will rather boast about my weaknesses, that the power of Christ may dwell in me." (II Corinthians 12:9) *The only way a believer will defeat the enemy in the area of spiritual temptation is through the power of God.* That power is appropriated through the believer's utter dependence upon Him.

Thus, we see in Ephesians six that our power comes through our close fellowship with the Lord. Paul goes on to say, "Put on the full armor of God..." Why should we put on this armor? "...that you may be able to stand firm against the schemes of the devil." The principles Paul is about to share with the Ephesians is for the purpose of helping them to avoid the crafty plans the devil devises to lead believers astray. When examining the various articles of armor, one can quickly see that most are defensive in nature: girdle, breastplate, shield, and helmet are all for the purpose of protecting oneself from the blows of the opponent. It could even be argued that the sword is defensive, in the sense that a person uses it to deflect the opponent's weapons.*

Again, the purpose for putting on the armor is so "that you may be able to stand firm against the schemes of the devil." In the thirteenth verse, Paul reemphasizes this by saying, "Therefore, take up the full armor of God, that you may be able to resist in the evil day..." The exhortation is repeated to exhort us to stand against the temptations presented by demons whatever the cost may be.

SLEEPING WITH THE ENEMY

While speaking with the disciples one day, Jesus said, "I will not speak much more with you, for the ruler of the world is coming, and he has nothing in Me." (John 14:30) Jesus revealed within this one statement the reason He was able to "stand firm against the schemes of the devil." He said the ruler of this world had *nothing* in Him. In other words, there was nothing in His life that was outside of the Father's will. There was no sin, rebellion, or secret habits. Satan did not have a "hook" in Jesus. There was nothing in which the devil had legal grounds to use against Him.

This is the place of refuge for the believer. If a Christian stays in God's will and remains obedient to Him, the enemy is unable to lure him into rebellion. Believers experience problems when they give in to foul spirits in small ways, making small alliances with those who are their enemies. If they have areas of common ground with the enemy, how will they stand? It is every believer's responsibility to keep himself untainted by the pollutions of this world system through the grace of God. The sinful nature may want to befriend unclean spirits, but by habitual acts of the will,

---

* A perfect picture of this is given us by the Lord Himself when He responded to the devil's temptations by quoting the Word of God (Matthew 4:4, 7, 10).

the man can choose to remain in fellowship with God by being obedient to Him; and as he does, the devil has nothing in him.

The armor of God is, in one sense, a protection to the believer from *himself*. As he establishes the principles of truth, righteousness, faith, and so on, he will grow spiritually and will be empowered to resist the temptations which appeal to his sinful nature. The real victory in the believer's life depends, not necessarily on how he responds to today's temptations, but on how willing he is to allow God to change him from the inside out. In much the same way that a championship baseball team is built by cultivating future stars through a good "farm system," so too the believer becomes victorious by allowing God to build maturity into his character. Although this growth does not come overnight, the process often must begin through one isolated experience.

PART FOUR

THE WAY OUT

thirteen

THE PLACE OF BROKENNESS AND REPENTANCE

I WAS INVITED TO DO AN INTERVIEW on one of the premier Christian radio talk shows about sexual addiction in the Church. During the days preceding the interview, I felt a growing conviction to convey to the radio audience the message that God changes people. I was determined to make the point that a man who is bound up in sexual sin has hope because of the transforming power of Jesus Christ.

However, the host of the program was equally determined to communicate his philosophy. His belief was that freedom from addiction rested upon the foundation of mutual accountability amongst others who are addicted. Each time I attempted to direct the conversation to the transforming power of Jesus, which can truly set all addicts free from their bondage, he would avert my efforts and emphasize the need for accountability. As we discussed in chapter four, accountability has its place in the restoration process, but it alone is not the solution to addiction. Its usefulness is short-lived for the person overcoming an addiction.

THE MAINTENANCE PROGRAM

The common philosophy of dealing with addictions that the

radio host, and countless others, advocate is that once a man is addicted to some vice, whether it is alcohol, drugs, gambling or sexual activity, he will *always* be addicted to it. This mentality is pervasive in various support groups where men open the meeting by going around the circle and saying, "Hi, my name is (Tim), I am a sexual addict." Though the man could have been walking in freedom for six years, he is still expected to identify himself with his past sin. Not only this, but he would also be expected to attend support group meetings for the rest of his life as his only means of escaping his addiction. He is a loser and must therefore always keep that in the forefront of his mind, lest he should go into delusion and return to his former lifestyle of sin.

Since most have little comprehension of or trust in God's power to change a person's life, their hope rests solely upon what they can do for each other; they are convinced that, to a degree, there is power within the "rooms" to maintain their sobriety. This "solution" has been termed "maintenance." It is based on the premise that an individual must learn to maintain his recovery from his sin. In other words, he must discover how to live his life in such a way that the sin is kept in abeyance. He is a victim of what is considered an invisible intruder that needs to be kept within certain boundaries. Instead of taking the wild beast out and mercilessly shooting it, it is respected and kept safely in a cage. The man attempts to control it, curb it, and stifle it, but he never becomes truly free of it. He is destined for a lifetime of a "white-knuckle" existence of being one step away from disaster, all the while professing a trust and belief in God.

Trying to "maintain" sin in this way keeps a person from being broken. Take Bob, for instance. He was a regular at the support group in his church for sexual addicts. He faithfully attended the meeting every Tuesday evening. He had been going for three years, admitting every time he would fall. He was always faithful to confess his failures, but it had become a routine of failure and confession. He never changed.

He later admitted that he had convinced himself that as long as he was going to the meetings and confessing his relapses with sin, God would be patient with him. His sin was not completely out of control as it had once been, but he had not gained any real victory over it. He had become comfortable with the arrangement.

The answer for believers is that God changes people from the inside out. This change occurs as the person sees his need for change, comes to grip with his sinful behavior, and experiences a genuine turning away from that lifestyle. Such a transformation does not merely involve quitting sin. It is much deeper than just abstinence. In order for God to get a person to the place where he is able to forsake the idols of his life, a tremendous upheaval of his entire inside world is necessary. He has cherished and protected his idol over the years because he loves and desires it. God's task is to gradually bring him to the place where he no longer desires it. Those who simply "maintain" their sin never truly learn to hate it. At best, they learn to keep it under control. Charles Spurgeon once wrote, "Men who only believe their depravity but do not hate it, are no further than the devil on their way to heaven."[1]

A revolution must take place before a person will hate his sin. A new King must be inaugurated. The old kingdom, under the reign of self, must be toppled. The person who becomes a follower of Christ and attempts to maintain control over his own life has not submitted himself to the lordship of Jesus Christ. All this person can ever hope for is to abstain from his besetting sin. On the other hand, the man who has allowed God to break down self rule, has a whole new set of values infused into his being. This is what Paul was referring to when he said, "Therefore if any man be in Christ, he is a new creature: old things are passed away; behold, all things are become new." (II Corinthians 5:17) He gave a fuller version of what he was expressing in his letter to the Ephesian church:

This I say therefore, and affirm together with the Lord, that you walk no longer just as the Gentiles also walk, in the futility of their mind, being darkened in their understanding, excluded from the life of God, because of the ignorance that is in them, because of the hardness of their heart; and they, having become callous, have given themselves over to sensuality, for the practice of every kind of impurity with greediness. But you did not learn Christ in this way, if indeed you have heard Him and have been taught in Him, just as truth is in Jesus, that, in reference to your former manner of life, you lay aside the old self, which is being corrupted in accordance with the lusts of deceit, and that you be renewed in the spirit of your mind, and put on the new self, which in the likeness of God has been created in righteousness and holiness of the truth. (Ephesians 4:17-24)

DEALING WITH SELF WILL

Every human being possesses an innate sense of self-determination and self-sufficiency. When a person becomes a follower of Christ, he has set himself on an unavoidable collision course with the will of God, regardless of the severity of his sin. Indeed, the very entrance into the kingdom of God is founded upon the person seeing that his way has been wrong and must therefore be changed. The biblical term used to describe the solution to this problem is called REPENTANCE.

Many suppose that when they first became Christians they experienced repentance and now they can move on to the more important things of the Christian life. Not only is the initial conversion experience for many very weak, as we shall soon see, but it is only meant to be the first in a lifelong series of such encounters with God. There is much that needs to be changed about the fallen human nature. God is not looking for more people who know how to appear religious or speak the latest "Christianese." He is looking to transform us from the inside out that we may bear the image of Jesus Christ to the unsaved world. True repentance then, is much more than aligning oneself with the Christian religion. The Greek word which we translate as repentance is *metanoia*. It is the combination of the words *meta* (after, following) and *noieo* (think). *Metanoia* means to reconsider, or to experience a change in one's line of thinking.

Before we discuss repentance of sexual sin, let us return to the matter of the human will. For a person to think that he can "repent" of any sin, and yet refuse to change his way of thinking is foolish. *Spiritual repentance is an experience whereby a person's will is altered for the express purpose of bringing it into line with God's will.*

Let me use a couple of stories out of the life of Jesus to illustrate the difference between real repentance and false repentance. One day Jesus noticed a young man intently listening to Him. He made that wondrous invitation for the young guy to follow Him. "I will follow You, Lord; but first permit me to say good-bye to those at home." Jesus replied to him, "No one, after putting his hand to the plow and looking back, is fit for the kingdom of God." (Luke 9:61-62) The man expressed his will: "I will; it is my express desire to follow You... but it is also my desire to spend time with loved ones first. I wish to be your follower, but it must be on my own terms." How different is the story of Zaccheus:

And He entered and was passing through Jericho. And behold, there was a man called by the name of Zaccheus; and he was a chief tax-gatherer, and he was rich. And he was trying to see who Jesus was, and he was unable because of the crowd, for he was small in stature. And he ran on ahead and climbed up into a sycamore tree in order to see Him, for He was about to pass through that way. And when Jesus came to the place, He looked up and said to him, "Zaccheus, hurry and come down, for today I must stay at your house." And he hurried and came down, and received Him gladly. And when they saw it, they all began to grumble, saying, "He has gone to be the guest of a man who is a sinner." And Zaccheus stopped and said to the Lord, "Behold, Lord, half of my possessions I will give to the poor, and if I have defrauded anyone of anything, I will give back four times as much." And Jesus said to him, "Today salvation has come to this house, because he, too, is a son of Abraham. For the Son of Man has come to seek and to save that which was lost." (Luke 19:1-10)

In this story, Jesus makes the invitation in a different way. He offers to be a guest in the home of Zaccheus. In such a simple offer, something powerful penetrated the heart of this greedy tax-collector. The change is immediately evident: "Behold, Lord, half of my possessions *I will* give to the poor, and if I have defrauded anyone of anything, *I will* give back four times as much." His will had been changed to conform to the will of God. This is the repentance the other one did not experience. Jesus later told a story to illustrate the difference between true and false repentance.

"But what do you think? A man had two sons, and he came to the first and said, 'Son, go work today in the vineyard.' And he answered and said, 'I will, sir,' and he did not go. And he came to the second and said the same thing. But he answered and said, 'I will not,' yet he afterward regretted it and went. Which of the two did the will of his father?" They said, "The latter." Jesus said to them, "Truly I say to you that the tax-gatherers and harlots will get into the kingdom of God before you." (Matthew 21:28-31)

In this passage of Scripture, the first son conveyed the impression that he would do the will of his father: "I will, sir," he stated. Though he represented himself as one who intended to do the will of his father, he failed to follow through. Perhaps he was the double-minded man who is unstable in all of his ways that James would later talk about; or perhaps he was someone who lived a facade of outward obedience without it being the reality of his life. Whatever the case may be, he did not obey his father.

The second son, on the other hand, refused from the onset. "It is my will not to do as you wish," he said. Later, having thought better of his decision, he changed his mind. Jesus said that he *regretted* his thinking. Perhaps the moral of the story could best be summed up in the words of Jesus during the Sermon on the Mount: "Not everyone who says to Me, 'Lord, Lord,' will enter the kingdom of heaven; but he who does the will of My Father who is in heaven." (Matthew 7:21) In other words, a mere verbal claiming of obedience does not carry the same weight as the actual performance of it.

The person who wishes to live a life of obedience but continually fails must deal with his will. He sees himself as under the power of some foreign entity (whether he considers it demonic or simply sin), but in reality he is under the power of his own will. He is much like the spoiled child who is continually naughty. There are times when he wants to be a good boy, but when something comes along that he wants to do, he does it regardless of the consequences. He is undisciplined. He is accustomed to having his own way. He, rather than his father, is the master of his life. The man in habitual sexual sin conducts himself in much the same manner. He does whatever he wishes to do. He commits acts of sexual sin because he enjoys it.

As we will discover in the remaining chapters, there are a number of aspects involved in a person coming into a life of freedom. One of the key elements of the process involves repentance: *having one's will altered to bring it into the will of God.* As Paul said, "For this is the will of God, your sanctification; that is, that you abstain from sexual immorality; that each of you know how to possess his own vessel in sanctification and honor, not in lustful passion, like the Gentiles who do not know God." (I Thessalonians 4:3-5)

Repentance describes the transforming of a person from being one who does his own (carnal) will, to one who does the will of his Father. At the beginning of His ministry, the first words out of the mouth of Jesus were, "Repent, for the kingdom of heaven is at hand." (Matthew 4:17) He then went on to give the fabulous Sermon on the Mount, which is a description of the initial experience of repentance and the lifestyle that emerges as a result. The Beatitudes contain all that is involved in the process of transformation. Those seven verses, Matthew 5:3-9, describe how a person is prepared for repentance, how it unfolds, and the life that accompanies it.

SEEING ONE'S NEED FOR CHANGE

Jesus opens His revolutionary sermon with the words, "Blessed are the poor in spirit, for theirs is the kingdom of heaven." (Matthew 5:3) These words describe the condition of an individual's heart who becomes aware of his great need for God's work in his life. The one who has a real conversion to Christ experiences the overwhelming sense of being utterly undone. A person, at least at this point in his life, comes to see that there is nothing he can possibly do to save himself. He realizes that only the blood of Jesus Christ can provide the atonement for his sin.

The man who is overwhelmed with a sense of complete powerlessness over his sin often has a sense of what it means to be poor in spirit. He has tried to quit his sinful behavior many times, making countless resolutions. He has tried with all his strength to change his life. When temptations would come along, like a little child being led by the hand, he would blindly follow the dictates of his lust. This person can see that his only hope for deliverance from the power of sin is the Savior.

Many understand, in a vague way, that they cannot overcome their sin but never experience true poverty of spirit. To be poor in spirit means that one truly sees no ability within oneself to overcome the power of sin without God's help. Those who try to "maintain" their sin have never come into a true sight of their helplessness. They will not acknowledge their need because they wish to remain in control of their own lives. When a person has truly seen his helpless condition, he is desperate for God's help no matter what it may cost him.

While there are many who never come to this place of poverty, others arrive and never go any further. They live their lives openly confessing their helplessness but continue to hinder the Lord from taking them through the process which will result in victory over sin. It is not enough that a man realizes he cannot overcome the sin on his own; something must take place inside him.

THE BREAKING OF SELF WILL

Once a person sees his sinful condition there is but one reasonable response: deep sorrow over how much he has disobeyed, offended, defied, and yes, even hurt his Lord. The second phrase Jesus uttered in His Sermon on the Mount was, "Blessed are those who mourn, for they shall be comforted." (Matthew 5:4)

When a person begins to experience true godly sorrow over his sin, a change begins to occur in his heart. He literally begins to hate his sin, realizing its evil, deceitful nature which has kept him out of real fellowship with God and other believers. Paul said of the Corinthians who finally repented, "I now rejoice, not that you were made sorrowful, but that you were made sorrowful to the point of repentance; for you were made sorrowful according to the will of God... For the sorrow that is according to the will of God produces a repentance without regret, leading to salvation; but the sorrow of the world produces death." (II Corinthians 7:9-10)

Throughout the years I have counseled many men who had only worldly sorrow. Jesus spoke of peace that the world gives. (John 14:27) There is also a sorrow that the world gives and the two are closely connected. Worldly peace depends upon favorable outward circumstances. The peace Jesus gives depends upon a sense of inner tranquility that only comes through being in an undisturbed relationship with God.

Worldly sorrow is the grief due to unfavorable circumstances. Sexual sin can quickly bring such circumstances about. Financial debts often pile up; a devastated wife may disappear with the children; or a secret life might be exposed on the job or even in the church. Some may even face criminal charges for their actions. Feeling tremendous remorse over one's actions because of the consequences that have followed is not uncommon. I truly empathize with the grieving, anguished men and what they must face because of their sexual misconduct. Nonetheless, such regret is common to any of the human race who encounter unfavorable circumstances. That is what is called by Paul, "worldly sorrow." It is not wrong to feel grief over these losses. It is only natural to feel badly when in an ill-suited predicament. The danger with worldly sorrow, however, is that it gives one a false sense of brokenness and repentance. Consequently, Paul says it leads to death.

I witnessed a tragic illustration of this recently. Jim and his wife, Sue, had gone through counseling with Pure Life Ministries some years ago. Jim would cry over his sin and then vow never to do it again. He would go to support group meetings, yet things never changed. He continued to frequent adult bookstores and massage parlors. He also had a terrible anger problem and would occasionally beat Sue and their two boys. Although we are typically very cautious about handing out such advice, we suggested that she get a legal separation from Jim. However, before it was all over, Sue remained in this abusive arrangement for over fifteen years. She finally decided to divorce him.

We had lost contact with Jim and Sue over the years but coincidently, I was invited to preach at their church. I was surprised to see them at this church and was happy to see Jim respond to the altar call that Sunday morning. He wept and wept at the altar. I was overjoyed to see his "repentance" until later the pastor talked to me. "Jim has been weeping for the last five years, ever since Sue divorced him," he informed me. "But Steve, he never changes. The sad thing is that he has been diagnosed with terminal cancer and has only a few months left to live." Right down to the very end, as far as I know, Jim was engulfed in worldly sorrow. I am not saying that his sin led to cancer, but one has to wonder.

How different is the man who experiences true godly sorrow! Yes, though he grieves the consequences of his sin, there is something different taking place inside of him. A deeper, more genuine remorse penetrates his heart which has been hardened for so long. He sees what his sin has done to his family. He becomes overwhelmed by the enormity of his selfish lifestyle. His pride stares at him glaringly. He is reminded of how unconcerned he has been about others. He realizes that he has grieved a loving God. He has repeatedly wounded the fragile spirit of his wife, and his actions have left an indelible impression upon his children. The pleasure of his sin has come at a tremendous price. Everywhere he turns he sees the devastation of his sin. This is not the selfish whining of a person in worldly sorrow. This man is being broken over *who he is*. The control he has had over his life has destroyed most everything of value to him. This is a person who can see all too clearly the price of self-will. True repentance is a profound and powerful experience (or on-going phenomena). How shallow in comparison those empty resolutions that many have made under the term repentance!

I have had numerous breakings in my life. Perhaps the one that affected me the most happened in 1991. I had been in ministry for five years at that time. Even though I had long since overcome habitual sexual sin and had even been used by the Lord to some extent, I was still very selfish and prideful. I was spending a couple of hours in prayer and Bible study every morning, but I could feel myself getting distant from the Lord. When I prayed it seemed as though God was a million miles away. The heavens had become brass to me. The Bible seemed dry and stale. I was growing increasingly cynical of others, hardened to the Lord, and cold to the needs of those to which I was called to minister.

Pure Life Ministries had recently purchased a larger piece of property (where we are currently located) and needed to find a new church for the men in the live-in program to attend. One Sunday, Kathy and I attended a small Pentecostal church out in the country, not far from the new facility. I was there to decide if it was the kind of church we would want the men to attend.

The pastor preached that day out of Luke chapter six. It was not so much what he was saying that moved me as it was that God was showing me that I was not living the Christian life. No, I was not stirred emotionally, but I felt convicted. At the end of the sermon he gave an altar call for anybody who felt that they needed to get right with God. In my prideful condition, the last thing I wanted to do was to respond to an altar call. I was there to check the church out, not to repent! In spite of my reluctance, I knew that I had to obey the Lord's voice.

As soon as my knees hit the floor at the altar, I began to weep. All I could see was how very prideful and arrogant I had been.

I saw the lack of mercy and love in my life. The more God showed me, the more I wept. Pretty soon deep sobs were wracking my whole frame. In front of this entire congregation, which I had been so concerned about impressing, I was blubbering like a baby! The more I cried, the more humiliated I felt. The more humiliated I felt, the more I cried.

It was a terrible experience in the flesh and yet was one of the greatest days in my life! My prideful thinking, selfish nature, and stubborn will were all dealt a severe, but precise, blow. Out of that experience came a new brokenness that completely transformed my thinking. It was not that I would never give in to pride or selfishness again; they just lost their uncontested power over my life.

This kind of brokenness is what the man in sexual sin desperately needs to experience. The strong will (like the spoiled child who always gets his way) must be dealt with severely by the Lord. God must be given His rightful position of authority in the man's heart. This dethronement of the "almighty self" can only take place through such brokenness.

Each time one is broken by God, self loses that much control over one's life. The old nature, which loves the pleasures of sin, must be crushed. This can only come about through the mighty hand of God. I will discuss this in more detail in the following chapter, but mention it now as an important part in the process of repentance.

The person who attempts to "maintain" his sin cannot have true victory because his *heart* has not changed! Those who tell you that you must spend the rest of your life in support groups and in therapy do not understand the transforming power of a repentant heart. Many of them will never know about repentance because they will not allow *themselves* to be broken by God. Thus, their own hardened, unbroken hearts establish the basis for what they teach others. Out of that stony ground comes the kind of teachings that promote weak repentance.

THE CONQUERED WILL

The third Beatitude we will discuss is, "Blessed are the meek, for they will inherit the earth." (Matthew 5:5 NIV) Meekness is the willing subjection of one person's will to the will of another. Jesus lived in absolute meekness. He was perfectly submitted to the Father. "For I have come down from heaven, not to do My own will, but the will of Him who sent Me," He told His followers. (John 6:38). In fact, on another occasion He said, "I can do nothing on My own initiative. As I hear, I judge; and My judgment is just, because I do not seek My own will, but the will of Him who sent Me." (John 5:30) Jesus was in such a state of submission to the Father that it was impossible for Him to have His own way.

Jesus did not need to be broken because He did not have a fallen human nature. He was born with His Father's sinless nature. It is a different matter for the sons of Adam. The only way we can come into meekness is through the breaking of our wills. A perfect picture of this is that of a stallion. It may be a beautiful and graceful animal, but it has no usefulness until it has been broken. However, once it has been broken, the powerful horse becomes controlled by the reins and verbal commands of its master. This is a picture of biblical meekness.

The Christian who has undergone the crushing of his will by his Heavenly Father has learned to have a healthy respect for the Master's whip. This is not the cowering fear an abused child has of a cruel father, but the proper reverence one has to One who commands respect. This man's will has been conquered so that he no longer sees his life as one in which he has the right to control. "Or do you not know that your body is a temple of the Holy Spirit who is in you, whom you have from God, and that you are not your own? For you have been bought with a price:

therefore glorify God in your body." (I Corinthians 6:19-20)

The fear of God establishes certain perimeters around the person, which helps to hinder any venturing into the unlawful territory of sexual sin. Righteousness is the result. "Blessed are those who hunger and thirst for righteousness, for they shall be satisfied," Jesus went on to say. The person who learns to live his life under the ever-present gaze of a holy God, longs to please Him. The Lord describes that longing as hungering and thirsting after righteousness. Such a desire to please God promotes a genuine hatred for sin and a willingness to overthrow all of one's idols.

Jesus proceeds to describe mercy, purity and peacemaking, which further characterize the life of a person who has experienced real brokenness and repentance. As the person's hardened, unmerciful heart is crushed, a new compassion and love for others replaces it. It is the new life which Paul described. However, this initial breaking by God is just the beginning!

fourteen

DISCIPLINED FOR HOLINESS

AFTER EXPLAINING THE PROBLEM of sexual addiction on a radio talk show, a lady called in to express what, no doubt, many of the listeners were thinking that day: "Just tell 'em to go take a cold shower!" In her simple understanding of the situation, these men were just "warm-blooded, American males" who needed to exercise a little self-discipline.

Although this dear woman did not fully comprehend the gravity of this issue, she was not that far off track. When you get right down to it, all sexual addicts lack self-discipline in one or more areas of their lives. Discipline is greatly needed in a sex addict's life, though the thought of it makes him cringe.

Discipline has been defined as, "Learning that molds character and enforces correct behavior... To discipline a person or a group means to put them in a state of good order so that they function in the way intended."[1] The Bible uses the term fool to describe a man who does not heed instruction nor receive "the life-giving reproof." Though discipline is the very thing which can help him out of the chaos he has created in his life, he refuses to receive it. Solomon said, "...Fools despise wisdom and instruction," (Proverbs 1:7) "hate knowledge" (Proverbs 1:22) and are "arrogant and careless." (Proverbs 14:16) "Do not speak in the hearing of a fool," he said, "for he will despise the wisdom of your words." (Proverbs 23:9) He also said, "A fool does not delight in understanding, but only in revealing his own mind." (Proverbs 18:2) Part of the reason a sexual addict is uninterested in receiving correction is because his mind "is in the house of pleasure." (Ecclesiastes 7:4)

Christian men whose lives have been ravaged by sin will humbly admit that these verses accurately describe the way they have been in the past. Many sought help, but were always looking for a painless, easy answer. They were drawn to "solutions" that required little and yet promised much. Of course, in today's society, there is never a shortage of self-proclaimed experts who boldly offer an easy way out of whatever issue or circumstance individuals commonly face in life.

Truthfully, there is no easy answer. Men who are determined to find an easy way out of their sin are simply wasting precious time groping around for what does not exist. *A life which has become out of control only comes back under control through the processes of God's discipline.*

BIBLICAL PRECEDENTS

Since childhood most of us have been bombarded with a lifestyle of instant gratification, selfish indulgence, superficial relationships, and shallow commitments. At some point, those who plan on living a genuine Christian life must come to grips with this un-Christlike way of living and face their need for change. Godly discipline allows a person to live a holy life in the midst of a decadent and perverse society such as ours.

Scripture has much to say about the concept of discipline. Chastisement, reproof, warning, correction, instruction, and training are all terms used under the general theme of discipline in the Bible. These may not be popular terms in our "anything goes" culture, but they all describe the way God deals with His children in all ages.

The Bible clearly expresses that human beings begin life off track spiritually. Solomon, speaking under a powerful anointing of wisdom, repeatedly counseled parents about the need to establish discipline in a child's life at an early age. "Foolishness is bound up in the heart of a child; the rod of discipline will remove it far from him." (Proverbs 22:15) "The rod and reproof give wisdom, but a child who gets his own way brings shame to his mother." (Proverbs 29:15) "Discipline your son while there is hope, and do not desire his death." (Proverbs 19:18) "He who spares his rod hates his son, but he who loves him disciplines him diligently." (Proverbs 13:24)

These are wise words for parents raising children in our day and age. Nevertheless, there is a spiritual truth that is much deeper than the practical truth being expressed here. Children come into a wicked world with a natural inclination toward sin and rebellion to God's prescribed way of living. Just as a baby's nature must be dealt with early on, so too must the new child of God learn about the hand of discipline from a loving, heavenly Father. Ministers who attempt to bypass this important aspect of spiritual growth are poor examples of what a spiritual parent should be. The writer of Hebrews said the following:

> You have not yet resisted to the point of shedding blood in your striving against sin; and you have forgotten the exhortation which is addressed to you as sons, "My son, do not regard lightly the discipline of the Lord, nor faint when you are reproved by Him; for those whom the Lord loves He disciplines, and He scourges every son whom He receives." It is for discipline that you endure; God deals with you as with sons; for what son is there whom his father does not discipline? But if you are without discipline, of which all have become

partakers, then you are illegitimate children and not sons. Furthermore, we had earthly fathers to discipline us, and we respected them; shall we not much rather be subject to the Father of spirits, and live? For they disciplined us for a short time as seemed best to them, but He disciplines us for our good, that we may share His holiness. All discipline for the moment seems not to be joyful, but sorrowful; yet to those who have been trained by it, afterwards it yields the peaceful fruit of righteousness. (Hebrews 12:4-11)

This wonderful passage of Scripture, which follows the great faith chapter of the Bible, presents a basic principle of the Christian life: "If you are without discipline," the writer of Hebrews asserts, "then you are illegitimate children and not sons." Though Christians might try to avoid God's discipline in their lives, if a person is truly a child of God, it is inevitable that he will face God's rod of correction. I sincerely question the salvation of those who never seem to face any godly discipline. The following is a letter from my wife's book, *When His Secret Sin Breaks Your Heart: Letters To Hurting Wives*. It expresses this truth perfectly.

Dear Lucy,

I'm so sorry to hear that your husband ran off with another woman. It must be crushing for you to hear how happy they are, especially since it seems as though everything in your life is crashing down around you. They are both making good money, going to church, living a prosperous life and seemingly without any troubles. How different your life must be. Your job hardly pays you enough to get by. The engine in your car must be rebuilt. You feel very alone. I can understand why you feel like God is blessing them and cursing you.

Lucy, has it occurred to you that these two may not even know the Lord? I realize they claim to be Christians, but their conduct seems anything but Christ-like to me. At the very least, they are terribly backslidden and in real delusion. Everything going well is not necessarily a sign of God's blessing on one's life. In fact, in a case like this especially, it appears to be a *lack* of God's hand on their lives.

Look at your life in comparison. You are a sincere believer, struggling to keep life together in the midst of grief and adversity. I have known much of this in my relationship with God. Allow me to share the words of Solomon with you: "My son, do not reject the discipline of the LORD, or loathe His reproof, for whom the LORD loves He reproves, even as a father, the son in whom he delights." (Proverbs 3:11-12)

I do not know enough about this situation to make any real judgments, but it looks as though your husband and his girlfriend are going their own way, without the slightest genuine concern about what God thinks. You, however, are being refined in the furnace of affliction.

Do not let their outward "happiness" fool you, Lucy. Happiness based upon favorable circumstances is only an inch deep. Solomon said, "...the way of transgressors is hard." (Proverbs 13:15 KJV) One day they will have to deal with the consequences of their actions; whether it be here on earth, or standing before a holy God.

The wonderful news for you is that God loves you enough to be extremely concerned about every aspect of your life. Though it seems He is far away during times like these He has never been closer. Turn to Him for the comfort that only He can give you.

THE REACTION TO DISCIPLINE

Many of us received the instruction Solomon gives in Proverbs 5 but simply refused to heed it:

Now then, my sons, listen to me, and do not depart from the words of my mouth. Keep your way far from (the adulteress), and do not go near the door of her house, lest you give your vigor to others, and your years to the cruel one; lest strangers be filled with your strength, and your hard-earned goods go to the house of an alien; and you groan at your latter end, when your flesh and your body are consumed; and you say, "How I have hated instruction! And my heart spurned reproof! And I have not listened to the voice of my teachers, nor inclined my ear to my instructors!" (Proverbs 5:7-13)

On a rare occasion, a young man will come into Pure Life Ministries seeking help before he throws his life away. However, most men who give over to sexual sin will suffer years of consequences before they are willing to allow God to begin a work of correction in their lives.

Sadly, there are also many who will never learn. They are like the man who broke his arm, but was unwilling to go to the doctor. He decided that he would rather live with a lame arm than to go through the pain of having it set. Sexual addicts are also broken up inside. Most must face the consequences of unhealthy childhoods or suffer the penalty for the poor decisions they have made. Every time the Lord draws close to bring the needed correction, they pull away. They feel that they cannot handle the pain of the reality of what they have been like. The real problem is that they, like the fool of Proverbs, only live life for today. Though the process of discipline would ultimately bring joy and freedom, they

Positive			Negative	
Verse	What he does	Result or reality	What he does	Result or reality
10:17	heeds instruction	on the path of life	forsakes reproof	goes astray
12:1	loves discipline	loves knowledge	hates reproof	called stupid
13:1	accepts discipline	called wise	does not listen	called a scoffer
13:18	regards reproof	will be honored	neglects discipline	poverty & shame
15:5	regards reproof	called prudent	rejects discipline	called a fool
15:10			forsakes the way	stern discipline
			hates reproof	will die
15:31	listens to reproof	dwell with wise		
15:32	listens to reproof	acquires understanding	neglects discipline	despises himself
29:1			hardens himself	beyond remedy

Figure 14-1

cannot see beyond what is easiest at the present moment.

That is why Solomon said, "A rebuke goes deeper into one who has understanding than a hundred blows into a fool." (Proverbs 17:10) He also said, "Though you pound a fool in a mortar with a pestle along with crushed grain, yet his folly will not depart from him." (Proverbs 27:22) There are those who refuse to learn, regardless the price of their folly. The man who will not receive instruction from the Lord is destined to repeat the same lessons over and over again. He is like the man described in Proverbs who did not want (1:25), would not accept, spurned (1:30), rejected, loathed (3:11), forsook (10:17), would not listen to (13:1) and even hated (5:12) the instruction of the Lord. Many, who have been this way in the past, are now learning to turn to (1:23), heed (10:17), regard (13:18), listen to (15:31-32), accept (13:1) and even love (12:1) God's reproof.

In Figure 14-1, we see a chart which outlines various verses from the Book of Proverbs regarding those who accept or reject the discipline of the Lord. It is a Hebraic way of writing to contrast good and evil, light and darkness, and/or foolishness and wisdom. In the verses listed, a comparison is given between a person who turns to God's process of correction and of one who turns away from it. From these passages one can readily distinguish between the wise and the foolish.

THE WAYS OF DISCIPLINE

God's discipline in the lives of His children is as diverse as the problems He must correct. For example, Peter's life is one which is characterized by a great deal of correction. Do you recall when Jesus asked the disciples who people supposed He was? Various notions were expressed; but then Peter, temporarily filled with a word from God, stood up boldly and exclaimed, "Thou art the Christ, the Son of the living God." What a declaration! This was one of those times you wish someone had been running a camcorder for all posterity! It was certainly one of Peter's greatest moments.

Jesus, never one to bypass an opportunity to bless someone, turned to Peter and said, "Blessed are you, Simon Barjona, because flesh and blood did not reveal this to you, but My Father who is in heaven. And I also say to you that you are Peter, and upon this rock I will build My church; and the gates of Hades shall not overpower it. I will give you the keys of the kingdom of heaven; and whatever you shall bind on earth shall be bound in heaven, and whatever you shall loose on earth shall be loosed in heaven."

Wow! How would it make you feel to have the Son of God say something like that to you in front of all your friends? I can just see Peter's head swelling. And, according to the law of gravity, what goes up must come down. A few minutes later, when Jesus disclosed what He would have to endure in Jerusalem, Peter rebuked Him. Imagine that! Peter, overflowing with pride, now thinks he is in a position to rebuke God!

Jesus whirled around and said to Peter authoritatively, "Get behind Me, Satan! You are a stumbling block to Me; for you are not setting your mind on God's interests, but man's." (Matthew 16:16-23) I do not understand how a man can be speaking by the word of the Lord one minute and speaking by Satan the next, but so it was. Peter received a piercing rebuke from Jesus. It is important to keep in mind that the Lord was not just venting frustration, as one of us might. His only concern was that Peter would learn to discern the difference between the voice of the Holy Spirit and the voice of the enemy. Peter was taught a lesson that day by the greatest Teacher known to man, and he probably never forgot it.

The Lord may also graciously correct His children through other believers. Paul describes an incident he had with Peter. Paul was facing constant opposition from the Judaisers, Jews who had supposedly converted to Christianity but wanted to retain the law. Peter had stood by Paul in the midst of the conflict. He could clearly see the hand of the Lord in Paul's work. Later, Peter came to Syrian Antioch where Paul's home church was located. Peter fellowshipped freely with the recently converted Gentiles *until* a group of Judaisers showed up from Jerusalem. Suddenly, he distanced himself from the Gentiles, probably making them feel as though they were rejected by the Lord. Paul confronted him publicly. "If you, being a Jew, live like the Gentiles and not like the Jews," the apostle stormed, "how is it that you compel the Gentiles to live like Jews?" (Galatians 2:14)

Sometimes a sharp rebuke is the very thing we need to get us back on track—to bring us down off our "high horse," so to speak. In this case, Peter's fear of man was exposed for all to see. God could have laid it on Paul's heart to take Peter aside and gently point out how he was being more concerned about what the Judaisers thought of him than he was about the welfare of the Gentiles. However, lessons that will create a restraining wall around a man in preparation for future temptations usually come at a tremendous price.

Other lessons are even more painful. Who can forget what Peter experienced the night Jesus was arrested? The Lord was sitting around the table eating the last supper with His disciples.

He decided it was time to tell them what was to take place that night; He would be betrayed, arrested, and then crucified. The overly-confident Peter could not bear to hear this kind of talk. "Lord, I will lay down my life for You," he said with undeniable self-assurance.

Jesus answered, "Will you lay down your life for Me? Truly, truly, I say to you, a cock shall not crow, until you deny Me three times."

Still full of his false confidence, Peter answered, "Even though all may fall away because of You, I will never fall away... Even if I have to die with You, I will not deny You," (A compilation of Matthew 26 & John 13).

Within a few hours, Peter learned the painful lesson of depending upon one's own strengths and abilities. After he denied him a third time, Jesus, who happened to be shoved out the door at that very moment, looked at His trusted disciple. One look from those eyes of love was enough to break Peter's heart. We are told that Peter "went out and wept bitterly." (Luke 22:62)

One might wonder why God is so hard on those He loves. I encourage you to spend some time reading the epistles of First and Second Peter. You will read the words of a man who had been through the process of God's correction for over thirty years. Peter did not become a man who God could speak such words of life through simply because he followed Jesus for three years. The life of Judas is clear evidence that just being around Jesus did not, in itself, produce such a life change. Peter had matured and had a deeper revelation of the things of God because he allowed the Lord to correct him. We might also consider the fact that if the Lord felt that a man like Peter needed to be regularly disciplined, how much more so those who are in habitual sin? Again, "For whom the LORD loves He reproves, even as a father, the son in whom he delights." (Proverbs 3:12)

DISCIPLINED FOR CHARACTER

Perhaps you are thinking, "Well, that's fine for Peter. He was one of the disciples. But I'm not going to be writing any books of the Bible, and I really don't want to go through God's discipline. I just want to live a normal life, free from this sin that keeps bringing me to ruin." The problem with this sort of thinking is that the person who will be loosed from sin must exhibit the character of someone who has indeed been set free. However, such character is not generated spontaneously but must be worked into him by the discipline of the Lord.

A number of years ago a well-known major league baseball pitcher participated in our live-in program. The pitching mound he built to practice on can still be seen by the barn. His minister had said to him, "Your talent got you to the top, but your life has been destroyed by a lack of character." It was true. He certainly had the ability. Actually, he could have been even more successful had he not destroyed himself with drugs and sex. God had tried to deal with him at various times, but he was too proud and unyielding. The following is a portion of his testimony he shared about what happened to him in the live-in program:

> Although I gave our Lord lip service and ostensibly worked or spear-headed Christian activities and causes, my life was secretly lustful, greedy, selfish, chaotic, and very ambitious. As I spent less and less time with the Lord, I began to rely more and more on myself. And by 1987 I was no longer even involved with Christian activities.
>
> Despite having my best year in 1988, I was no longer interested in anything. At the height of my career I gave myself over to every pleasure I wanted. At first every-

thing went my way, on and off the field. But soon many problems started and quickly my life was falling apart in every area. I no longer really cared, and although I tried to "tow the line," I was soon a prisoner of my own devices and began to be very cynical. I began to try counseling because my marriage had been on the rocks. I tried "Christian" psychology, twelve-step groups, clinics, rehabs, and books, but my arrogance and the deep hold of sin were too much.

It wasn't until I came to Pure Life Ministries that I was shown how to successfully walk with God again. The people there know God and believe that Jesus Christ alone can and will help us out of whatever problems have made our lives so dysfunctional. Seeking God and instruction on prayer along with loving support and discipline are constantly taught...

His story is a ringing testimony to the truth of what Solomon said, "Poverty and shame will come to him who neglects discipline, but he who regards reproof will be honored." (Proverbs 13:18) The Hebrew word for honored is a very interesting term. It literally means to be heavy or weighty but is seldom used in a literal way. "From this figurative usage it is an easy step to the concept of a 'weighty' person in society, someone who is honorable, impressive, worthy of respect."[2] The process of God's discipline will eventually make a man into "a 'weighty' person in society, an honorable, impressive person who is worthy of respect.

This is almost unimaginable for those bound in sexual sin. Though they may display a confident, even arrogant exterior, deep within them there is much shame and guilt over their hidden life. I can remember secretly thinking of myself as someone who was seedy, shifty, and disgraceful. I guess it could be said that I was a "light-weight" morally. As we discussed in the first chapter, the more sin a person gives over to, the more his character will be gutted of anything of real substance.

Some sexual addicts see their sin as a minor quirk in an otherwise impeccable character. Such thinking is sheer fantasy! A person's behavior in secret is where character—or the lack of it—is revealed. A man cannot be compartmentalized. He can only act out of the substance of what he consists of as a man. Secret sexual sin is not a fluke; it is a direct by-product of a man's character. A man's secret behavior will only change as his character changes.

Take Henry, for instance. He is the charismatic man mentioned in chapter four who had become the director of one of the most successful drug rehab ministries in the country. As mentioned earlier, the truth came out that he was having numerous affairs with married women and prostitutes and had began abusing drugs again. Outwardly, he seemed to be a man of real character. However, the real man inside was exposed when he secretly acted out his sin behind the scenes.

Henry came to Pure Life Ministries a broken man. The staff loved him, but they were not impressed with, nor taken in by, his charismatic personality. He was not going to be able to smooth his way through this program. He eventually graduated. He began his graduation speech by naming a number of the aspects of the program that he did not like. A flat pillow, leaky shower head, and a roommate who snored, were all mentioned. Then he said something that has stuck with me all these years later. "This program was absolutely perfect for me. In fact, it was tailor made by God. He knew exactly what I needed. If I would have had my way, everything would have gone smoothly. I wouldn't have had any problems. I wouldn't have had to face any difficulties. Everything would have gone just the way I wanted it to go. But I thank God that He crossed my will almost everyday in this place. Because if everything would have gone perfectly, I would still be the man I was who was sneaking around in sin."

Others simply try to create honor for themselves. They believe that if they carry themselves with a lot of confidence, they can make themselves seem honorable to those around them. And indeed, there are many who "judge according to appearance" (John 7:24) and are taken in by these "Christian" deceivers. Jesus discerned this brassy approach with some of those around Him.

And He began speaking a parable to the invited guests when He noticed how they had been picking out the places of honor at the table; saying to them, "When you are invited by someone to a wedding feast, do not take the place of honor, lest someone more distinguished than you may have been invited by him, and he who invited you both shall come and say to you, 'Give place to this man,' and then in disgrace you proceed to occupy the last place. But when you are invited, go and recline at the last place, so that when the one who has invited you comes, he may say to you, 'Friend, move up higher'; then you will have honor in the sight of all who are at the table with you. For everyone who exalts himself shall be humbled, and he who humbles himself shall be exalted." (Luke 14:7-11)

Being a man of honor does not come about by acting as if one deserves to be treated as such. Substance comes as God builds a person's character. Henry left the Pure Life Live-In Program with a degree of moral and spiritual weightiness he had never before possessed. Yet, it did not come about until his false character was exposed for what it was and God was able to begin building real character in him. Perfectly describing Henry's life, Solomon said, "A man's pride will bring him low, but a humble spirit will obtain honor (or weightiness)." (Proverbs 29:23)

Still others think that they can find some quick, painless way to achieve the same results. You can observe them streaming into revival meetings,* looking for that one prayer by the evangelist that is going to change everything in their lives. Others flock to deliverance sessions, hoping to be set free of the devil that is causing them to sin. Yet others, perhaps a little closer to the truth, hope that one experience of brokenness will turn everything around for them. All of these things might have their place in the believer's life, but the Christian life is not formed through one experience. In the words of a friend, "God can change a man in an instant, but it takes time to build character." That sums it all up.

DISCIPLINED FOR HOLINESS

The last thing I want to touch on, regarding the process of discipline the Lord takes the believer through, is the holiness that comes forth out of it. Perhaps you remember our passage in Hebrews 12, "...He disciplines us for our good, that we may share His holiness."

God does not discipline a man because He is angry with him. He does it because He has a purpose in mind for that person's life. He is looking for holiness. Our friend Peter, who experienced much scourging at the hands of his Heavenly Father, helps us see what God is doing, "As obedient children, do not be conformed to the former lusts which were yours in your ignorance, but like the Holy One who called you, be holy yourselves

---

* Revival meetings can be a wonderful opportunity for God to bring a person into much needed brokenness, but spiritual maturity takes time.

also in all your behavior; because it is written, "YOU SHALL BE HOLY, FOR I AM HOLY." (I Peter 1:14-16)

Holiness does not come from reading a good book. It does not come about by being in a powerful meeting. Holiness comes by the Lord's purging out of us our love for sin and for self. This process takes time.

fifteen

WALKING IN THE SPIRIT

IN PAUL'S LETTER to the church in Galatia, he wrote,
"...Walk in the Spirit, and ye shall not fulfill the lust of the
flesh." (Galatians 5:16 KJV) After dealing with thousands of
Christian men in sexual sin (including many ministers), I have yet
to find any evidence to dispute this statement. A man can go to
psychologists, support groups, or deliverance services. He can
be prayed for by a famous evangelist or commit himself to
a sexual addiction clinic; but if he wants to overcome habitual
sin, he must learn to walk in the Spirit. Since the Bible is truly the
inspired Word of God, then this conditional promise becomes
one of extreme importance to the sexual addict in search of
freedom.

I think we would all agree that the phrase "lust of the flesh"
accurately characterizes the nature of sexual sin. A few verses
later Paul gives a catalogue of "the works of the flesh" which
begins with "adultery, fornication, uncleanness, lasciviousness,
idolatry..." (Galatians 5:19-20a KJV) Sexual sin and idolatry are right
at the top of the list. How much more so when sex *is* the idol of
a person's life? It is one thing for someone to dabble in
immorality, but it is another matter when the person is a regular
worshipper *At The Altar Of Sexual Idolatry*. He is spiritually

bankrupt and desperately needs a way out. Paul gives the escape route with this obscure formula:

"IF... ye walk in the Spirit, THEN.... ye shall not fulfill the lust of the flesh."

This conditional promise is so significant that each phrase must be examined carefully so that the full meaning of what is being expressed may be understood and then applied to one's life.

To Walk

It was Jehovah Himself who first used the term "walk." Through His servant Moses, He said, "If you walk in My statutes and keep My commandments so as to carry them out, then I shall give you rains in their season, so that the land will yield its produce and the trees of the field will bear their fruit." (Leviticus 26:3-4) In a dream, He said to Solomon, "And if you walk in My ways, keeping My statutes and commandments, as your father David walked, then I will prolong your days." (I Kings 3:14) Through Asaph He exclaimed, "So I gave them over to the stubbornness of their heart, to walk in their own devices. Oh that My people would listen to Me, that Israel would walk in My ways!" (Psalm 81:12-13) By the prophet Isaiah the Lord declared, "I have spread out My hands all day long to a rebellious people, who walk in the way which is not good, following their own thoughts." (Isaiah 65:2) Several hundred years later Jesus used the same illustration when He said, "I am the light of the world; he who follows Me shall not walk in the darkness, but shall have the light of life." (John 8:12)

In the Bible, the term "walk" describes a certain way one lives his life. In our modern day vernacular the term "lifestyle" would be used. This word is not simply describing the kind of day, or even week, someone is having. It is certainly not referring to someone who feels spiritual on Sunday while being in the flesh the rest of the week. When Paul says to "walk in the Spirit," he is describing an on-going condition of a person's life. If a person is living his life "in the Spirit," he will not succumb to the desires of his flesh.

To Walk in the Flesh

I am amazed at how a man can be in the most despicable sin and really believe that he is close to God. We can safely assume that if a person is living his life under the dictates of the flesh he is not one who is walking in the Spirit. In fact, I will go even further to say that if a person is fulfilling the lusts of the flesh he is indeed walking in the flesh. Thus, we can use the opposite terminology to say, "If you walk in the flesh, you will fulfill the lusts of the flesh." In Galatians 5, Paul gives a comprehensive definition to what it means to walk in the flesh, "Now the deeds of the flesh are evident, which are: immorality, impurity, sensuality, idolatry, sorcery, enmities, strife, jealousy, outbursts of anger, disputes, dissensions, factions, envying, drunkenness, carousing, and things like these, of which I forewarn you just as I have forewarned you that those who practice such things shall not inherit the kingdom of God." (Galatians 5:19-21)

A tenderhearted person who reads this passage of Scripture will immediately examine his heart, point by point. "Do I give in to impure thoughts? Does the desire for pleasure occupy a strong place in my heart? Do I have any idols in my life? Do I have a problem with my temper? Do I ever feel jealous or envious over other people? How often do I find myself embroiled in disputes with others?" Affirmative responses to these questions are all tell-tale signs of a person who is not walking in the Spirit. However, the one who quickly scans the list with a superficial glance, claiming to be free of such a lifestyle is only deceiving himself. Likewise, so is the person who wrangles over every term, trying to avoid the truth of what is being expressed.

Jesus said, "If you abide in My word, then you are truly disciples of Mine; and you shall know the truth, and the truth shall make you free." (John 8:31-32) This is also a conditional promise. The person who lives out the words of Jesus in his daily life will know the truth when he sees it, and that truth will bring him into liberty. If a person is going to experience real freedom, it is imperative that he becomes open and brutally honest with himself.

TO WALK IN THE SPIRIT

There are many who have an occasional experience with God, feel His presence in a church service, or even see Him at work in their lives, and believe they are walking in the Spirit. To walk in the Spirit means that a person's life is dominated, controlled, and guided by the Holy Spirit. Just as the list of "the deeds of the flesh" defines what it means to be in the flesh, the following list of "the fruit of the Spirit" defines what it means to be in the Spirit.

Paul says, "But the fruit of the Spirit is love, joy, peace, patience, kindness, goodness, faithfulness, gentleness, self-control; against such things there is no law. Now those who belong to Christ Jesus have crucified the flesh with its passions and desires. If we live by the Spirit, let us also walk by the Spirit." (Galatians 5:22-25) Again, the person who is willing to be honest with himself will examine this list and ask the difficult questions: "Am I really as devoted to the lives of others as I am to myself? Do I have the patience to endure difficult people and trying circumstances without losing the sense of God's presence? How kind am I to those who cross my will? Am I truly living in subjection to the Holy Spirit everyday?"

As the fruit of the Spirit grows in a person's life, it helps the other person mature in other areas of his life as well. As a person grows in faith, he will be strengthened to grow in meekness also. A good gauge for a person to use to examine where he is spiritually is to examine his weakest point. For addicts, the lack of self-control is a glaring manifestation of a deeply-rooted problem.

If you walk in the Spirit, you will not fulfill the lusts of the flesh. At first glance, one would think the key word in this phrase is either "walk," or "Spirit." However, the primary term we want to focus on here is "in." As considered earlier, just as the spirit of this world creates an atmosphere a person can abide in, so too does the Spirit of God.* A person who lives his daily life in an atmosphere of God is not going to give in to or pursue lusts that may still lie dormant within his nature.

The apostle John said, "And you know that He appeared in order to take away sins; and in Him there is no sin. No one who abides in Him sins; no one who sins has seen Him or knows Him... And the one who keeps His commandments abides in Him, and He in him. And we know by this that He abides in us, by the Spirit whom He has given us." (I John 3:5-6, 24) These verses do not suggest that a person lives in sinless perfection—only that there is no sin which is *ruling* his life. The Spirit and grace of Jesus Christ sustains him at a level above dominating sin. This way of living within the control of the Holy Spirit does not happen over night; it is developed within a believer's life as he matures.

THE DAILY SUSTENANCE OF PRAYER

The key to walking in the Spirit is found in the words of Jesus, "I am the true vine, and My Father is the vinedresser... Abide in Me, and I in you. As the branch cannot bear fruit of itself, unless it abides in the vine, so neither can you, unless you

---

* The truth of the matter is that the enemy counterfeits what God does.

abide in Me. I am the vine, you are the branches; he who abides in Me, and I in him, he bears much fruit; for apart from Me you can do nothing." (John 15:1, 4-5)

There are a number of elements involved with entering into this kind of fellowship. First and foremost is prayer. The very essence of the Christian experience is entering into and maintaining an intimate relationship with God. It is for this purpose that we have been saved from our sins. Yet, how few devote themselves to such blessed intimacy. Attending church is important, but our connection to the Vine must be maintained daily. Imagine what it would be like to have a marriage which was based on nothing more than a formal meeting once or twice a week.

Having a time of prayer each day is essential to the life of a believer. Prayer ushers in the life-changing power of the Holy Spirit. Just as God speaks to us through His word, we talk with Him through prayer. Prayer is simply talking to God. One should not be concerned about being eloquent. The Lord is looking for *real* conversation! He is our dearest Friend and that is how the believer should communicate with Him.

Just as it is with any new spiritual habit, developing a prayer life may be difficult initially. It begins by having a firm conviction that prayer is an essential part of the daily life. The person who sets himself on the course of cultivating a regular devotional time may find that time seems to drag by slowly at first. This will gradually change as the habit takes root. The person will soon find himself looking forward to his morning devotions. Before long, the length of time dedicated to communing and fellowshipping with God will grow.

There are at least three keys to a successful prayer life. First, a person must determine what his *style* of prayer will be. Some like to sit in a room where they can feel free to talk to God without concern about anyone else hearing them. Others like to write their prayers, as it helps them keep their thoughts focused on the Lord. Personally, I have always found it easiest to concentrate and talk to the Lord while walking. Wherever I may be, whether at home in Kentucky or in some distant city, I have the same ritual every morning. I have a cup of coffee and study the Bible for an hour, and then I go for a prayer-walk for another hour. Each person has to determine for himself what works for him.

Another key element is choosing *when* to pray. If at all possible, it is always best to pray in the morning. The Lord should get the first fruits of the day. Most people set their alarms only to allow themselves just enough time to get ready for work. The believer who is serious about developing a time with God will begin the routine of early to bed, early to rise. Trying to cram prayer time into an already hectic morning schedule will never work. It will soon fall by the wayside.

The last thing that must be considered is how much time to spend in prayer. Basically, the more time spent with the Lord, the better. What is spoken to God is not as important as just being with Him. Relationships are not established merely on words alone; they are also built on non-verbal communication. For instance, my wife and I can sit in the same room, not saying a word, and just enjoy each other's company. This is what God desires. He longs to spend time with those He loves. As we have already mentioned, building a devotional life is not easy. The man who is just beginning to develop a prayer life should avoid overburdening himself. It is much better to be faithful with ten minutes a day than to sporadically spend an hour at a time. The habit is never established in the person's life who is inconsistent. Until prayer is a regular part of one's daily routine, it will always be a drudgery. Once it has become grounded as a consistent element at the start of each day, it becomes effortless. It becomes a good habit!

As the person begins this new adventure, it is also important that he does not make the mistake of watching a clock; time will appear to slow down. Personally, I always glance at my watch as I am leaving on my walk. When it seems as though it has been about an hour since the time I left, I will look again just to make sure that I am not coming back too soon. I will often spend longer than an hour in prayer, but it is very important to me that I do not spend less than an hour. Those who are sitting in a room should turn the clock around so that it cannot be seen. Some might want to set their wrist watch (or even a cooking timer outside the room) which will inform them that their time is up.

As this daily routine becomes a part of the person's life, he will soon discover that it is no longer a chore to pray. In fact, he will soon discover that ten minutes goes by too quickly, and that he will need to pray for fifteen minutes in order to cover all his concerns. As this important spiritual discipline is established, God will begin to give him a burden for the souls of those around him. At this point his prayer life begins to enter into a new phase. He is penetrating the powerful realm of intercession.

As the person's devotional life progresses, he will also begin to spend more time worshipping the Lord. This is an integral part of growing in our love for God. Some people worship while listening to Christian music they enjoy. However, it is important to remember that simply singing songs that one enjoys is not the same as truly entering into the spirit of worship. Jesus said, "But an hour is coming, and now is, when the true worshipers shall worship the Father in spirit and truth; for such people the Father seeks to be His worshipers. God is spirit, and those who worship Him must worship in spirit and truth." (John 4:23-24) If the person is truly worshiping God, there is something flowing from his heart toward the Lord. This is what Jesus meant when He talked of worshiping "in spirit and truth." However, there are groups such as Vineyard, Hillsong, Maranatha, and Hosanna which seem to have a real anointing for praise and worship. Some people can benefit greatly by spending time being immersed in this type of Christian music.

Something very powerful occurs in the spiritual realm when a person begins truly praising God. Heart-felt praise cleans out the atmosphere of demonic activity. I remember standing in chapel service while in Bible college once. We spent time singing every morning, but this particular day we seemed to enter into a higher level of worship. As I closed my eyes, a picture formed in my mind. High above us was the presence of a holy God, and between the students and the Lord was a thick cloud of satanic darkness. This evil presence was keeping us from Him, but as we lifted up our voices in praise, that ugly cloud separated and soon dissipated. Our praise opened up a direct avenue to God!

Randy Sager tells the story of when he and others used to go into the worst districts of San Francisco to witness to the unsaved. Before going into the streets and engaging others in conversation, the small group would gather in the street and spend time singing and praising the Lord. One night, as he was walking down the street, a filthy-looking, "homeless" man came out of an alley and called Randy over to him. The man showed him a badge and told him that he was an undercover officer. He said, "I don't know what you people are doing, but every time you come down here the crime rate drops to zero!"

On another occasion, an angry crowd of militant homosexuals showed up and started hurling insults at the tiny band of believers. The situation became super-charged with hatred. As it appeared that the gay activists were going to attack them, Randy started quietly singing a song of praise. Soon the other Christians caught on and joined in with him. The rage of the mob diminished, and they left the scene quietly. There is no question that true worship helps to bring a person into the Spirit.

FOOD FOR THE SOUL

Spending time in prayer and worship helps the believer to live in the presence of the Holy Spirit each day. There is another aspect to our spiritual equation which is equally important. The Word of God is the source of the believer's spiritual sustenance.

It has the inherent power to impute life into a saint's being. A Christian needs God's nourishment regularly lest he "dries up." (John 15:6) However, when it comes to wielding the Sword of the Spirit, it is absolutely essential that the believer is "handling accurately the word of truth." (II Timothy 2:15) One problem sexual addicts face is that their thinking has been warped through years of abuse and damage caused by their exposure to pornography and lewd fantasy. I have used the illustration of the company spy who broke into the computer room of his chief competitor and messed up the circuitry in their main frame computer. This is a picture of what the devil has done to men who have gotten involved in sexual sin. The enemy has fouled up their inner circuits in such a way that nothing inside them works as it should. Nevertheless, the Word of God has the power to transform a person from the inside out. Over a period of time, the Word will gradually rewire the believer's circuits if he remains faithful and spends time in the Bible every day. To help us to see what regular Bible study will do for the struggling saint, we will turn to the words of James.

Therefore putting aside all filthiness and all that remains of wickedness, in humility receive the word implanted, which is able to save your souls. But prove yourselves doers of the word, and not merely hearers who delude themselves. For if anyone is a hearer of the word and not a doer, he is like a man who looks at his natural face in a mirror; for once he has looked at himself and gone away, he has immediately forgotten what kind of person he was. But one who looks intently at the perfect law, the law of liberty, and abides by it, not having become a forgetful hearer but an effectual doer, this man shall be blessed in what he does. (James 1:21-25)

In this inspired passage of Scripture, there are several

concepts which can play a vital role in the life of the believer. The first one mentioned is the importance of repentance: "putting aside all filthiness and all that remains of wickedness..." I have known men over the years who have spent hundreds of hours in the Bible and yet have only grown increasingly indifferent to the Lord. There must be a sincere repentance experienced before the Word can be implanted. The unrepentant person who spends time in Scripture only grows more calloused in his heart.

Next, we are to approach the Word humbly. Many who spend time reading the Bible are doing just the opposite. Rather than allowing the Word to penetrate and search their hearts and to bring conviction, they use it only to fortify doctrinal opinions or to show others how much they know. The book of Hebrews said, "For the word of God is living and active and sharper than any two-edged sword, and piercing as far as the division of soul and spirit, of both joints and marrow, and able to judge the thoughts and intentions of the heart."

This is a phenomenal statement which the Bible makes about itself. Jesus said that His words were "life and spirit." (John 6:63) It is "the rod of (the) mouth and the breath of (the) lips" of "the living God." (Isaiah 11:4) There is a divine energy which goes forth as the Scripture is approached *in the right spirit*. The quickened Word has the power to pierce the most intimate recesses of a man. It can divide the carnal thoughts and intentions of the soulish realm from the Christ-like thinking which emanates from the spirit. It dissects one from the other, thereby bringing to an end the chaos and confusion that results from the deceitfulness of sin. Every motive, attitude, or thought pattern is methodically and systematically exposed by the Word for what it really is. The entire fallen nature is pierced with the double-edged sword of the Spirit. With frightening reality John Calvin speaks of those who shut out the truth of Scripture:

Nothing of this kind is found in the reprobate; for

they either carelessly disregard God speaking to them, and thus mock him, or glamour against his truth, and obstinately resist it. In short, as the word of God is a hammer, so they have a heart like the anvil, so that its hardness repels its strokes, however powerful they may be. The word of God, then, is far from being so efficacious towards them as to penetrate into them to the dividing of the soul and the spirit. Hence it appears, that this its character is to be confined to the faithful only, as they alone are thus searched to the quick. The context, however, shows that there is here a general truth, and which extends also to the reprobate themselves; for though they are not softened, but set up a brazen and an iron heart against God's word, yet they must necessarily be restrained by their own guilt. They indeed laugh, but it is a sardonic laugh; for they inwardly feel that they are, as it were, slain; they make evasions in various ways, so as not to come before God's tribunal; but though unwilling, they are yet dragged there by this very word which they arrogantly deride; so that they may be fitly compared to furious dogs, which bite and claw the chain by which they are bound, and yet can do nothing, as they still remain fast bound.[1]

The person who is sincerely looking for God to expose and put to death the sin which is still lodged within him rejoices to see the Sword of the Spirit. He can trust what it reveals because it is held by the nail-pierced hand. This is not the flailing sword of the person Solomon wrote about "who speaks rashly like the thrusts of a sword." (Proverbs 12:18) This is the meticulous work of the loving Surgeon extracting the cancer of sin which has entwined itself throughout the patient's inner being.

It is called by James, "the perfect law." The man who approaches the Word in a humble spirit realizes that it is the only source of truth with absolute credibility. Unfortunately, many have become increasingly cynical about the Bible. They are busy running all over the country looking for "the latest word," missing what has been sitting under their noses all along—*the Eternal Word.* If the Bible does not seem convincing enough for someone, rest assured that Satan will make sure something else takes its place. *Anything else!* The enemy would rather see a believer spend hours reading self-help books than to spend five minutes in God's revealed Truth. This is why there are bookstores loaded with alternatives.

HOW TO APPROACH SCRIPTURE

Furthermore, James spoke of looking "intently at the perfect law." The Bible deserves our most devoted interest. There are different ways to approach Scripture. Some people like to read vast sections of the Bible at a time. Perhaps they have a system for reading the entire Bible through in a year. I must admit that I question this superficial approach. I would not go so far as to say that it is wrong; I just wonder how deeply the words penetrate the heart of a person who "speed reads" chapters at a time.

Personally, I prefer to study the Bible verse by verse, chapter by chapter, and book by book. I will typically spend weeks studying one book of the Bible. I will take a chapter at a time, read it with different translations, study key words, and read what several commentators have to say about that chapter. By the time I am done, that book is "mine." The words are written on the "tablet of my heart." It is in me. I may not cover much of the Bible quickly, but what I do study becomes embedded within me. To date, I have done in-depth studies of just about every book in the Bible.

Someone else might prefer to "meditate" on Scripture by taking sections of Scripture and carefully mulling over every word. This involves reading those particular sections repeatedly, asking the Holy Spirit to bring the Word "alive" to him. This is often how God reveals precious nuggets of truth to His followers. Dr. Jenson discusses what this approach did in his own life:

> The new habit pattern that had gradually developed in me was not like any other. To become "transformed by the renewing of your mind" (Rom. 12:2) means getting God's Word on the inside to saturate our lives, thoughts, attitudes, emotions, and actions, so that we are conformed from the inside out into the likeness of Jesus Christ.
>
> I am convinced that I had to go through that biblical process of meditation just as I had meditated on lewd pictures and thoughts for years, building them into my system. The only way to counteract that was to be transformed by the actual renewing of my mind—by meditating on the Word of God...[2]

He later compares biblical meditation to a cow "chewing her cud." The cow swallows the food, regurgitates it, chews it some more, and eventually it is completely digested. This illustrates how one meditates on the Word of God.

And lastly, there are those who spend time memorizing sections of the Bible. To illustrate the value of Scripture memorization, let me relate the fascinating testimony of a young man I met years ago. Phil was raised in a Christian home and always had a desire to be in the ministry. He entered Bible college and upon graduating, joined the staff of a large church. However, Phil also had a problem with pornography that nobody, including his new wife, knew about. It was not long, however, before her awareness began growing. When she discovered him with pornography, she confided in the senior pastor of their church. He immediately set up a conference with them and confronted

Phil about the problem. Phil describes what happened next:

> As I sat before the pastor and my wife, a tremendous battle raged within me. On the one side a reluctance to abandon all the pleasures of my sinful habits; yet on the other side, a love for my wife and a desire to save my marriage.
>
> Then the Lord spoke clearly to my heart and let me know that it was time to make a decision about my life. "There is healing in my Word..." He seemed to say. "Wash yourself in it!"
>
> I left there realizing that I had no alternative but to obey the Lord, or lose all! Even though I now had deeply desired this change, I found my heart still to be deceptive and sinful. For several weeks after, I floundered with no plan or direction with which to overcome my problem. But the words of the Lord kept coming back to me, "There is healing and cleansing in my Word!"
>
> Hesitatingly at first, I began to memorize Scripture. I started with the book of I Peter and grew increasingly more aggressive in my approach. The first few verses were the most difficult to learn, but the more I memorized the easier it became. I started each day by learning a few verses. I would repeat them over and over until I had them memorized and then I would review the ones that I had learned previously. Every idle moment throughout the day became opportunities to review verses. Soon I began carrying with me a copy of the page in the Bible I was working from. Whether driving down the road, sitting in a doctor's office, taking a walk; no matter where I was, I would try to keep God's Word in my thoughts.
>
> The change in my heart started almost immediately! I found that all the usual temptations that would come to me were absolutely powerless! The "fiery darts" the

enemy threw had no sting! At first it was a difficult choice, as each thought would come, to choose whether I would pick the thoughts of fantasy or just start quoting God's Word. But as I chose Scripture, the temptation melted away.

As I continued doing this, I discovered that I was experiencing absolute victory in this area of my life, day after day, week after week. The Word not only touched my life in the area of lust, but has begun healing in every area of my life... my marriage, business, self-image, confidence, love, faith... and the list goes on!

I cannot emphasize enough the importance of soaking up God's Word. The person may not be changed overnight, but the change will come in time. As I have said to men in the past, "If you don't want to be in the same condition two months from now, you better get right on it! Every day that you prolong starting is that much longer that you will be going through this suffering." Jay Adams talks about the importance of the Word of God in changing habits:

> The Spirit works through His Word; that is how He works. So to help a counselee to discipline himself toward godliness, a counselor must insist upon the regular study of God's Word as an essential factor.
>
> It is by willing, prayerful, and persistent obedience to the requirements of the Scriptures that godly patterns are developed and come to be a part of us... He does not promise to strengthen unless they do so; the power often comes in the doing...
>
> Using the Bible every day disciplines. Disciplined, biblically structured living is what is needed. Structure alone brings freedom. Discipline brings liberty. People have been brainwashed into thinking the opposite. They

think freedom and liberty come only by throwing over structure and discipline.

Liberty comes through law, not apart from it. When is a train most free? Is it when it goes bouncing across the field off the track? No. It is free only when it is confined (if you will) to the track.

Then it runs smoothly and efficiently, because that was the way its maker intended it to run. It needs to be on the track, structured by the track, to run properly. Counselees need to be on the track. God's track is found in God's Word. In God's round world the counselee cannot lead a square life happily; he always will get the corners knocked off. There is a structure necessary for the commandment-oriented and motivated life; that structure is found in the Bible. Conforming to that structure by the grace of God enables Christians to change, to put off sin, put on righteousness, and thus to become godly men.

This, then, is the counselor's biblical answer: regularly read the Scriptures, prayerfully do as they say, according to schedule, regardless of how you feel.[3]

Doing the Word

The last thing that we should gather from our section of Scripture in James is that we should "abide" by the Word, becoming an "effectual doer" of it. As the person's mind becomes re-programmed with Scripture, living by a biblical standard will become easier. The truth of the matter is that a person really only "knows" the Word to the degree that he is living it. Again, this takes time. As the believer immerses himself in biblical teaching, he will find that it is affecting the hundreds of decisions he makes throughout the course of a given day.

The first nine chapters of Proverbs deal almost exclusively

with the power that the Word of God bestows upon a man who encounters sexual temptation:

"For wisdom will enter your heart, and knowledge will be pleasant to your soul... To deliver you from the way of evil, from the man who speaks perverse things." (Proverbs 2:10, 12) "My son, give attention to my wisdom, incline your ear to my understanding... For the lips of an adulteress drip honey, and smoother than oil is her speech." (Proverbs 5:1, 3) "For the commandment is a lamp, and the teaching is light; and reproofs for discipline are the way of life, to keep you from the evil woman, from the smooth tongue of the adulteress." (Proverbs 6:23-24) "My son, keep my words, and treasure my commandments within you... That they may keep you from an adulteress, from the foreigner who flatters with her words." (Proverbs 7:1, 5) "Now therefore, my sons, listen to me, and pay attention to the words of my mouth. Do not let your heart turn aside to her ways, do not stray into her paths." (Proverbs 7:24-25)

As the thoughts of God are implanted within a person's being, a boundary is erected around him which helps him during times of temptation to *do* what is pleasing in the sight of God.

Perhaps this is why James called the Word "the law of liberty." It sets people free! The Psalmist said that those who are established in the Word would stay pure, (Psalm 119:9-11) have a reverence for God, (119:38) a hatred of sin, (119:53) a life of liberty, (119:45) and that sin could have no dominion over them. (119:133) David said that the man who has the Word hidden in his heart will not slip. (Psalm 37:31) Joshua said that those who meditate on it will become prosperous. (Joshua 1:8) Paul said that our faith comes from hearing the Word of God, (Romans 10:17) while the writer of Hebrews proclaimed that it is impossible to please God without faith. (Hebrews 11:6) And finally, Jesus said that those who abide in His Word, would be set free. (John 8:31-32) How much plainer can it be? If you believe God's Word, then you can have hope that it truly will liberate you!

As long term, effectual changes occur within you through the Word, spending time in the presence of God daily will help you to "walk in the Spirit." Thus, both your mind and heart will be transformed by the power of God. As Jesus said, "Abide in Me, and I in you. As the branch cannot bear fruit of itself, unless it abides in the vine, so neither can you, unless you abide in Me. I am the vine, you are the branches; he who abides in Me, and I in him, he bears much fruit; for apart from Me you can do nothing." (John 15:4-5)

sixteen

OVERCOMING LUST

IN 1983, I WAS A STUDENT in Bible school and consumed with lust. The splendid conversion I had experienced just a few months before had been gutted of all its glory by the sexual sin I had fallen back into. I was desperate for help but did not know to whom or where to turn. One day, however, the pastor of the church I was attending announced that next week he would speak on the subject of lust. I was overjoyed! I could not wait until the following Sunday. On that long awaited day, after what seemed like the longest worship service I had ever attended, the pastor stepped up to the podium and began his message. For the next forty-five minutes the congregation received a pounding message about why it is wrong to lust. I knew it was wrong; I needed answers to how to overcome the lust in my life! I left church more discouraged than ever. Since then God has made it very clear to me how lust can and should be overcome in the life of the Christian. Jesus addressed the subject in His Sermon on the Mount:

> You have heard that it was said, 'you shall not commit adultery'; but I say to you, that everyone who looks on a woman to lust for her has committed

adultery with her already in his heart. And if your right eye makes you stumble, tear it out, and throw it from you; for it is better for you that one of the parts of your body perish, than for your whole body to be thrown into hell. And if your right hand makes you stumble, cut it off, and throw it from you; for it is better for you that one of the parts of your body perish, than for your whole body to go into hell. (Matthew 5:27-30)

Unfortunately, this passage of Scripture has been very disconcerting to some. However, Jesus is not telling struggling believers to start gouging and hacking at their bodies. The real problem being addressed is in the mind. If the mind becomes corrupted with lust, it will require some sacrificial severing to repair the damage. Lust will not just disappear. The man who is serious about walking in purity must take some drastic measures. The serious implications of the Lord's statements here should serve as an added incentive. There are three aspects to lust which must be addressed in the believer's life. Each of these elements carries with it a weapon with which to attack the problem.

CONDITIONS CONDUCIVE TO LUST

The spirit of this world creates spiritual atmospheres conducive to lust. The apostle John said, "Do not love the world, nor the things in the world. If anyone loves the world, the love of the Father is not in him. For all that is in the world, the lust of the flesh and the lust of the eyes and the boastful pride of life, is not from the Father, but is from the world. And the world is passing away, and also its lusts; but the one who does the will of God abides forever." (I John 2:15-17)

The world is full of lust. In practical terms, the spirit of this world capitalizes upon the fact that humans have carnal desires which are innate within them: the lust for pleasure, the lust for gain, and the lust for position. The enemy constantly attempts to create certain atmospheres which are tailor-made for the particular lust within us. Hence, the devil is called "the prince of the power of the air." For instance, if one were to go to a mall, he would find an atmosphere there which promotes coveteousness. Women especially are vulnerable to the displays in the clothing stores. There is a spiritual climate there which provokes people to want more and more and more. Another example would be going to a boxing match. This environment incites pride, anger and ultimately, violence. These things can actually be felt "in the air." If one goes into a bar, the ambience puts him in a partying mood. Nevertheless, it is the enemy at work in each of these settings.

For men involved in sexual perversion, there must be a constant awareness of the atmospheres which tend to provoke sexual lust. For instance, it is not advisable for a sex addict to go to the beach or spend time browsing at a magazine rack. It does not simply depend upon whether or not there are scantily clad girls to gawk at, but one must become sensitive to *any* place which has a sensuous ambience where seducing spirits lurk.

Even the home must be carefully guarded. Television, as we have already discussed, is a way the enemy can bring a lustful atmosphere right into your living room. The best approach is to get rid of it. At the very least, the man should limit how often he views television and be extremely selective in which shows he views. Other items within the home which must be seen as potential traps are magazines, catalogues, and newspapers. One does not necessarily have to cut them out completely, but at least be careful as to what is in the house. The internet is also a possible trap of the enemy. Pornography sites on the web are by far the largest money-makers through internet commerce. It is important to ruthlessly root out anything in the home which the devil might use in a time of weakness. The person who is going to get the victory over lust must do everything within his power to minimize the enemy's ability to affect him spiritually. Sacrificial decisions such as these are what Jesus was referring to when He spoke about tearing out eyeballs and cutting off one's hands.

QUENCHING THE FLAMES OF HELL

Who can adequately describe the hell of living in the spirit of lust? To be driven with a whip but never satisfied... To commit humiliating and degrading acts... To strive with all one's heart for some experience and then once it has been accomplished, find it to be empty and unsatisfying... To have one's thinking become dark, evil, and even insane... To hurt loved ones again and again... To experience a life of misery, despair, and hopelessness... To find oneself drifting further and further away from God... Anyone who has lived this kind of life knows more about the flames of hell than he may realize.

Lustful living is hellish living. Again, lust is demanding and never satisfied. The more one feeds the beast, the more ravenous it becomes. Perhaps the allergic reaction to poison ivy would illustrate the intense craving for immorality some are consumed by. The body becomes covered with a rash which incites intense itching. If the person scratches the infected area, he risks the possibility of making it worse and spreading it to other parts of his body. If he does not scratch it, he feels as though he might go insane! Yet, even if he grated it with a metal file, a few minutes later it would itch all the more.

In the second chapter, we noticed that one of the first things that happens to the person who goes down the path into a lifestyle of sexual sin is that he becomes ungrateful. *The Spiral of Degradation* is a horrifying reality for many. However, the good news is that if one retraces his steps, he can climb right out of that pit! *Gratitude quenches the fire of lust.* A thankful spirit destroys the driving passion for sex because it creates contentment within the man's heart. It soothes the beast, smothers the flames, and medicates the itch. The message behind lust is, "I want! I want! I want!" The feeling lodged within the grateful heart is, "Look at all I have! Thank You Lord, for all that You have done for me and given me. I don't need anything else." A grateful heart is a full heart. When a person is content with life, he will not be driven by the lust for what he should not have. For example, the other night I ate a big Mexican dinner. Afterwards, if the waiter would have brought me a rack of delicious ribs or a thick filet mignon steak, I would not have wanted either. I was full; I was content. My appetite was completely satisfied; I did not *want* anything else.

There are those who would say, "What do I have to be grateful for? My life is nothing but a total mess. I am absolutely miserable. I feel pressured to quit habits that I can't seem to quit. My wife has had it with me. I'm not happy in the world, but I'm also not happy as a Christian. What exactly do I have to be grateful for?" It has never occurred to them that a large part of the reason they are in such a predicament is because of their unthankful, stingy spirit. What a different outlook than that of the little old lady living in poverty who looked down at the scrap of dry bread and cup of water sitting on the table in front of her and exclaimed, "What, all this and Christ too?!"

It reminds me of the story of two little boys, both nine years old. Johnny's daddy is an affluent attorney in a big city. At Christmas time he purchased his son a large number of gifts. The one he was most excited about was the new Super Nintendo system he bought for his boy. On Christmas eve, he was careful to put it all the way in the back of the tree so that it would be the last present Johnny would open. The following morning the nine-year old impatiently opened and tossed aside all his presents. His dad's anticipation was mounting as Johnny finally grabbed the last package. He tore off the wrapping paper, discovered the Nintendo, and threw it down. "I wanted the new Sony Playstation!" he yelled, storming off to his bedroom, slamming the door behind him.

Meanwhile, down in the heart of Mexico there is an orphanage where unwanted little boys and girls are abandoned. Life in the dilapidated facility is all that little Juan has ever known. On this same Christmas morning, an American pastor showed up with a truckload of used toys he had collected at the church. He began handing out assorted toys to all the children. He could not help but notice Juan standing off to the side. He went into the truck and pulled out a bike: broken spokes, bent handle-bars and all. Wheeling it down the ramp to Juan, he said, "Here little guy, this is for you." The little boy looked up at him in amazement. Nobody had ever given him anything. He could not believe it. "Go ahead, Juan. It's for you." At that, the backward youngster jumped on the bike and began riding around the parking lot laughing and crying with joy.

These two boys represent the attitudes we can choose to have in life. We have so much to be grateful for in America. God has truly shed His grace upon our country. Besides the outward prosperity we enjoy, is all that God has done for us as believers. A quick breeze through Scripture reveals just a few things which God gives His children. He parted with His Son, the most precious gift He had to offer, to die on the cross for us. (John 3:16) He bestows eternal life, (Romans 6:23) and gives all things pertaining to life and godliness. (II Peter 1:3) He hands us the keys to the kingdom, (Matthew 16:19) and bestows upon us the power to tread upon serpents. (Luke 10:19) He distributes spiritual gifts. (I Corinthians 12) He imparts to us the power to become sons of God. (John 1:12) He gives us a Spirit of power, of love and of a sound mind. (II Timothy 1:7) He makes it possible for us to have victory through Jesus. (I Corinthians 15:57) He provides us with all of the wisdom we need. (James 1:5) He gives us the Holy Spirit. (Acts 2:38) For Christians, there is no limit to our gratitude lists. If a believer is not grateful it is because he willfully chooses not to be.

Gratitude is a disposition of life that must be encouraged and nurtured. If a believer waits until he feels like being thankful, it might never happen. He must make it a priority to develop a habit of being grateful regardless of his circumstances. There are two basic things one can do which will help. First, the person needs to repent of complaining. This means he asks the Lord to forgive him for his spirit of ingratitude. He must make a commitment to quit grumbling. He will have to repent of self-pity because it is the underlying disposition which fosters thanklessness. He must also repent of being demanding and selfish in life. Christians should strive to be in the spirit Juan was in, rather than the attitude Johnny displayed.

Secondly, he must learn to start expressing gratitude. He should regularly thank the Lord for all that He has done in his life. God has certainly been extremely patient with those of us who have struggled with sexual sin. We have much to be thankful for! Another practical exercise one can do is to make gratitude lists. For instance, a believer can make a list of all the things he can think of that he is grateful for in his life. Perhaps the following week he will make one about his job. Of all of the gifts I have ever given my wife, one of her favorites is a framed list of thirty-five things I love about her which I gave to her on her 35th birthday. To this day she absolutely adores it.

Doing gratitude lists will have an unbelievable effect on what spirit a man is in. For those who are especially ungrateful, perhaps they should have their wives go to the local video store and rent *A Christmas Carol!* The message of that movie is certainly appropriate to the miserable man who is never satisfied with his life and cannot find anything to thank God for.

CLEANSING THE CUP

In the fourth chapter I spoke about the need to pull down the facades of holiness and to expose the true nature of one's heart. In the fifth chapter we looked at the mind of the man given over to sin, which is full of wickedness and so on. This same terminology is used by Jesus when speaking about the Pharisees. One day He was eating with the Pharisees when one of them criticized Him for not ceremonially washing His hands before eating. This would be comparable to a Christian not bowing his head and making a show of saying grace before dinner. Jesus turned to them and said, "Now you Pharisees clean the outside of the cup and of the platter; but inside of you, you are full of robbery and wickedness. You foolish ones, did not He who made the outside make the inside also? But give that which is within as charity, and then all things are clean for you." (Luke 11:39-41)

I have dealt with thousands of men in sexual sin over the last fifteen years. Many had learned to clean the outward life. They faithfully attended church. They quit their past life of partying and carousing. They had repented of the open rebellion they had once lived in toward God. Outwardly they seemed to be doing fairly well. However, it was another matter inwardly. Although they had cleaned the outside of the cup, their inside world was still full of wickedness, and, as the Lord said of the Pharisees on another occasion, "self-indulgence." (Matthew 23:25)

Jesus did not scold the Pharisees for cleaning up their outward lives. It is pleasing to God for us to go to church and to repent of that outward visible evidence of wickedness. He was trying to teach them that it is just as important to cleanse the inside life as well. Many men who have been controlled by a driving lust have managed to overcome the outward acts of sexual sin, but are still consumed by lust inside. Something must change in the inward life.

Jesus gave the answer to the Pharisees that day. "...*give* that which is within as charity, and then all things are clean for you." In that one word He put His finger right on the problem. In their hearts the Pharisees were not *givers* but *takers*. How opposite was our Savior! He spent His entire ministry doing for others. His life was one devoted to doing acts of mercy. He constantly sacrificed for the sake of others, always showing kindness, healing, delivering, teaching, and *giving*. What was within Him came out in the form of mercy, love, and compassion.

In that one word, *giving*, He provides the answer to the person who has learned how to do the outward things of religion and yet is still filled with wickedness. This one word, which is used some two thousand times in Scripture, describes the fundamental nature of God and consequently what it means to be godly. It also describes why many remain defeated. The steps outlined in this book will lead the struggling man toward victory. He can close the avenues he has opened up to the devil. He can allow God to deal with his flesh and go through His mighty process of discipline. He can avoid the schemes of the enemy. He can see what he is like and go through a real breaking over it. He can develop a wonderful devotional life. However, if he is going to be cleansed on the inside, a transformation will have to take place within. He must take less and give more!

Lust is a passion—a selfish passion. To leer over another's body is to seek to take something from that person for self. Sexual desire completely revolves around the gratification of one's own flesh. It is utter selfishness. There is another passion available to the child of God. It is what drove Jesus to lay down His life at the cross of Calvary. Luke called it His "passion." (Acts 1:3 KJV) There is a heavenly flow a person can immerse himself in in order to meet the needs of other people. It is the holy fire in which God lives—a passion to help those in need. For the man who has lived his entire life in self-centeredness, this concept seems completely foreign. "Look, pal, I just want to get rid of this lust problem. I'm not looking to turn the world upside-down." Yet, this is the answer that Jesus gave to those who needed a great inner purging. He said to give. It is the opposite spirit of wanting to take for self.

What exactly did Jesus mean when He stated the second

greatest commandment—one of the two commandments upon which the entire Bible rests? When He said that we should love our neighbors as ourselves, did He mean, as the worldly teachers claim, that we need to first learn to love ourselves? No! If there is one thing that is true about those in sexual sin, it is that they have done a thorough job of loving themselves. In fact, they have been in such a passion to please themselves that they have hurt every person who has been close to them. Certainly, Jesus must have meant something different than this! For anyone who makes more than a cursory examination of New Testament living can surely see that the foundation of the Christian life involves doing good to others. Loving others is not a suggestion, but a commandment! If one were to look at the "Ten Commandments," he would find that the first four deal with our love for God and the last six with our love for others. In fact, let me take that a step further. Every time a person sins, he is sinning against God and/or another person.

Jesus said, "A new commandment I give to you, that you love one another, even as I have loved you, that you also love one another. By this all men will know that you are My disciples, if you have love for one another." (John 13:34-35) Paul said, "owe nothing to anyone except to love one another; for he who loves his neighbor has fulfilled the law." (Romans 13:8) Peter stated, "Above all keep fervent in your love for one another, because love covers a multitude of sins." (I Peter 4:8) And finally, John declared, "We love because He first loved us. If someone says, 'I love God,' and hates his brother, he is a liar, for the one who does not love his brother whom he has seen, cannot love God whom he has not seen." (I John 4:19-20)

To love others in the power of God is not some vague, mystical concept. In simplest terms, it means to give of oneself. Jesus said, "...give that which is within as charity, and then all things are clean for you." As the person learns to become a giver in his heart, he will begin to view everything in life differently. He will be cleansed inside.

On a practical level, one sure way into this heavenly passion is to begin seeing the needs of others. Sexual sinners are experts at taking extremely good care of their every need and desire. How little interest they have shown in the lives of others. Paul expressed what love is in a practical way: "Let nothing be done through strife or vainglory; but in lowliness of mind let each esteem other better than themselves. Look not every man on his own things, but every man also on the things of others. Let this mind be in you, which was also in Christ Jesus." (Philippians 2:3-5 KJV)

Unquestionably, this is the mind that Jesus has had toward us. He has been patient and extremely merciful to each one of us. He has tried to do everything within His power to do good to us. However, many are like the slave who was forgiven a great debt but quickly forgot the mercy done to him, and therefore, showed a lack of mercy to his brother. To him the king said, "'You wicked slave, I forgave you all that debt because you entreated me. Should you not also have had mercy on your fellow slave, even as I had mercy on you?" (Matthew 18:32-33)

Jesus said, "Heal the sick, raise the dead, cleanse the lepers, cast out demons; freely you received, freely give." (Matthew 10:8) In other words, go out and meet the needs of others. Start seeing other people as God sees them. As you do this, the Lord's compassion will begin to grow within you. A gradual change will occur in your heart. Rather than seeing people as objects to use for your own selfish purposes, you will begin to see them as people with problems, struggles, and hurts. You will begin to invest your life in theirs for *their* good. This is the normal Christian life. Anyone can claim to be a follower of Christ, but those who truly have the Spirit of God within them will eventually be compelled to love other people. Oswald Chambers said:

"When the Holy Spirit has shed abroad the love of

God in our hearts, then that love requires cultivation. No love on earth will develop without being cultivated. We have to dedicate ourselves to love, which means identifying ourselves with God's interests in other people."[1]

Jesus said to give that which is within. If the sin is in the heart, would not the best place to deal with it be in the heart? "All these evil things proceed from within and defile the man," Jesus said. (Mark 7:23) The key is to turn one's heart into one of goodness by praying for others. As the man learns to truly intercede for the needs of other people, a transformation will occur. He will become a giver in his heart instead of a taker. God wants a spirit of blessing to be within His people all the time. The more a man prays for others, the less he will become irritated, offended and provoked by them; and yes, the less they will appeal to him sexually.

Praying for others is definitely a huge step in the right direction. The change will soon break out of the heart into outward actions. The old stinginess will be replaced with a new spirit of giving. Just like the transformation ole' Scrooge went through, the person will soon be looking for opportunities to meet needs. He will delight in giving his time, money, and possessions. More importantly, he will give his life away: just so others may prosper and be blessed.

The best way to begin this process is to find a need and fill it. I can remember when I was in my early days of freedom. The Lord laid a burden on my heart to begin giving out bags of little necessities to the homeless people on skid row in Sacramento. I took my own money and went to thrift stores and bought every satchel, tote bag and gym bag I could find. Then I filled the bags with all kinds of little goodies that I thought would be a blessing to these men who were living on the streets. I did this for several weeks until the Lord told me it was time to stop. What a wonderful opportunity to do mercy to others expecting nothing in return. It was the first time I truly understood what Jesus meant when He said, "It is more blessed to give than to receive." (Acts 20:35)

The possibilities of getting involved in the needs of others are limitless. Nursing home ministries are always looking for volunteers to help the elderly who have often been forgotten and abandoned by family and friends. What a wonderful place to live out the mercy which God has shown to you. Jail ministries need men who will take an interest in those behind bars. Boys need Sunday school teachers who will take an interest in their lives; and soup kitchens need people who will come out and serve unselfishly. If nothing else, one can go to his pastor and offer to serve in whatever capacity is necessary to help the ministry. Most pastors are inundated with pastoral obligations and various problems concerning members of their congregation and have very few people willing to give of their time.

It is very important that one does not get into situations which will bring glory to one's self. Men who have been involved in sexual sin must first learn to become *servants*. To become involved in a leadership position where one is noticed by others will defeat the entire purpose. Jesus said, "Beware of practicing your righteousness before men to be noticed by them; otherwise you have no reward with your Father who is in heaven." (Matthew 6:1) *A person has to unselfishly serve or nothing will change inside him.*

If the man will get out of himself, he will soon come to understand the blessed life of being a giver. There is not a devil in hell that can stop him from living out God's love to other people. Until he begins to do this, he will remain imprisoned behind the walls of his own selfishness.

Close every avenue the enemy might have to affect your soul; develop and nurture a thankful spirit; and learn to be a giver instead of a taker. These spiritual exercises will transform the way you see other people; you will begin to see them through the eyes of the One who laid down His life for both you and them.

seventeen

HOW TO BE A GREAT LOVER
(A CHAPTER FOR MARRIED MEN)

> A new commandment I give to you, that you love one
> another, even as I have loved you, that you also love one
> another. By this all men will know that you are My
> disciples, if you have love for one another. (John 13:34-35)

OUR SOCIETY PLACES a tremendous emphasis on
sex. Don Juan and Casanova are exalted as heroes even
though they were both sex addicts obsessed with the
next conquest. Hollywood is unfailing in its portrayal of the hero
as the great lover who has numerous women at his disposal.
Rarely is the leading man happily married and devoted only to his
wife. The message conveyed by the film industry is that it is good
and acceptable to be sexually active with many partners. The
world's presentation of a great lover masks the reality of the self-
centered gigolo who moves from woman to woman, desperately
trying to fill an empty spot in his life.

Perhaps the reason Hollywood so readily promotes the
adulterer is because it has such a superficial idea about what love
is. In the movies, love is a tidal wave of emotion which overtakes
a person almost against his or her own will. How many movies
are there where the married woman helplessly "falls in love" with
another man? She knows it is wrong, but she just cannot seem

to help herself. Of course, the husband is always made to appear to be some monster so that everyone cheers when the anguished wife finally gives in to her feelings and commits adultery.

The world's concept of love is extremely shallow and goes no deeper than the emotions one is feeling at any particular time. Since each person is expected to consider his own interests before those of others, love is no more substantial than the super-charged feelings of a new relationship. Hollywood's concept of love is, in reality, nothing more than sexual lust. Based on this notion, one's emotions are the foundation for love. One can then safely say that commitment is only as secure as a person's fluctuating passions. Consequently, it is no great surprise that the divorce rate has sky-rocketed in America during the last forty years because the level of devotion and the sense of commitment people have for each other has steadily declined.

Biblical Love

The Bible renders the correct meaning of the word love. Love is not based upon mysterious feelings which overwhelm some hapless person. It is a premeditated, willful decision, as well as an unselfish act of treating another person with kindness and respect. "We know love by this," the apostle John said, "that He laid down His life for us; and we ought to lay down our lives for the brethren. But whoever has the world's goods, and beholds his brother in need and closes his heart against him, how does the love of God abide in him? Little children, let us not love with word or with tongue, but in deed and truth." (I John 3:16-18)

A husband's commitment level to his wife comes, in large part, because he has dedicated himself to the unselfish lifestyle of Christianity. Good feelings may come and go, but a Christian's commitment to his wife is for life. This level of devotion to another person is not difficult for the man who is living his life with a sincere concern for the needs and feelings of other people, especially his wife and family.

The foundation of biblical love is based upon one's behavior, rather than one's feelings. When a man is being kind to his wife, for instance, he is loving her; thus, when he is being unkind to her, he is not loving her. Since love is a behavior which a person can choose to do, his emotions must always be secondary to his conduct. This is why Jesus could command His followers to love their enemies. He did not expect them to have warm and fuzzy feelings when others mistreated them. He gave them practical instructions in how to handle such situations:

> But I say to you who hear, love your enemies, do good to those who hate you, bless those who curse you, pray for those who mistreat you. Whoever hits you on the cheek, offer him the other also; and whoever takes away your coat, do not withhold your shirt from him either. Give to everyone who asks of you, and whoever takes away what is yours, do not demand it back. And just as you want people to treat you, treat them in the same way. (Luke 6:27-31)

The man who wishes to be a great lover according to biblical standards has the wherewithal to do so; not simply because it is a choice he can make, but because the Holy Spirit resides within him and will love others through him. The same principles taught in Scripture about how a believer should treat others must also apply to one's mate. In fact, when Jesus said to "love your neighbor as yourself," one must come to the conviction that his closest neighbor is his wife! For the purposes of our study here, it would be helpful to examine Paul's dissertation on love from I Corinthians 13.

> Love is very patient and kind, never jealous or envious, never boastful or proud, never haughty or

selfish or rude. Love does not demand its own way. It is not irritable or touchy. It does not hold grudges and will hardly even notice when others do it wrong. It is never glad about injustice, but rejoices whenever truth wins out. If you love someone you will be loyal to him no matter what the cost. You will always believe in him, always expect the best of him, and always stand your ground defending him... love goes on forever. (I Corinthians 13:4-8a Living Bible)

In this portion of Scripture the married man has been given a wealth of information on how to be a "great lover." Let us examine these different elements of love in the context of marriage. Paul begins his teaching by saying that true love is patient with the other person. This is a big problem for many husbands. Most men, who have been involved in sexual sin, tend to approach the marital bed with a lack of genuine concern about the feelings of their wives. They often view their wives merely as objects to be used to meet their sexual needs. The needs of the wives are largely ignored. It is simply a fact that women warm up sexually at a much slower rate than men. The man who is involved in a filthy lifestyle often does not have the patience to show concern about his wife's sexual needs. Just when she is warming up to him sexually, he has already finished and is ready to roll over and go to sleep. This blatant act of selfishness is very unfortunate because it is a wonderful opportunity for him to put her needs above his own and to show her the love which will help to hold the marriage together.

Equally important is the need for kindness. The true biblical lover is a man who is kind and gentle to his wife. He cannot scream at his wife during dinner and then expect her to be "in the mood" that night! Many wives have been emotionally beaten down for years by abusive and controlling husbands. Women are very sensitive and fragile. They need to be treated with gentleness. Indeed, a husband must learn to be a "gentleman." As the husband learns to treat his wife with tenderness, the walls she has constructed over time will eventually come down. Typically, a woman would love to do more to please her husband, but his harshness leaves her fearful. As trust is gradually restored, however, she will be able to "come out of her shell." "There is no fear in love; but perfect love casts out fear..." (I John 4:18) the apostle John said. If the husband can restore the trust that he has shattered, the love life between him and his wife can be reestablished.

Other characteristics of "agape love" is that it is not jealous or envious. Due to the tremendous amount of guilt sexual addicts carry around, they are often subconsciously fearful that their wives are being unfaithful. They become jealous of their wives, imagining all sorts of things—pure paranoia. It is usually just a projection of their own guilt. As they begin to emerge from the small, selfish world they have lived in for so long, these insecurities will gradually dissipate.

The biblical lover is also never haughty nor arrogant. When I was deep in sin, I really thought my wife was tremendously lucky to have me! I developed such an attitude over the years because I felt confident I could always find another girl to love me. At the time, I failed to see what an ugly person I was inside. It was not my wife who was lucky but I was the fortunate one! This became real to me when she left me and filed for divorce. Suddenly, I realized that the likelihood of my finding another woman who loved God and her husband was remote. Mercifully, the Lord restored my relationship with my wife, and my attitude was never the same again. One of the things I have learned over the years is how much a woman respects humility in a man. I had always thought of meekness as something that would cause a woman to lose respect for her husband, but just the opposite is true.

This brings us to the most important feature of love. Paul said that true love does not demand its own way. I can vividly remember how self-centered I was with my wife. Looking back, it seems that everything in our lives revolved around what I wanted, how I wanted things to be, what made me happy, and so on. My wife was forced to eke out whatever pleasures she could in life, much like a dog under the table hoping for a few measly scraps of food. This selfish way of life carried over into the bedroom as well. Sex was primarily for my pleasure only. It did not occur to me that my wife would also like to enjoy herself and experience true intimacy with her husband.

Fortunately, as I began to mature in my faith and take responsibility for my actions, I was forced to face the fact that I had been extremely self-centered in every area of my life. As we saw in the last chapter, if the inward man is to be cleansed a great transformation must take place: he must be changed from being a taker into being a giver. That is exactly what the Lord began to do inside me. Inner conviction about my selfishness opened my eyes to my wife's needs. I started to realize that she, as a woman, had emotional needs which were meant to be met within times of intimacy. I also learned to put her desires above my own. I began to ask myself questions like, "What can I do to please her?" "What would she enjoy?"

As I became less selfish in bed, our times of intimacy became more enjoyable. It was no longer necessary to entertain myself with lavish fantasies to consummate the act. Gradually, the pleasure of having a *healthy* sex life with my wife was enough to keep me satisfied. Not only did my lust for other women diminish, but my love for my wife increased. She began to respond to me as she saw the change which was occurring within me. As our love grew, the walls of protectiveness came tumbling down, and we started working together instead of against each other, as a married couple ought.

Furthermore, the person who has true love is not irritable or touchy. He does not hold grudges against those who have seemingly offended him. Gradually, he learns to get out of himself and to see the importance of those around him. What a hellish life it is to be constantly consumed with one's own rights. C.S. Lewis said, "We must picture Hell as a state where everyone is perpetually concerned about his own dignity and advancement, where everyone has a grievance, and where everyone lives the deadly serious passions of envy, self-importance, and resentment."[1]

As already discussed, the man in sexual sin has lived a life of deception. Once he begins coming out of this darkness, he starts to have a new appreciation for truth—even if it is at his own expense. When he takes responsibility for what he has been like and abandons his double life, his wife will sense the life of deception and denial crumbling and will be flooded with great hope. However, if the husband involved in immorality continues to blame-shift or minimize his sin, the wife will not feel as though she can trust him. Admitting to his sinful nature brings the man out of the darkness and into the light.

As Paul finished up his discourse, it seems as though the adjectives came rushing out of him. "You will always believe in him, always expect the best of him, and always stand your ground defending him... love goes on forever." Many married sexual addicts demand this kind of love from their wives but have given very little of it themselves. The wife will respond to what the husband has given her. It is his responsibility to love her first. (Ephesians 5:25) As she feels loyalty and commitment from him, she will usually respond accordingly. If he shows that he believes in her, her faith in him should begin to grow.

A Different View of One's Wife

Many, many times through the years at Pure Life we have been in the unfortunate position of having to console a repentant man about the loss of his wife. It is always such a sad situation. Finally, the man has come to his senses and is sincerely taking the steps into a real repentance, but alas! It is too late. The wife has been hurt too many times and has decided that she has had enough. Once that decision has been made in her heart, it is almost impossible for her to change her mind. Something inside has clicked. She has closed her heart to him and has chosen to continue her life without him.

Other men are more fortunate. Their wives have not yet reached such a state. These men have begun the process of repentance before it was too late. They are now in the enviable position of having a wife who can help them through the process of restoration. Solomon understood the value of having a wife in the midst of this struggle. After warning men about the consequences of giving in to sin, he attempts to reason with husbands to be ravished by their own wives, rather than chasing other strange women:

> Drink water from your own cistern, and fresh water from your own well. Should your springs be dispersed abroad, streams of water in the streets? Let them be yours alone, and not for strangers with you. Let your fountain be blessed, and rejoice in the wife of your youth. As a loving hind and a graceful doe, let her breasts satisfy you at all times; be exhilarated always with her love. For why should you, my son, be exhilarated with an adulteress, and embrace the bosom of a foreigner? For the ways of a man are before the eyes of the LORD, and He watches all his paths. His own iniquities will capture the wicked, and he will be held with the cords of his sin. He will die for lack of instruction, and in the greatness of his folly he will go astray. (Proverbs 5:15-23)

There are three action words I want to look at briefly in this section of Scripture. First, Solomon says that the man should rejoice with the wife of his youth. This is the spirit of gratitude that we spoke of earlier. Instead of having a complaining attitude about what God has given him, he should develop a thankful heart for his wife. She is a wonderful blessing from God for him.

Next, Solomon instructs the man to be satisfied with the breasts of his wife. This is obviously bedroom talk. It is the contentment which comes from having a grateful heart. Satisfaction is available for the man who is willing to allow God to change him.

Lastly, he exclaims "be exhilarated always with her love. For why should you, my son, be exhilarated with an adulteress?" Perhaps I can rephrase it this way, "Be exhilarated with your own wife. If the Lord can help you be thrilled with her love, why would you want to go to bed with some prostitute?"

This points to the workings of God that the carnal man cannot comprehend. God has the power to enable a person to be satisfied with what he has been given. This requires patience and obedience. As the man obeys God, it enables the Lord to help and bless him. This takes time.

A wonderful picture of this concept is brought to us through the story of the Israelites (as mentioned before) in the wilderness with Moses. We touched upon this story earlier when we were showing how God will give someone over to what they have insisted that they want. Let us return to this story so we may gain further understanding of God's help in the battle with the flesh. We will only need to look at a small portion of the narrative to get the point.

> And the rabble who were among them had greedy desires; and also the sons of Israel wept again and said, "Who will give us meat to eat? We remember the fish which we used to eat free in Egypt, the cucumbers and the melons and the leeks and the onions and the garlic, but now our appetite is gone. There is nothing at all to look at except this manna." (Numbers 11:4-6)

This story illustrates both the spirit of lust and how God attempts to provide an escape. The children of Israel were wandering in the wilderness because the Lord was trying to purge the love of Egyptian idolatry out of them before He sent them into the Promised Land. Everything in God's plan hinged upon whether or not they would allow Him to transform them from wicked idolators into a godly nation. The "greedy desires" which drove the Israelites to rebellion are very comparable to the lust which has driven many Christians into the same miserable situation. Men keep themselves in bondage to the memory of the sexual encounters of the past. They are constantly trying to relive those experiences—to recapture the feeling. They have been unwilling to surrender them and accept God's plan for their lives. They want to live in the shadow of Mt. Sinai but are unwilling to let go of Egypt. Therefore, a constant murmuring and unrest takes place inside their hearts.

The manna is a picture of the man's wife. God has given him an answer to the appetite in his loins. However, manna is boring to the man who is accustomed to eating from the tree of variety. He is unwilling to allow himself to be satisfied. God has an answer for those who sincerely want it. It is found in the words of complaint from the murmurers: "...but now our appetite is gone. There is nothing at all to look at except this manna." *If a man will learn to love his wife, in spite of how he may feel inside, God will take away the appetite he has for other women and will give him in its place a desire for his wife.* "Be exhilarated with your own wife. If I can help you be thrilled with her love, why would you want to go to bed with some prostitute?"

God will help the man to be thrilled with the love of his wife if he will learn to love her as He does. It is my testimony that this is what God has done in my life. *I am satisfied.* Just like the "rabble" in the wilderness, each one will have to decide if he *wants to be* satisfied.

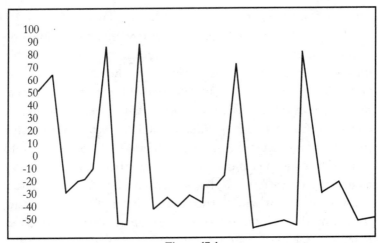

Figure 17-1

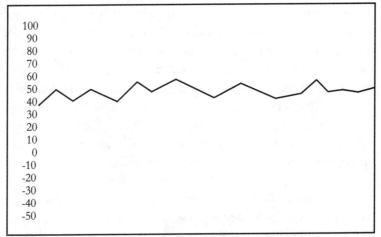

Figure 17-2

Part of the problem with sexual addicts is that they have lived in the fast lane of sexual experiences for so long they can hardly handle the slow lane and doing the speed limit. If a man is accustomed to driving 80 m.p.h., 55 seems like a snail's speed. It drives the flesh crazy. However, if he will get in the slow lane and force himself to stay there, the frenzy he feels inside will eventually subside, and 55 m.p.h. will seem fast!

The problem with trying to live life at 80 m.p.h. is that no one can maintain that level. Life was not meant to be lived at such a pace. Figure 17-1, on the previous page, shows the life of the typical sexual addict. He is unwilling to live in the 40-60 m.p.h. range with everyone else. He is continually looking for greater experiences, new conquests, and baser sin. Since there is such a price with sin, once he has culminated his lust, he plummets into the depths of despair and hopelessness. He believes the only way to escape depression is to boost himself up with a new sexual experience. It is what Solomon was referring to when he said, "For why should you, my son, be exhilarated with an adulteress?" It is the exhilaration of fantasy.

Figure 17-2, on the previous page, shows the life of a man who is content with the love of his wife. His life is not characterized by extreme peaks and valleys. Since he does not experience the despair of sin, he does not feel a need to pump himself up with the false high of illicit sex. He is content to live his life at 50 m.p.h. What is wrong with that? If God can make him satisfied with his own wife, wouldn't that be better than trying to live at a pace he was not created for? This seems unattainable to some but only because they are accustomed to living life by their feelings rather than by faith.

I will end this chapter with a cute story my friend Mike Broadwell once told me. His young niece was watching a gold fish swimming back and forth in its tank. This greatly saddened the little girl because it seemed like such an empty life, swimming back and forth in the same old tank. Everything was always the same; nothing ever changed. The poor fish would never have anything else to look forward to in life. This seemed tragic to the sensitive little girl. Uncle Mike knew just what to say, "Annie, God created that gold fish with a tiny memory. By the time he swims to the end of the tank he has completely forgotten where he just was and when he turns around, it's all new territory to him!" God has the power to do the same miracle in the human heart! As the man takes himself out of the fast lane of sexual activity, the Lord will instill within him a newfound desire for his wife.

eighteen

THE POWER OF GOD'S GRACE

THE LASH OF THE EGYPTIAN WHIP had not dispelled Jonadab's memories of the many nights he had spent in the temple of On. He knew the stories about the mystical encounters his descendants had supposedly had with Jehovah, the great God of the Hebrews. However, he had always preferred the fertility goddesses of Egypt. "The goddess Ipsis knows how to reward her worshippers," he would often quip to himself after a night with a temple prostitute.

One would think that the unforgettable events which occurred in the past year would have had more of an impact on Jonadab. He had been an eye witness to the destruction of the greatest kingdom on earth. Wave after wave of Nature's fury pounded away at Pharaoh's empire until there was nothing left but the wail of grieving parents. If that were not enough, he had also been among the Israelites who had crossed the Red Sea on dry ground. But a year later, these were but vague memories. Not even the thundering voice of Jehovah from Sinai could quiet the memories of those unforgettable rendezvous in the temple of On. They were always in his mind.

One day Jonadab's friend Nahshon told him about a young woman who was married to one of the elders of the tribe of

Issachar. "She's a real beauty, Jonadab!" he had told him, "and I hear she's a little on the wild side!" Jonadab became obsessed with the thought of having this woman. Every chance he had, he would make his way over to her tent and strike up conversations with her. Finally, she invited him in to her abode. Unfortunately for both of them, an elderly neighbor had seen him enter the tent. By the time the old woman had returned with the tribal leaders, the two were engulfed in the passions of adultery.

With several eye witnesses, it was a brief trial. Jonadab was hauled outside the camp, near the refuse pit, and stoned by the leaders of the offended husband's tribe. Jonadab shrieked in terror as the merciless shower of stones pounded him into the dust of the Sinai. His lust-filled life was finally brought to an abrupt end.*

In the six thousand years of mankind's existence, there were only fleeting periods when God's judicial system was put into effect in the lives of humans. Yet, each season when the Almighty's presence dwelled amongst His people, was a picture of what it is like when God controls the affairs of men. Under His judicial system, if you sinned, you had to face the penalty of the law. In God's kingdom, the punishment for every transgression was clearly stated in the Law of Moses. There were no misunderstandings, nor any exceptions.

Those of us who have only known the dispensation of grace must continually face the temptation to disregard God's judicial system in our lives. "That doesn't apply to us anymore," one might say, "we are not under the law." Yes, that is true. Nevertheless, "the law," Paul tells us, "has become our tutor to lead us to Christ..." (Galatians 3:24) In other words, coming to an understanding of how God views sin will lead us into a revelation of Jesus Christ. God sending His Son to die a cruel, horrible

---

* A fictional account based on life under Jehovah's rule.

death on the Cross does not mean He no longer hates sin and has disregarded His judicial system. It simply means that His Son's death provided an atonement for our sin. We are no longer required to pay the full penalty for our transgressions. God now only requires that we confess our sins and repent of them. His grace means that those of us who have lived perverted lives should now dwell in the grateful awareness that we are criminals who deserve to be administered the same death penalty which Jonadab experienced, but have been given a pardon because the Judge ordered His Son to suffer the punishment on our behalf.

Unfortunately, a sinister and flippant attitude has crept into the Church. Our perspective of the horrible nature of sin has become so distorted by humanism that if God dealt with a man today as He did with Jonadab, we would feel that He had been too harsh and unmerciful. If a modern day Ananias and Sapphira were struck dead by our holy God, we would literally become unraveled. By and large the Church is quite comfortable with the very thing that this holy Being hates: SIN.

Grace Is Not a Synonym for Patience

One day, high up on the lonely crags of Mt. Sinai, God revealed Himself to Moses. As He passed in front of the old prophet, He proclaimed, "The LORD, the LORD God, compassionate and gracious, slow to anger, and abounding in lovingkindness and truth; who keeps lovingkindness for thousands, who forgives iniquity, transgression and sin; yet He will by no means leave the guilty unpunished, visiting the iniquity of fathers on the children and on the grandchildren to the third and fourth generations." (Exodus 34:6-7) One could easily spend a lifetime studying this self-portrait painted by the Lord and never exhaust its full meaning.

The phrase which holds a special interest to the man in habitual sin is "slow to anger." Eight times this description is repeated in the Old Covenant about the Lord. Its New Testament equivalent, *makrothumeo*, is translated loosely as patient or longsuffering. This Greek term is used to describe one of the fruits of the Spirit. *Vine's Expository Dictionary* says the following of this term: "...to be patient, longsuffering, to bear with... 'Longsuffering is that quality of self-restraint in the face of provocation which does not hastily retaliate or promptly punish; it is the opposite of anger, and is associated with mercy...'"[1]

For the man who has continually failed to live up to the requirements of a holy life, it is "good news" indeed to find out that God does not get easily angered over his transgressions. I, myself, can attest to the fact that the Lord is extremely patient. Over the years, my repeated acts of rebellion and utter lawlessness warranted His immediate wrath and judgment. However, what I received in return was His love, compassion, and mercy. Although He has "chastened me sore," (Psalms 118:18) and dealt severely with my sinful nature, The Lord has patiently bore me all the while. In describing this word, *makrothumeo*, Matthew Henry captured the essence of God's heart: "It can endure evil and provocation without being filled with resentment or revenge. It will put up with many slights from the person it loves, and wait long to see the kindly effects of such patience on him."[2]

It is unquestionable that God exhibits tremendous patience towards man's open rebellion to His commandments. Nonetheless, we must understand that even though God is patient there will be a season of reaping for one's past indiscretions. God's patience should never be confused with His grace. Although they work together, they are two different aspects of His character.

The *Theological Dictionary Of The New Testament* says the following about *makrothumeo*: "The majestic God graciously restrains his righteous wrath, as in his saving work for Israel... He does so in covenant faithfulness but also out of regard for human frailty... Forbearance, of course, is not renunciation but postponement with a view to repentance."[3]

God is patient in regards to a man's sin, but *His patience is for the purpose of giving a person time to repent.* Regarding the second coming of the Lord, the apostle Peter said, "The Lord is not slow about His promise, as some count slowness, but is patient toward you, not wishing for any to perish but for all to come to repentance. But the day of the Lord will come..." (II Peter 3:9-10a) He then went on to say, "Therefore, beloved, since you look for these things, be diligent to be found by Him in peace, spotless and blameless, and regard the patience of our Lord to be salvation..." (II Peter 3:14-15a)

It is extremely dangerous for an individual involved in habitual sin to assume that because he has not yet had his "day of reckoning" for his misconduct that there will be no forthcoming judgment to face. The people of Israel made this error. They repeatedly provoked the Lord through their blatant disobedience and unbelief. Isaiah conveyed the grief and frustration which the Lord felt over His people's waywardness:

My well-beloved had a vineyard on a fertile hill. And He dug it all around, removed its stones, and planted it with the choicest vine. And He built a tower in the middle of it, and hewed out a wine vat in it; then He expected it to produce good grapes, but it produced only worthless ones. "And now, O inhabitants of Jerusalem and men of Judah, judge between Me and My vineyard. What more was there to do for My vineyard that I have not done in it? Why, when I expected it to produce good grapes did it produce worthless ones? So now let Me tell you what I am going to do to My vineyard: I will remove its hedge and it will be consumed; I will break down its wall and it will become trampled ground. And I will lay it waste; it will not be pruned or hoed, but briars and thorns will come up. I will also charge the clouds to rain

no rain on it." For the vineyard of the LORD of hosts
is the house of Israel, and the men of Judah His delight-
ful plant. Thus He looked for justice, but behold,
bloodshed; for righteousness, but behold, a cry of dis-
tress. (Isaiah 5:1-8)

Jesus used the same illustration to portray the salvation
experience. He said, "I am the true vine, and My Father is the
vinedresser. Every branch in Me that does not bear fruit, He
takes away; and every branch that bears fruit, He prunes it, that
it may bear more fruit... By this is My Father glorified, that you
bear much fruit, and so prove to be My disciples." (John 15:1-2, 8)
Again, God is extremely patient with His people. He will "put up
with many slights from the person (He) loves, and wait long to
see the kindly effects of such patience on him." But it is
important that we understand that He has a vineyard for the
express purpose of growing fruit. As any experienced vinedresser
who has spent years cultivating a crop, He expects to one day
reap a fruitful harvest. May God's hatred of sin never be
forgotten nor minimized.

GRACE IS NOT A SYNONYM FOR LOVE

Love is a biblical term used to describe the Lord which
often becomes blurred in the minds of believers. God is love,
and the depth, the height, and breadth of His love is immeasurable. I will limit what I have to say about it to one great,
two-fold truth: God is in a passion to demonstrate His love
to us, and He expects love to be returned to Him.* Jesus said

---

* The Lord expects us to return His love, but He is not like the selfish person who
will not love another unless his love is returned. God's love is unselfish, giving, and
sacrificial in nature. However, God's love is a lot like electricity; there must be a circuit
for it to be complete. He loves people tremendously, but if that love is not returned,
it will eventually be taken back.

that the greatest commandment God gave to man was that he love Him with all his heart, soul and mind. (Matthew 22:37-38) The entire Bible rests upon this divine mandate.

However, love is not the same as grace. They are two distinct concepts. Allow me to illustrate the difference between love and grace with a story from the life of Jesus. He was walking along one day when a wealthy, young man asked Him what he must do to be saved. Imagine the penetrating eyes of our Savior bearing into your inmost being! Mark records the story:

> "You know the commandments, do not murder, do not commit adultery, do not steal, do not bear false witness, do not defraud, honor your father and mother. And he said to Him, "Teacher, I have kept all these things from my youth up." And looking at him, Jesus felt a love for him, and said to him, "One thing you lack: go and sell all you possess, and give to the poor, and you shall have treasure in heaven; and come, follow Me." But at these words his face fell, and he went away grieved, for he was one who owned much property. And Jesus, looking around, said to His disciples, "How hard it will be for those who are wealthy to enter the kingdom of God!" (Mark 10:19-23)

Many Christians, including myself, have had awesome experiences in which the love of God became so real that it was almost tangible. I have been in worship services when it seemed as though God's presence could be felt washing over the congregation as gentle waves upon a seashore. The Lord has an enormous love for people. However, one must be careful not to confuse His love with His grace. God's love for mankind is a powerful force. It is easy to get carried away with the feelings produced by that love and to corrupt it into something it is not meant to be. His love does not negate His commandments; He will not simply overlook sin. In fact, if anything, His love demands that we obey Him and turn away from our sin. After the encounter with the rich young ruler, Jesus said to His disciples:

> "If anyone loves Me, he will keep My word; and My Father will love him, and We will come to him, and make Our abode with him. He who does not love Me does not keep My words; and the word which you hear is not Mine, but the Father's who sent Me." (John 14:23-24)

The dangerous thing about savoring God's love while in a state of unrepentant sin is that a person can actually be deceived, thinking he is in true fellowship with the Lord. Notice in the story concerning the rich, young ruler that Jesus' love did not determine this man's eternal destiny. Yes, Mark tells us that Jesus did indeed love him. I am sure His love manifested itself as a powerful passion which emanated from His very Being. Nonetheless, this man's eternity depended upon *his response* to that ardent love. Would he obey the words of Jesus or not? As Jesus is faithful to do with all those who follow Him, He mercifully brought this man to a crossroad—Choose today whom you will serve, God or mammon!

This story is not meant to be a command to give all of one's possessions away. Jesus saw the idolatry in this man's heart, and therefore, He brought him to a fork in the road: If you wish to be My follower, you must forfeit your "idol." I ask you, has the Lord changed? If He laid down this condition to a man regarding money, how much more so those who have made sin their idol?

You will notice also, that once this man made his decision, Jesus did not (as so many Christian leaders today might do) run after him trying to work out some kind of compromise: "Listen, uh, I didn't mean to come on quite so strongly. You probably just need some time to work up to this kind of a commitment. Why don't you follow Me for awhile and hopefully later you can give away some of your money. After all, nobody is perfect. We are all sinners saved by grace. God understands."

Grace Is Not a Synonym for Licentiousness

Jesus continually compelled His followers to respond to His words (i.e. make a decision). He was not content to allow them to follow Him outwardly while not making a real surrender inwardly. He saw right into the core of men's hearts and confronted them about their attitudes.

Jesus not only disregarded the social protocol that one finds in today's "user friendly" churches, but He was actually a stumbling block to many "declared" followers. Take, for instance, the major "social blunder" He made, as described in the sixth chapter of the Book of John. The incident began on a very promising note. Jesus fed five thousand people with only two fish and five loaves of bread. The people were so astonished that one even exclaimed, "This is of a truth the Prophet who is to come into the world." (John 6:14) He openly acknowledged what others were afraid to say, that Jesus was the Messiah.

Surely this was a crowd ripe for a tremendous revival service! They were (literally) eating out of His hand. Yet, after that, it was as if He could not say anything right. He began by claiming to be the "bread of heaven." Now, surely He could see that these people needed to be gradually led up to a grand statement such as this. After all, claiming to be the "bread of heaven" to a crowd of simple, country folk was extremely risky. Then, to make matters worse, He went on to tell them that if they wanted to have eternal life they would have to eat His flesh and drink His blood! John tells us that "as a result of this many of His disciples withdrew, and were not walking with Him anymore." (John 6:66) The interesting element to this story is what happened next. Not at all intimidated by the crowd's response, He turned around to His twelve disciples and asked them, "You do not want to go away also, do you?" Simon Peter answered Him, "Lord, to whom shall we go? You have words of eternal life. And we have believed and have come to know that You are the Holy One of God."

Unlike many preachers today who are obsessed with having an enormous congregation, Jesus was interested in those who would pursue Him regardless of the cost. He understood that most would not follow Him, yet He never tempered the piercing truth of God's Word. He loved those people, but He refused to submit a compromised version of what God was offering to all sinners.

This uncompromising stance was maintained by His disciples over the next thirty years. In spite of this, others, whose teachings were characterized by a weak position on sin, came into prominence in the Church. Jude, speaking in the fire of God's Spirit, warned the body of Christ to beware of those "who turn the grace of our God into licentiousness..." (Jude 4).

I am convinced that what many people today are accepting as grace is really nothing more than *the presumptuous license to sin*. Dietrich Bonhoeffer was a godly man who could see this tendency beginning to form within the Church even back in the 1930's. He lived in Germany and his status as a national, religious leader could be comparable to Billy Graham in our day and age. He was fearless in his preaching, and it eventually cost him his life at the hands of the Nazis. Before the beginning of World War II, he penned these immortal words in a book that has become a classic, *The Cost Of Discipleship*:

Cheap grace is the deadly enemy of our Church. We are fighting today for costly grace.

Cheap grace means grace sold on the market like cheapjacks' wares. The sacraments, the forgiveness of sin, and the consolations of religion are thrown away at cut prices. Grace is represented as the Church's inexhaustible treasury, from which she showers blessings with generous hands, without asking questions or fixing limits. Grace without price; grace without cost! The essence of grace, we suppose, is that the account has been paid in advance; and, because it has been paid, everything can be had for nothing. Since the cost was infinite, the possibilities of using and spending it are infinite. What would grace be if it were not cheap?..

Cheap grace is the preaching of forgiveness without requiring repentance, baptism without church discipline, Communion without confession, absolution without personal confession. Cheap grace is grace without discipleship, grace without the cross, grace without Jesus Christ, living and incarnate...

Costly grace is the treasure hidden in the field; for the sake of it a man will gladly go and sell all that he has. It is the pearl of great price to buy which the merchant will sell all his goods...

Such grace is *costly* because it calls us to follow, and it is *grace* because it calls us to follow *Jesus Christ*. It is costly because it costs a man his life, and it is grace because it gives a man the only true life.[4]

In a book written primarily to those who are continuing to wallow in a lifestyle of ongoing, flagrant sin, it is very important to touch on what the Bible teaches about this matter of grace. Allow me to assure you that this is not a discussion involving the age-old argument about the preservation of the saints. It concerns the clear scriptural mandate as to what it means to be a true follower of Christ. John MacArthur, a staunch advocate for the doctrine known as "eternal security," said the following:

The contemporary church has the idea that salvation is only the granting of eternal life, not necessarily the liberation of a sinner from the bondage of his iniquity. We tell people that God loves them and has a wonderful plan for their lives, but that is only half the truth. God also hates sin and will punish unrepentant sinners with eternal torment. No gospel presentation is complete if it avoids or conceals those facts. Any message that fails to define and confront the severity of personal sin is a deficient gospel. And any "salvation" that does not alter a life-style of sin and transform the heart of the sinner is not a genuine salvation.[5]

Whether you believe that unrepentant sinners have never had a true conversion, or you simply believe that they are backslidden, what the New Testament teaches about the eternal destiny of those who die in habitual sin is exceedingly clear and absolutely irrefutable. In order that you fully understand the penalty for ANY sinner who WILL NOT REPENT and turn from his sin, let us examine the following statements made by Jesus and other God-inspired writers. In no way is this meant to be a "scare tactic," but rather it will hopefully serve as a sobering reminder to all of us how God views sin and the judgment that will fall upon all those who die in their sins.

Jesus spoke these words in the Sermon on the Mount:

"...but I say to you, that everyone who looks on a woman to lust for her has committed adultery with her already in his heart. And if your right eye makes you stumble, tear it out, and throw it from you; for it is better for you that one of the parts of your body perish, than for your whole body to be thrown into hell." (Matthew 5:28-29)

Paul told the Galatians:

"Now the deeds of the flesh are evident, which are:

immorality, impurity, sensuality, idolatry... of which I forewarn you just as I have forewarned you that those who practice such things shall not inherit the kingdom of God." (Galatians 5:19-21)

He also warned the church at Corinth:

"Or do you not know that the unrighteous shall not inherit the kingdom of God? Do not be deceived; neither fornicators, nor idolaters, nor adulterers, nor effeminate, nor homosexuals, nor thieves, nor the covetous, nor drunkards, nor revilers, nor swindlers, shall inherit the kingdom of God." (I Corinthians 6:9-10)

The writer of Hebrews said:

"For if we go on sinning willfully after receiving the knowledge of the truth, there no longer remains a sacrifice for sins, but a certain terrifying expectation of judgment... How much severer punishment do you think he will deserve who has trampled under foot the Son of God, and has regarded as unclean the blood of the covenant by which he was sanctified, and has insulted the Spirit of grace? For we know Him who said, 'Vengeance is Mine, I will repay.' And again, 'The Lord will judge His people.' It is a terrifying thing to fall into the hands of the living God." (Hebrews 10:26-31)

In the first epistle of Peter we read:

"For if after they have escaped the defilements of the world by the knowledge of the Lord and Savior Jesus Christ, they are again entangled in them and are overcome, the last state has become worse for them than the first. For it would be better for them not to have known the way of righteousness, than having known it, to turn away from the holy commandment delivered to them." (II Peter 2:20-21)

And finally, the apostle John stated:

"The one who says, 'I have come to know Him,' and does not keep His commandments, is a liar, and the truth is not in him. Little children, let no one deceive you; the one who practices righteousness is righteous, just as He is righteous; the one who practices sin is of the devil... No one who is born of God practices sin, because His seed abides in him; and he cannot sin, because he is born of God." (I John 2:4; 3:7-9)

In spite of the overwhelming evidence to the contrary, there are those who simply will not accept what the Bible clearly teaches. Motivated by a false notion of the mercy of God, these well-intentioned teachers wish to open wide the gates of heaven to anyone who gives the slightest commitment to Christianity. However, just because there are some who pass along this perverted, anemic gospel does not make it so. When a man stands before God with a life of carnality, selfishness, and unrepentant sin, his doctrinal opinions will no longer matter. His dead faith, which he exercised here on earth, will be exposed for what it is, and he will discover, to his horror, that he has sentenced himself to an everlasting place of torment—HELL!*

One of the key reasons people remain in sin is because they

---

* I do not mean to infer that one can ever become good enough or do anything to earn his way into heaven. However, the one who has a real, saving faith in God does not remain in habitual sin. He has undergone the genuine repentance discussed in the thirteenth chapter. It does not mean that he will not have struggles; but he has a living, vibrant faith which cannot be held in the shackles of habitual sin.

lack a fear of God. Any attempt to override the voice of the Holy Spirit's conviction in a sinner's life is dangerous. Solomon had much to say about the fear of the Lord:

"The fear of the LORD is the beginning of knowledge; fools despise wisdom and instruction." (Proverbs 1:7) "Do not be wise in your own eyes; fear the LORD and turn away from evil." (Proverbs 3:7) "The fear of the LORD prolongs life, but the years of the wicked will be shortened." (Proverbs 10:27) "In the fear of the LORD there is strong confidence, and his children will have refuge. The fear of the LORD is a fountain of life, that one may avoid the snares of death." (Proverbs 14:26-27) "By lovingkindness and truth iniquity is atoned for, and by the fear of the LORD one keeps away from evil." (Proverbs 16:6) "The fear of the LORD leads to life, so that one may sleep satisfied, untouched by evil." (Proverbs 19:23) "Do not let your heart envy sinners, but live in the fear of the LORD always." (Proverbs 23:17)

It is right to fear the Lord. A healthy reverence for God stands as a mighty fortress against the attack of the enemy through temptation.

Grace That Saves From Sin

One of the ways we have gotten off track doctrinally in this century is that there has been a gradual but definite decline in the awareness of the evil nature of sin. Those who have a weak comprehension of the horror of sin will take a weak stand against it. I do not possess a doctorate degree in theology, yet, for many years, I have studied the teachings of the men of God of past centuries, and there is a marked difference in their approach to sin than what is virtually commonplace in the Church today.

This corporate loss of the shame of sin has been promoted by the "hyper-grace" teachings which have flourished during our time. Dr. Michael Brown writes the following:

> There is an ocean of grace waiting for us, inviting us to dive in and swim. There's no end to its depth or length, and even through endless ages of eternity, we will stand in awe at the wonder of it all. The tragedy is that many preachers and teachers today have unintentionally misrepresented God's grace, practically turning it into a license to sin. And in doing this, they have cheapened its power and demeaned its value. They have polluted the holy waters flowing from the heavenly throne.
>
> Can I be totally honest with you? I believe that grace is one of the most misunderstood subjects in the contemporary Church. On the one hand, there are legalists who seem to forget that salvation is by grace through faith and not by works. They turn Christianity into a lifeless religion plagued by futility and marked by always-failing human effort.
>
> On the other hand, there are leaders who seem to forget that salvation by grace includes freedom from sin as well as forgiveness of sin. They turn Christianity into a religion that "saves" but doesn't transform. Both positions are wrong. Dead wrong.[6]

When dealing with church-going men who are unsaved and/or backslidden, it is important to understand that God's grace is there to empower His people to overcome sin. In fact, one of the prophecies about Jesus was that He would come to "save His people from their sins." (Matthew 1:21)

Having a proper, biblical understanding of God's grace is not a problem unless a person wishes to cling to his sin.

Unfortunately, there are many who do not want to be saved from their sins; they only wish to be saved from hell. In the words of an old-time Baptist preacher, "That's like the unrepentant thief who went before the judge pleading not to be sent to prison. He had no intention of quitting the behavior that got him into his predicament. He only wanted to be spared a prison sentence."

As I mentioned earlier, God has graciously set aside the demands of the law. He now is only looking for confession and repentance from the heart. As stated by the apostle John, "If we confess our sins, He is faithful and righteous to forgive us our sins and to cleanse us from all unrighteousness." (I John 1:9) Those who imagine that they can remain in unrepentant sin are saying, *"I don't want to be cleansed; I just want to be forgiven."*

William Barclay said the following:

> Grace is not only a gift; it is a grave responsibility. A man cannot go on living the life he lived before he met Jesus Christ. He must be clothed in a new purity and a new holiness and a new goodness. The door is open, but the door is not open to the sinner to come and remain a sinner, but for the sinner to come and become a saint.[7]

GRACE PROVIDES AN ATMOSPHERE OF ACCEPTANCE

One of the most important aspects to the grace of God is that it provides a safe haven for the repentant sinner. When a habitual sinner repents, he does not need to punish himself further with condemnation. He does not have to earn his way back into the Father's "good graces." When he confesses the wrongness of his actions and turns from them, he is instantly restored. One of the wonderful stories Jesus told was that of the prodigal son. To understand the proper context of what He was

explaining, we will include His two smaller stories which precede
it:

And He told them this parable, saying, "What man
among you, if he has a hundred sheep and has lost one
of them, does not leave the ninety-nine in the open
pasture, and go after the one which is lost, until he finds
it? And when he has found it, he lays it on his shoulders,
rejoicing. And when he comes home, he calls together
his friends and his neighbors, saying to them, 'Rejoice
with me, for I have found my sheep which was lost!' I tell
you that in the same way, there will be more joy in heaven
over one sinner who repents, than over ninety-nine
righteous persons who need no repentance.

"Or what woman, if she has ten silver coins and loses
one coin, does not light a lamp and sweep the house and
search carefully until she finds it? And when she has
found it, she calls together her friends and neighbors,
saying, 'Rejoice with me, for I have found the coin which
I had lost!' In the same way, I tell you, there is joy in the
presence of the angels of God over one sinner who
repents."

And He said, "A certain man had two sons; and the
younger of them said to his father, 'Father, give me the
share of the estate that falls to me.' And he divided his
wealth between them. And not many days later, the
younger son gathered everything together and went on
a journey into a distant country, and there he squandered
his estate with loose living.

"Now when he had spent everything, a severe
famine occurred in that country, and he began to be in
need. And he went and attached himself to one of the
citizens of that country, and he sent him into his fields
to feed swine. And he was longing to fill his stomach

with the pods that the swine were eating, and no one was giving anything to him. But when he came to his senses, he said, 'How many of my father's hired men have more than enough bread, but I am dying here with hunger! 'I will get up and go to my father, and will say to him, "Father, I have sinned against heaven, and in your sight; I am no longer worthy to be called your son; make me as one of your hired men."'

"And he got up and came to his father. But while he was still a long way off, his father saw him, and felt compassion for him, and ran and embraced him, and kissed him. And the son said to him, 'Father, I have sinned against heaven and in your sight; I am no longer worthy to be called your son.' But the father said to his slaves, 'Quickly bring out the best robe and put it on him, and put a ring on his hand and sandals on his feet; and bring the fattened calf, kill it, and let us eat and be merry; for this son of mine was dead, and has come to life again; he was lost, and has been found.' And they began to be merry.

"Now his older son was in the field, and when he came and approached the house, he heard music and dancing. And he summoned one of the servants and began inquiring what these things might be. And he said to him, 'Your brother has come, and your father has killed the fattened calf, because he has received him back safe and sound.' But he became angry, and was not willing to go in; and his father came out and began entreating him. But he answered and said to his father, 'Look! For so many years I have been serving you, and I have never neglected a command of yours; and yet you have never given me a kid, that I might be merry with my friends; but when this son of yours came, who has devoured your wealth with harlots, you killed the fattened calf for him.' And he said to him, 'My child, you have always been with me, and all that is mine is yours. 'But we had to be merry and rejoice, for this brother of yours was dead and has begun to live, and was lost and has been found.'" (Luke 15:3-32)

These stories wonderfully illustrate the grace of God. Though they almost need no comment, allow me to make a few observations. First, they were told to a group of scowling, self-righteous Pharisees who were upset with Jesus for being in the company of "tax gatherers" and "sinners." Jesus was emphasizing how delighted God is when a sinner repents. This point was masterfully driven home in the parable of the lost son (Luke 15:11-32) by the contrasting sentiment of the older brother who had no joy over his own brother's repentance. He could only see his brother's past failures and disappointments.

Secondly, notice the atmosphere of acceptance that the father's love created. One of the primary aspects of God's grace is that *He will always accept the penitent heart*—no matter how horrendous the sin! From what I have been told, Ted Bundy and Jeffrey Dahmer both repented and therefore are in heaven this day. When a sinner comes to God in repentance, it does not matter what he has done, the slate is wiped CLEAN! No condemnation; no guilt trips. There is only joyful acceptance from God the Father.

The third thing I will make note of is that the father did not run after his son in an attempt to work out a compromise: "Listen son, let's talk about this thing. Why don't you stay at home. You would be safer here. I know you're going through a difficult time right now. I won't interfere with your personal affairs. I love you. You can have your vices, just please come home." Instead, the father let him go and gave him what he wanted. However, as his son was returning, the father rushed to embrace and welcome him home where he belonged. After immediately restoring him back to his rightful place, the father explained to his confused and merciless older son, "we had to be merry and rejoice, for this brother of yours was dead and has begun to live, and was lost and has been found."

GRACE GIVES THE POWER TO BREAK FREE FROM SIN

Just as the apostle Paul was gearing up to deliver his fabulous treatise on righteousness, he made this statement: "...but where sin increased, grace abounded all the more." (Romans 5:20) It is very important for the man whose life is characterized by lustful acts to know that as much as he has indulged in sin, God has an even greater measure of grace to overcome that sin. As we have already seen, the reason Jesus came was to break the power of sin over the believer's life. Paul said it this way: "For the grace of God that brings salvation has appeared to all men. It teaches us to say "No" to ungodliness and worldly passions, and to live self-controlled, upright and godly lives in this present age." (Titus 2:11-12 NIV)

Yes, it is true: grace is the means whereby salvation is available to all of mankind. Yet, it is even more than that. Grace is also a teacher, and its primary subject of instruction is how to live a life pleasing to God. When that temptation arises for something ungodly, grace is there to teach us to say "No." When an opportunity comes to give over to some worldly passion, grace instructs us to deny it. Not only does it help us during those times of temptation, but God's daily grace is an active force in the life of the believer "to live self-controlled, upright and godly lives in this present age."

It is exactly what Paul spoke of when he said, "No temptation has overtaken you but such as is common to man; and God is faithful, who will not allow you to be tempted beyond what you are able, but with the temptation will provide the way of escape also, that you may be able to endure it." (I Corinthians 10:13)

It is God's grace that empowers us to withstand the overwhelming desire for sin. In other words, *the atmosphere that provides acceptance and forgiveness when we repent, is the same godly atmosphere which provides a way through every temptation of sin.*

It is my testimony that for the past fifteen years it has been God's grace that has kept me from giving in to the powerful lust for women that once dominated my life. Just to give one example of a number I could share, I will tell of an incident that happened to me in 1988. At that time, I had only been out of habitual sin for three years. I was in Texas holding a conference on the subject of overcoming sexual addiction. There was an attractive female doctor there who seemed very interested in Pure Life Ministries. She was asking a number of questions and seemed reluctant to leave after the conference.

The man who I was travelling with had other appointments and asked her to give me a ride back to the house where we were staying. I did not think anything of it at the time. She seemed to have an interest in becoming involved with Pure Life Ministries, so I was glad to have the opportunity to talk with her. During the drive across town though, I started becoming aware of her physically. When we arrived at the house, I felt an overwhelming lust for her overtake my mind. It was the same black, demonic cloud I had experienced in the car going to Bakersfield earlier that year. As I was experiencing this intoxicating desire for her, she made it clear to me that she was available. Just then, at that critical moment, even more overpowering than the lust came a fear that I would get caught if I committed adultery. This all-encompassing fear was all I needed to get out of the situation.

What an example of God's wonderful, sustaining grace! Had I been left to myself, I would have thrown away all that the Lord had accomplished in my life over the previous three years. I would have shattered the trust that had been so painstakingly reestablished with my wife. I would have ruined Pure Life

Ministries before it even got off the ground. Indeed, I would have plummeted into the depths of sin once more. Nevertheless, I was not left to myself! God's grace was there to provide a way of escape.

If His grace is there for the believer, why do some men continually cave in to their temptations? I believe the key is found in what we discussed in the fifteenth chapter.* Though I do not all together understand, abiding *in* Christ enables God's grace to sustain the believer. As John said, "And you know that He appeared in order to take away sins; and in Him there is no sin. No one who abides in Him sins... And the one who keeps His commandments abides in Him, and He in him." (I John 3:5-6,24)

Allow me to illustrate how this works in a practical way. I have done quite a bit of travelling. I was once in Heathrow Airport outside of London; there is a moving walkway that goes right down the middle of the terminal for probably a half of a mile. There are various shops, restaurants, and bars lining each side. If a person wishes to find sin, it is there for the taking.

Using that airport as an illustration of the Christian journey of life, the escalator would be the object which would represent God's grace. As I abide in Christ, it somehow keeps me safe from all the temptations and trappings of this world. My responsibility is to stay attached to the Vine; God's job is to empower me to overcome the temptations of life that come along. Maintaining a dependent relationship upon the Lord every day through prayer and Bible study, keeps me securely attached to the Vine and spiritually nourished. These are the mediums which the Lord uses to infuse His power into my life. The moving walkway is an illustration of God's grace transporting me through some very hellish places. It is not my own self effort that is getting me

---

* I should add to this that I believe that many church-going men have never had a true conversion to Christ. They are attempting the impossible: "...those who are in the flesh cannot please God," (Romans 8:8).

through. It is God's power alone. He will receive all of the glory when I arrive in heaven because I am fully aware that I do not have the strength within myself to withstand such temptations. Yes, if I were bent on committing sin, I could climb over the escalator handrail at any moment during my transit and could go into a bookstore that offers pornography. Yet, there is a spiritual handrail called the fear of the Lord which has been established within me. It is an added, protective feature built into me which is just enough of a barrier to keep me from wandering toward the ever-present allurements provided by the spirit of the world. Those whose fear of God has been paralyzed by the teachings of "sloppy grace," do not enjoy this added protection. In even worse trouble are those who wander around free of the discipline and spiritual strength that comes through maintaining a daily devotional life.

I have a better understanding of His wonderful grace because I have been kept by it for a long time. I have seen it at work on my behalf many times over the years. Earlier in my walk with the Lord, I did not understand grace so well. In fact, as astonishing as it may seem when considering the depth of sin that I had once been involved in, I became quite a Pharisee when I first started walking in victory over sexual sin. I gave myself much undeserved credit for my freedom. I became remarkably similar to the Pharisee in Luke eighteen who said, "God, I thank Thee that I am not like other people: swindlers, unjust, adulterers, or even like this tax-gatherer. I fast twice a week; I pay tithes of all that I get." (Luke 18:11-12) I was continually comparing myself favorably to others. Just as this Pharisee, I was doing many things right. My zeal for the Lord was intense. I was willing to live a "sold-out" life for God, sacrificing everything else to serve Him. My devotional life was firmly in place, but I had lost sight of what a wretch I had been and all that the Lord had done for me. I had become very prideful and self-righteous.

God continued dealing with me. He was unwilling to leave

me in such a terrible state. One day in 1991, the Lord helped me in a quite unexpected way. I was due to make an appearance on *Focus On The Family* the following week. I was preparing to share my testimony on this show, knowing that perhaps millions of people would hear it. Deep down inside I was anxious to share with the world how *I* had overcome sexual sin. God will share His glory with no other, however.

During that time, I was preaching in various churches around the country. This particular weekend, I was scheduled to hold services in a church in Michigan. We live in Kentucky, and normally my wife would travel with me on such a trip, but she had developed a back-ache and decided to stay home. I would have to make the six-hour drive by myself. There was no lack of confidence within me.

I made the long drive that day, struggling at times with the temptation to go into some city and look for pornography, or worse. But I managed to quell those incessant thoughts and made it into Michigan. After filling up my gas tank at a truck stop, I went in to the store to use their facilities. Making my way through the store (To properly appreciate what happened next, it might be helpful to imagine me walking through in all my pharisaical garb!), I noticed a man standing at the magazine rack looking at a "girlie" magazine. I walked by him, peering over his shoulder hoping to see flesh. Sure enough, the magazine was opened to a pornographic layout of some chosen beauty for that month.

That one glimpse of flesh haunted me all weekend. Somehow, I made it through Sunday services and on Monday morning I started home for Kentucky. As soon as I left the parsonage, my mind quickly drifted back to that truck stop. "No! I will not stop and look at that magazine!" I exclaimed to myself. No matter how strong of a stance I tried to take, the picture of the girl continued to plague me. I eventually reached the sign indicating that the off-ramp was one mile away. "I will not stop! I am going on with God!" I shouted. "Glory, hallelujah!"

When the turn-off appeared, I exited the freeway, drove straight to that gas station, went in and saturated my mind with the pictures in that magazine. My heart was thumping wildly as I scrambled through the pages. Just then, a tiny voice inside me yelled, "Run!"

Knowing it to be the Holy Spirit, I left immediately and made the long, guilt-filled trip back to Kentucky. For the next several days, I continually berated myself. One morning, my self-condemnation reached its peak. "How could you be so stupid! Here you are about to go on national radio, and you have looked at pornography! Stupid!" On and on the self-imposed tirade went.

Before finishing the story, I must refer to an incident that happened to me ten years prior. I was a cadet in the Los Angeles Sheriff's Academy. The 18-week training was drawing to a close. I was one of the fortunate ones who had endured the rigorous academy. A third of the class of one hundred and fifty cadets had dropped out. Those of us who made it lived in a certain degree of fear of doing anything that might cause us to be disqualified.

This particular day the cadets were bussed out to the Pomona Fair Grounds to participate in a two-day intensive driving school. There was a high-speed course that was set up with orange parking cones in the vast asphalt area. My turn finally arrived. The first thing I noticed about the squad car was that it was equipped with a roll cage. A helmet sat on the driving seat awaiting me. "Get in, put on your helmet and take off," said the fearless instructor sitting in the passenger seat.

I did exactly what I was told. I was driving fairly fast when, to my surprise, the instructor yelled out, "faster!" I immediately responded by increasing my speed even more. I was flying around the curves and accelerating on the straight-a-way's. Coming to one particularly difficult curve, I lost control for a second and was forced to drive off of the track. I immediately barreled through the cones again, getting back on the roadway and finished out the course. I sat in silence as the instructor filled out his paperwork. Knowing I had gotten off of the track, I moaned, "I guess I failed the course." I was sick inside thinking it might affect my graduating the academy.

"Failed? Why do you think you failed?" he asked.

"I missed that turn and drove right off the track," I lamented.

"Yeah, but you jumped right back on! You did great!" He exclaimed.

Ten years later, as I was on my morning prayer-walk, beating myself for viewing the pornography in the gas station, God spoke to me. (Tears well up in my eyes all these years later as I recall this incident.) In one of those crisp, eternal moments, I relived the incident that occurred a decade before in the squad car. Now it was the Lord speaking. "Steve, you made one little mistake. But you've been doing great! You've been in prayer everyday. You've been pressing in to Me. You've been in the Word faithfully. Yes, you got off track for a moment, but you jumped right back on!"

I had come into a true revelation about the grace of God. From that day on, I understood that my victory over sin was not because of my efforts but because of God's fabulous grace!

BIBLIOGRAPHY

CHAPTER THREE

1. Harris, Archer & Waltke, *Theological Wordbook Of The Old Testament,* Moody Press, Chicago, 1980, p. 742.
2. Frank Worthen, *Steps Out Of Homosexuality,* Love In Action, P.O. Box 2655, San Rafael, CA 94912 1984, p. 79.

CHAPTER FOUR

1. As reported in New Creation Ministries' December, 1999 newsletter.

CHAPTER FIVE

1. Merlin Carothers, *What's On Your Mind?* The Foundation Of Praise, Escondido, CA 1984, p. 30.
2. Adam Clarke, *The Bethany Parallel Commentary* on the New Testament, Bethany House Publishers, Minneapolis, MN, 1983, pps. 39-40.
3. Charles Spurgeon, *Commentary on Matthew,* as cited in AGES Digital Library, AGES Software, Albany, OR, 1996, p. 53.
4. Spiros Zodhiates, *The Complete Word Study Dictionary,* New Testament, AMG Publishers, Chattanooga, TN, 1992, p. 1087.

5. Marvin R. Vincent, D.D., *Word Studies in the New Testament*, as cited in AGES Digital Library, *ibid*, Vol. 3, p. 57.
6. Frank Worthen, *Love In Action Newsletter*, January, 1983.
7. S. Conway, *The Pulpit Commentary*, *Vol. XXII*, The Book of Revelation, McDonald Publishing Co., McLean, VA; p. 83.

Chapter Six

1. C. Jerdan, *The Pulpit Commentary*, *Vol. XXI*, *ibid*, The Book of James, pps. 12-13.
2. Thomas A Kempis, as cited in *The Pulpit Commentary*, *ibid*.
3. *Bethany Parallel Commentary On The New Testament*, *ibid*, p. 1346.
4. Frank Worthen, *ibid*, p. 46.
5. Ronald A. Jenson, *Biblical Meditation*, I.C.B.I. Press, Oakland, CA 1982, p. 39.
6. Dietrich Bonhoeffer, *Temptation*, SCM Press, London, 1964, p. 33.
7. Adam Clarke, *Clarke's Commentary on the Old Testament*, as cited in AGES Digital Library, *ibid*, Vol 3, p. 1694.

Chapter Seven

1. Warren Wiersbe, *The Best Of A.W. Tozer*, Baker Publishing House, Grand Rapids, MI, 1978, p.176.
2. Charles Spurgeon, *unknown origin*.
3. C.S. Lewis, *Mere Christianity*, Collier Books, NY, 1943, p.108.
4. William Gurnall, *The Christian In Complete Armour*, The Banner of Truth Trust, p. 205.
5. Thomas A Kempis, *Of The Imitation Of Christ*, Baker Book House, 1973, p.17.
6. Martin Luther, *Inspiring Quotations*, Thomas Nelson Publishers, Nashville, TN, 1988, p. 92.
7. Andrew Murray, *Humility*, Whitaker House, 1982, pp. 24, 12.

Chapter Nine

1. Frank Worthen, *Love In Action Newsletter*, January, 1983.

2. Steve Gallagher, *Living In Victory,* Pure Life Ministries, P.O. Box 410, Dry Ridge, KY, 41035, 1997, pps. 137-138.

CHAPTER TEN

1. Charles Hodge, *Commentary On The Epistle To The Romans,* as cited in AGES Digital Library, *ibid,* p.304
2. Worthen, *Steps Out Of Homosexuality, ibid,* p. 4.
3. Nelson E. Hinman, (as recorded on) *Never Beyond What's Written,* Heart Talk Ministry, Sacramento, CA.
4. Jay E. Adams, *The Christian Counselor's Manual,* Presbyterian and Reformed Publishing Co., Phillipsburg, NY, 1973, pp. 180-188.

CHAPTER ELEVEN

1. Erwin W. Lutzer, *Living With Your Passions,* Victor Books, Wheaton, IL, 1983, p. 31.
2. Sumrall, *60 Things God Said About Sex,* Thomas Publishers, New York, NY, 1981, p. 53.
3. Warren Wiersbe, *ibid,* pp. 85-86.
4. Tim LaHaye, *The Battle For The Mind,* Fleming H. Revell Co., 1980, pp. 25-26.
5. *Webster's New Collegiate Dictionary,* G. & C. Merriam Co., Springfield, MA, 1960, p.615.
6. David Wilkerson, *Set The Trumpet To Thy Mouth,* World Challenge, Inc, Lindale, TX, 1985, pp.53-55.
7. Ronald A. Jenson, *ibid,* pps.15-18.
8. Frank Mankiewixz & Joel Swedlow, *Remote Control,* Ballantine Books, NY, NY, 1978, pp.187-189.
9. Donald E. Wildmon, *The Home Invaders,* Victor Books, 1985, pp. 45-46.

CHAPTER TWELVE

1. Merril C. Tenney, *Demons In The World Today,* Tyndale House, Wheaton, IL, 1971, pp. 113-114.

2. *ibid.*
3. Merlin Carothers, *What's On Your Mind?, ibid,* pps. 12-13, 17-18.

CHAPTER THIRTEEN
1. Charles Spurgeon, *Inspiring Quotations,* ibid, p170.

CHAPTER FOURTEEN
1. *Baker Encyclopedia of the Bible,* Vol. 1, Baker Book House, *ibid,* 1988, page 631.
2. *Theological Wordbook Of The Old Testament, ibid,* p.426.

CHAPTER FIFTEEN
1. John Calvin, *The Commentaries on the Epistle of Paul to the Hebrews,* as cited in AGES Digital Library, *ibid,* pp. 90-91.
2. Ronald A. Jenson, *ibid.*
3. Jay E. Adams, *ibid.*

CHAPTER SIXTEEN
1. Oswald Chambers, *Oswald Chambers The Best From All His Books,* Thomas Nelson Publishers, Nashville p204

CHAPTER SEVENTEEN
1. C.S. Lewis, *The Quotable Lewis,* Tyndale House Publishers, Wheaton, IL, p. 291.

CHAPTER EIGHTEEN
1. W.E. Vine, *VINE'S Expository Dictionary of Old and New Testament Words,* Fleming H. Revell Co., Old Tappan, NJ, 1981, Vol. 3, p. 12.
2. Matthew Henry, *The Bethany Parallel Commentary on the New Testament, ibid,* p. 1029.
3. Gerhard Kittel and Gerhard Friedrich, *Theological Dictionary Of The New Testament,* William B. Eerdman's Co., 1985, p. 550.
4. Dietrich Bonhoeffer, *The Cost of Discipleship,* Collier Books,

New York, 1949, pps. 45-47.

5. John F. MacArthur, Jr., *The Gospel According to Jesus*, Word of Grace, Panorama City, CA, 1988, p. 60.

6. Michael L. Brown, *Go and Sin No More*, Gospel Light, Ventura, CA, 1999, pps. 213-214.

7. William Barclay, cited in *Go and Sin No More*, *ibid*, p. 224.

Other Books Available by
PURE LIFE MINISTRIES

IRRESISTIBLE TO GOD — *NEW FROM STEVE GALLAGHER!*

Before a person can come into intimate contact with a Holy God, he must first be purged of the hideous cancer of pride that lurks deep within his heart.

"This book is a road map that shows the arduous but rewarding way out of the pit of pride and into the green pastures of humility. Here is the place of blessing and favor with God."
—Steve Gallagher

Humility is the key that opens the door into the inner regions of intimacy with God. *Irresistible to God* unfolds the mystery that God is indeed drawn to the one who is crushed in spirit, broken by his sin, and meek before the Lord and others.

WHEN HIS SECRET SIN BREAKS YOUR HEART — *KATHY'S NEWEST BOOK!*

What can be more devastating for a wife than to discover her husband has a secret obsession with pornography and other women? Yet, this is what countless Christian wives face every day. Kathy Gallagher has been there; she understands the pain of rejection, the feelings of hopelessness and the questions that plague a hurting wife.

In this collection of letters, Kathy imparts heart-felt encouragement by providing the practical, biblical answers that helped her find healing in the midst of her most trying storm. The 30-day journal offers wives a place to prayerfully reflect and meditate upon Kathy's letters.

AT THE ALTAR OF SEXUAL IDOLATRY — *OUR BESTSELLER!*

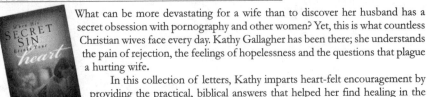

Sexual temptation is undeniably the greatest struggle Christian men face. Here's a book that digs deep and has the answers men are looking for—the kind that *actually* work. *Sexual Idolatry* draws back the curtain and exposes how sexual sin corrupts the entire man, something Steve Gallagher understands: having lived in the bondage of it for over twelve years. Help men put an end to the mystery of lust and maximize God's power in their lives with the proven answers that have helped thousands. *Spanish translation available as well. Sexual Idolatry Workbook also available.*

AT THE ALTAR OF SEXUAL IDOLATRY AUDIO BOOK (4 CDs)

Now you can benefit from the piercing truths contained in *Sexual Idolatry* without actually picking up the book. Whether you are on the go, working at your computer or simply relaxing at home, this moderately abridged audio version of our bestseller will impart God's answers as you listen.

LIVING IN VICTORY

The secret to victorious living is to tap into God's great storehouse of mercy for one's own needs, and then act as a conduit for that power, directing it toward the lives of others. Overcoming habitual sin is important, but real victory occurs when a person becomes a weapon in the hands of a powerful God against the legions of hell. That is Living in Victory!"
—Steve Gallagher

BREAK FREE FROM THE LUSTS OF THIS WORLD

Break Free is by far Steve Gallagher's best writing; its strength is his sobering deliverance of the unvarnished truth to a Church rife with sensuality and worldly compromise. In a time when evangelical Christians seem content to be lulled to sleep by the spirit of Antichrist, *Break Free* sounds a clarion wake-up call in an effort to draw the Body of Christ back to the Cross and holy living. Those with itching ears will find no solace here, but sincere believers will experience deep repentance and a fresh encounter with the Living God.

THE WALK OF REPENTANCE

The Walk of Repentance is a 24-week Bible study for any Christian that desires to be more deeply consecrated to God. Each week of this easy-to-use curriculum has a theme, addressing the everyday challenges believers face one step at a time. Its simplicity is its strength, using only the Word of God—and occasional stories of saints of old—as its content. Experience the times of spiritual refreshing that follow repentance; go deeper in God as you allow His Word to take root in your heart.

VIDEOS

BREAKING FREE FROM HABITUAL SIN

People try all kinds of methods to break sinful habits, but God has only given one answer to habitual sin: Repentance. Find the freedom you seek; allow the Lord to tear down your old way of thinking and loose the chains that bind you.

OVERCOMING INSECURITY

Insecurities… how many of us have felt their paralyzing effects; yet, how few of us recognize them as the blight of pride? Allow the Lord to dismantle those crippling defense mechanisms that keep you from the abundant Christian life.

WHEN THE TEMPLE IS DEFILED

Christian men in sexual sin often need a wake-up call, a message that pins them to the floor in repentance. This sermon, filmed at Zion Bible Institute during a day of prayer and fasting, describes what happens to those who desecrate their inner being with pornography and sexual sin. God's presence was very strong and used this message to spark great repentance.

AUDIO

BREAKING FREE FROM THE POWER OF LUST — *OUR MOST POPULAR SERIES!*

The insidious beast of lust can entrap a person to the point of hopeless despair. But the Lord has given answers that work! The biblical revelations imparted in this series will break the power of lust in the believer's heart. (Four Tapes)

Pure Life Ministries

Pure Life Ministries helps Christian men achieve lasting freedom from sexual sin. The Apostle Paul said, "Walk in the Spirit and you will not fulfill the lust of the flesh." Since 1986, Pure Life Ministries (PLM) has been discipling men into the holiness and purity of heart that comes from a Spirit-controlled life. At the root, illicit sexual behavior is sin and must be treated with spiritual remedies. Our counseling programs and teaching materials are rooted in the biblical principles that, when applied to the believer's daily life, will lead him out of bondage and into freedom in Christ.

Biblical Teaching Materials

Pure Life offers a full line of books, audiotapes and videotapes specifically designed to give men the tools they need to live in sexual purity.

Residential Care

The most intense and involved counseling PLM offers comes through the **Live-in Program** (6-12 months), in Dry Ridge, Kentucky. The godly and sober atmosphere on our 45-acre campus provokes the hunger for God and deep repentance that destroys the hold of sin in men's lives.

Help At Home

The **Overcomers At Home Program** (OCAH) is available for those who cannot come to Kentucky for the Live-In program. This twelve-week counseling program features weekly counseling sessions and many of the same teachings offered in the Live-in Program.

Care For Wives

Pure Life Ministries also offers help to wives of men in sexual sin. Our wives' counselors have suffered through the trials and storms of such a discovery and can offer a devastated wife a sympathetic ear and the biblical solutions that worked in their lives.

Pure Life Ministries

P.O. Box 410 • Dry Ridge • KY • 41035
Office: 859.824.4444 • Orders: 888.293.8714
info@purelifeministries.org
www.purelifeministries.org